GADABOUT GUIDES

MALDIVES

STUART BEVAN

Text copyright © Stuart Bevan, 1994.
Copyright © Gadabout Guides, an imprint of CIS Publishers.
First published in 1982, 1985 and 1987 by Other People Publications.

This edition published in 1994 by
Gadabout Guides A.C.N. 053 515 156
245 Cardigan Street, Carlton Vic 3053.

All rights reserved. No part of this publication may
be reproduced or transmitted in any form or by any means,
electronic or mechanical, including photocopying, recording,
storage in an information retrieval system, or otherwise,
without the prior written permission of the publisher,
unless specifically permitted under the Australian
Copyright Act 1968 as amended.

Edited by Virginia Greig.
Maps by Cliff Watt.
Design by CIS Publishers.
Typeset by Kim Bear.
Printed in Singapore by PH Productions Pte Ltd.

Bevan, Stuart, 1951–
  Maldives.
  4th ed.
  Bibliography.
  Includes index.

  ISBN 1 875633 25 1.

  1. Maldives—Guidebooks. 1. Title.

915.49504

CONTENTS

Introduction	2
Formation and History	5
The islands	6
Atoll formation, weather patterns, vegetation and fauna, and an environmental update	
History	23
Chronicles of history, aborigines, Arabs, Ali Rajas, Portuguese, British and Borahs, Sultans and Sultanas	
The 20th century	29
An overview of major events from 1900 until the present	
Island Life	41
People	42
Social classes, marriage and divorce, Islam, festivals and holidays, arts and crafts, music and dance	
Government	63
The political system — from the Citizen's Majlis to administrative atolls and Islamic law	
Economy	65
Fish and tourism	
Food	67
Teashop temptations and local recipes	
Language	70
Dhivehi and Thaana, a pronunciation guide, useful phrases and place names	

Facts for the Visitor — 83
Getting there — from anywhere — 84
At the airport — facilities — 85
Formalities — visas, permits, customs and currency — 86
Things to do — from scuba diving to cultural tours — 89
Places to stay — resorts, hotels, boats and guesthouses — 90
Getting around — by air and sea — 97
General information — from health precautions to shopping tips — 100

Kaafu — 115
Male' — 116
Initial impressions of this island capital, what to do and see, places to stay and where to eat

Male' Atoll — 137
A tour of the resorts and fishing villages

Central Atolls — 155
Alifu — 156
An outer atoll with some far-flung resorts

Vaavu — 161
Spectacular diving destinations

Meemu to Laamu — 164
The central atolls rarely visited by *dhon meehun* (white people) — Meemu, Faafu, Dhaalu, Thaa, and Laamu

Northern Atolls — 177
Lhaviyani — 178
At the centre of the fishing industry

Baa and Raa — 180
The realm of criminals and carpenters

Noonu to Haa Alifu   186
Existing at the mercy of the Indian Ocean — the northernmost atolls of Noonu, Shaviyani, Haa Dhaalu and Haa Alifu

Southern Atolls   199

Gaafu Alifu to Seenu   200
Equatorial Maldives — the southern atolls of Gaafu Alifu, Gaafu Dhaalu, Gnyaviyani and Seenu

Additional Information   209

Travel directory   210
A survival kit of rates, addresses, telephone and facsimile numbers for travel agencies, tourist hotels and resorts

Further reading   226
Gadabout Guides   229
Glossary   235
Dhivehi dictionary   243
Index   257
Photo credits   265

Maps

Indian Ocean	1	Central atolls	168
Maldive archipelago	8	Lhaviyani	179
Male'	120	Baa	182
Kaafu: North Male'	139	Raa	184
Kaafu: South Male'	143	Northern atolls	188
Alifu	158	Southern atolls	202
Vaavu	163		

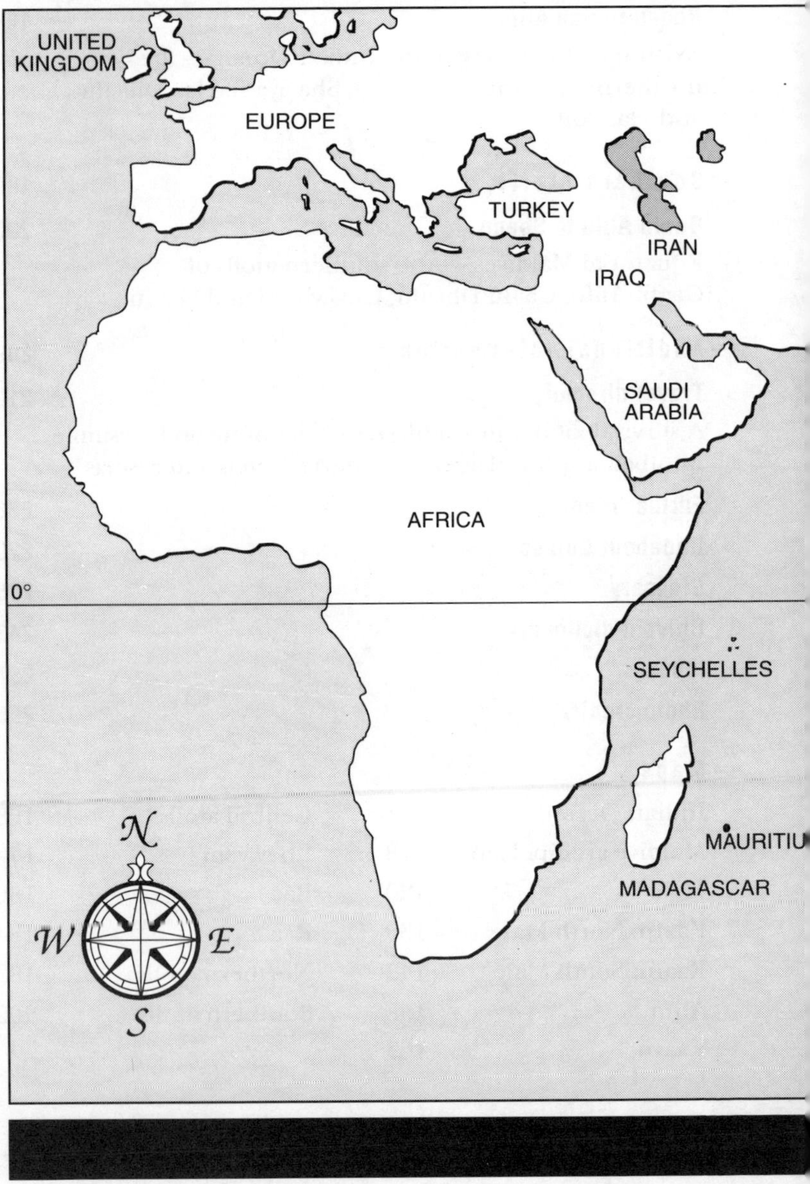
UNITED KINGDOM
EUROPE
TURKEY
IRAN
IRAQ
SAUDI ARABIA
AFRICA
0°
SEYCHELLES
MAURITIU
MADAGASCAR
N
W
E
S

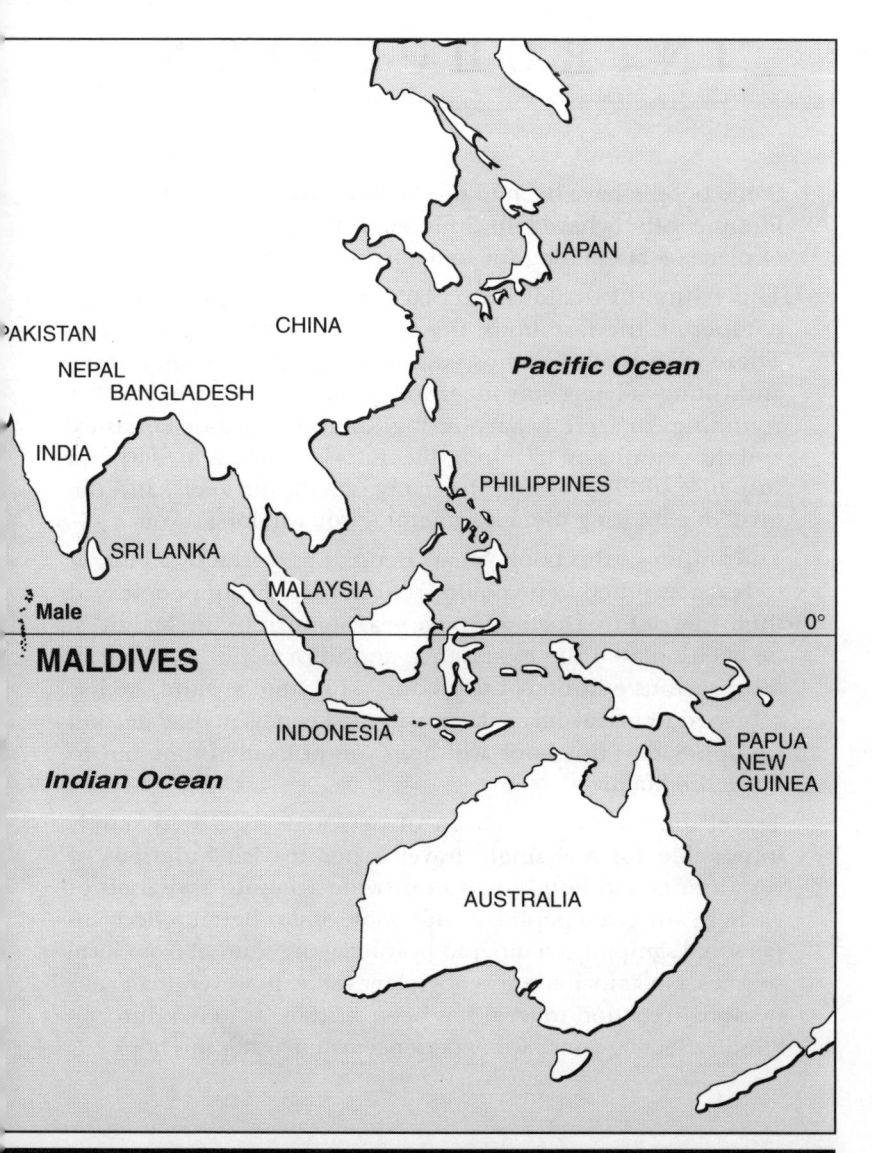

INDIAN OCEAN

INTRODUCTION

Some people have been to the Maldives for a visit and stayed a lifetime, others have left within days. The Maldives is that sort of place — fascinating for some, frustrating for others.

This nation of islands is no place for the frail or fragile, the pampered, the fastidious, the gourmet or the nightclubber. These islands are for those who are adventurous, inquisitive and young-at-heart, anyone who is exhilarated by tropical surroundings or secretly harbouring Robinson Crusoe fantasies, and those unfussed by minor discomforts. There is mystery and suspense hidden among the many islands and reefs, and the thrill of exploring them is something you will long savour.

The author of this book, Stuart Bevan, was driven by a hunger to learn as much as he could from the Maldivian people and their way of life. During his five-year sojourn in the Maldives, he accumulated the experience and information recalled in the previous editions of this book. This time around, he has returned to his favourite destination to keep us up-to-date, and he hopes that this book will help you not only to see but to know the Maldives.

Travel guides are reflections of personal taste. It is simply impossible for any single travel writer to visit hundreds of restaurants and hotels, and to provide accurate appraisals of each, in any given period. In this book, Stuart Bevan reflects his personal samplings tempered by intelligent counsel from local sources. No contribution is of greater value, however, than your personal reaction to what has been written, as well as information reflecting your own experiences while using this book.

Acknowledgments

Hassan Maniku, former Director of the Department of Information and local academic and author, offered a wealth of informative literature. Ibrahim Manik, Minister of the newly formed Ministry of Information and Culture, helped edit this edition.

The Ministry of Tourism continually provided up-to-date details about resorts, guesthouses and matters relating to visitors to their country. Aminath Shaaheen, in particular, cast her meticulous eye over the content of this edition to ensure its accuracy.

French-born Philippe Metois, a long-time resident of Vanuatu and major contributor to Gadabout Guides' Vanuatu travel book, provided a fresh look at the Maldives through the lens of his camera.

Jo Cormack worked in Male' for some years as a voluntary teacher. During her stay she uncovered an amazing stream of data from an equally amazing array of sources.

Onny Martin also worked for some time in Male'. His photographic library and local contacts were invaluable sources of reference.

Ibrahim Hameed returned to the Maldives, having graduated from a New Zealand university, and helped prepare the language section of this book.

Hasan Ramiz, a Swiss traveller, married a woman from the southern atolls and wishes for little more than 'a poor but human and relaxing lifestyle'. His keen insight into many aspects of local life were of great help.

Sultan Mohammed Imaduddeen VI on board HMS Pomon

FORMATION AND HISTORY

The islands 6
History 23
The 20th century 29

THE ISLANDS

Few countries have a landscape as remarkable as that of the Maldives (pronounced Morl-*dives*, as in *gives*). Ancient travellers once knew it as Maladiv, meaning 'a garland of islands'. Now the inhabitants call it Maldive Islands.

The Maldives is an archipelago of some 1190 islands (locals are used to discovering newly risen islands every now and then) that span the equator about 650 km south-west of Sri Lanka. On a map, the islands resemble a cartographer's error, a spray of ink. They are, in fact, scattered in a chainlike formation which extends 820 km from north to south and 130 km at the widest point.

The islands are dispersed over 26 atolls (the word 'atoll' was derived from the local term *atholhu*, meaning a ringlike coral formation enclosing a lagoon). As the water becomes shallower on approach to an island, the deep blue of the Indian Ocean seeps into seemingly harmless, warm and idyllic turquoise lagoon waters. But don't be fooled — ancient mariners likened the Maldives to a wall in the middle of the sea. Entry can be made only via a few narrow channels and this part of the Indian Ocean is renowned for shipwrecks. In fact, it is foolhardy to navigate the archipelago without an experienced local traveller close at hand.

Atoll formation

It is still a matter of debate as to when and how these atolls were formed. In 1842, Charles Darwin proferred the first acceptable theory of atoll formation. He suggested that atolls were created when a volcanic land mass subsided slowly into the ocean, while coral built up and out around the plateaux. Darwin noted in a postscript, however, that the Maldives were somehow different and quite unlike the atolls he had examined in the Pacific and Atlantic Oceans.

Not until 1962 were the peculiarities of the Maldivian atolls studied. Hans Hass, an eminent German scientist, made a diving expedition through the archipelago and concluded that, '... the inner structure of certain coral reefs is not compact but porous and unstable, hence extended reef platforms invariably sag in the centre. The depth of the lagoons may be explained by crystallisation and perishing of the coral substance, reinforced by the cumulative effect of the tides ... '

In other words, changing sea levels, tectonic activity and an amazing coral evolutionary process has created, over milleniums, a series of reefs along the peaks of the vast submerged mountain range which extends through the centre of the Indian Ocean. By raising the reef a fraction of a centimetre each year, the coral finally pierces the surface of the ocean and begins to form a platform. According to Hass, the centre of the platform eventually subsides due to perishing of the coral (it suffocates when food and oxygen are scarce) and the massaging effect of the tides. Around the rim of the atoll, where the coral has built hardest and highest, sand and debris accumulate, vegetation takes hold and islands begin to form.

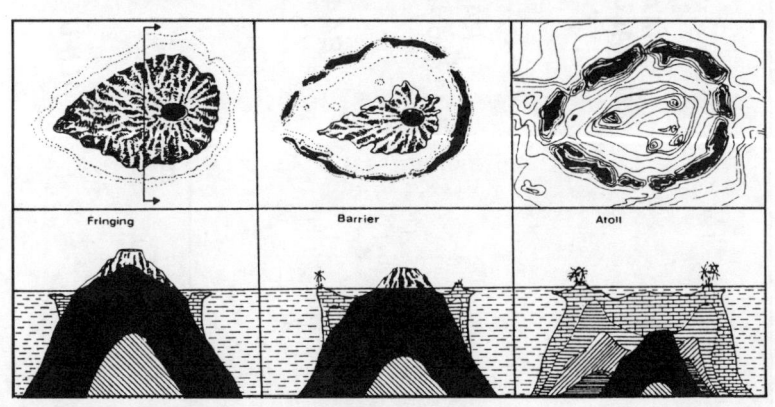

Atoll formation

Maldives — 8 —

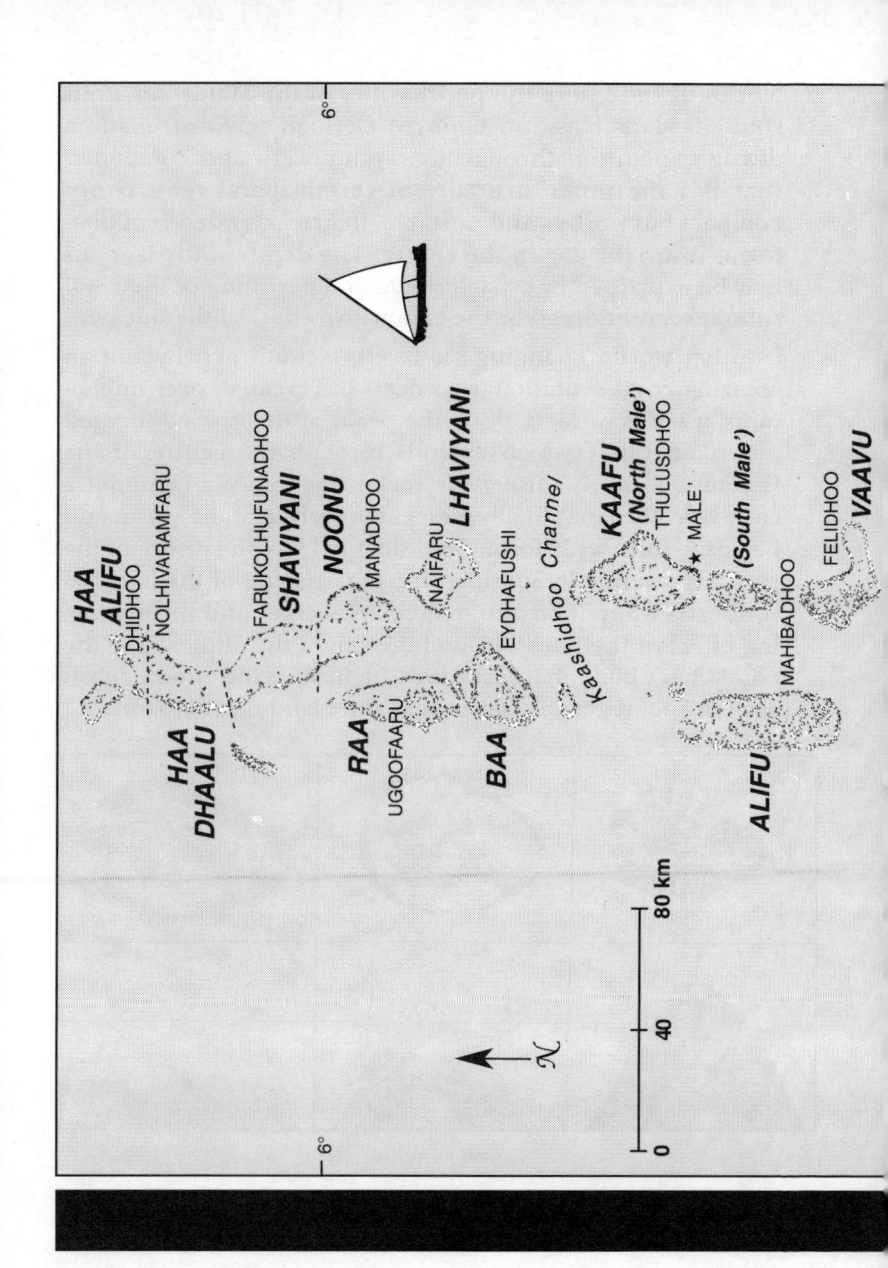

MALDIVE ARCHIPELAGO

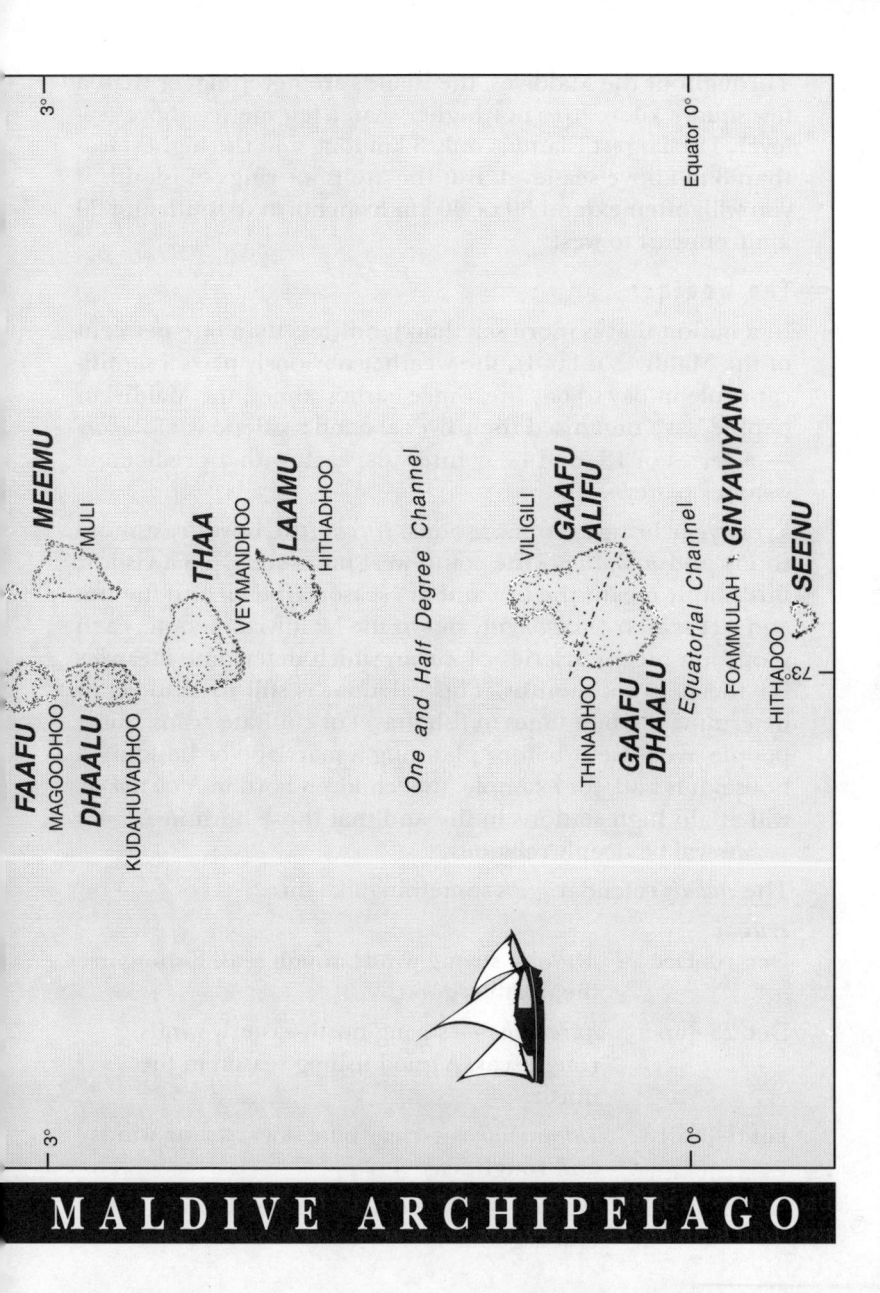

3°

FAAFU
MAGOODHOO

DHAALU
KUDAHUVADHOO

MEEMU
MULI

THAA
VEYMANDHOO

LAAMU
HITHADHOO

VILIGILI

GAAFU ALIFU

GAAFU DHAALU
THINADHOO

One and Half Degree Channel

Equatorial Channel

FOAMMULAH · **GNYAVIYANI**

SEENU
HITHADOO

73°

Equator 0°

0°

— 9 — *Formation and history*

Throughout the Maldives, the islands are never bigger than a few square kilometres nor higher than a few metres above sea-level. The largest island is only 8 km long and the highest less than 3 m above sea-level. But the atolls, or rings of islands if you will, often extend 30 or 40 km from north to south and 20 km from east to west.

The weather

In a nation that is more sea than land (less than one per cent of the Maldives is land), the weather obviously plays a significant role in day to day life. Since earliest times, the Maldivian people have organised their lives around a calendar of *nakaiy* — a series of 13- or 14-day intervals, each with a predictable weather pattern.

Every year brings two monsoons, *iruvai* (the north-east monsoon) and *hulhangu* (the south-west monsoon). To a visitor, this simply means the hot and dry season (*iruvai*) and the hot and wet season (*hulhangu*). But to the Maldivian people, each monsoon means a series of *nakaiy* which determine lifestyles for the next six months. This calendar is still used today to determine the best times to fish, travel or cultivate crops. Some people even use it before planning a marriage or building a house. It is said, for example, that children born in *Maa nakaiy* will attain high stations in life and that those born in *Uthura nakaiy* will be deeply religious.

The *nakaiy* calendar goes something like this:

Iruvai

Dec 10–Dec 22   *Mula* — strong winds, rough seas. Fishing in the north is good.

Dec 23–Jan 5   *Furahalha* — strong north-easterly winds, rough seas. A good fishing season in the north.

Jan 6–Jan 18   *Uthurahalha* — clear blue skies, strong winds and rough seas.

Jan 19–Jan 31   *Huvan* — calm seas, blue skies. Fishing in the east is good.

Unloading tuna, Male' harbour

Above: Making limestone for building houses
Below: A typical coral house

Kurumba Village

Put yourself in the picture

Contact Sunland Travel - your complete host.

- Resort/hotel reservations
- Camping and fishing tours
- Inbound and outbound tour operation
- Diving safaris, sailing excursions
- Filming expeditions
- Individual and group tours
- Incentive packages

sunland travel (pvt) ltd

Owners and operators of Makunudhu Island

Asrafee Building 3F, 1/44 Chandani Magu, Male' 20-03. PO Box 20145
Republic of Maldives. Telephone: (960) 324658/324758 Facsimile: (960) 325543
Telex: (896) 77064 SUNLAND MF Cable: SUNLAND/MALDIVES

Feb 1–Feb 13   *Dhinasha* — north-easterly winds, moderate seas, plenty of sunshine.

Feb 14–Feb 26   *Hiyaviha* — seas are calm, days and nights are hot.

Feb 27–Mar 11   *Furabadhuruva* — frequent, short sharp bursts of thunder and lightning. Small plants and bushes are cut down, left to dry and then burnt.

Mar 12–Mar 25   *Fasbadhuruva* — usually clear blue skies. If thunder is frequent during this period, local lore says the yam harvest will be good for the year.

Mar 26–Apr 7   *Reyva* — if storms occur they may be severe. Fishing is good in the north. Some trees are cut down and burnt.

Hulhangu

Apr 8–Apr 21   *Assidha* — begins with a storm, then becomes hot and dry. People allow themselves to be wet by the first rains, believing it will bring them good luck. Fishing is poor, millet and trees are planted.

Apr 22–May 5   *Burunu* — begins with a storm and strong winds, then becomes calm. Fields are cleared, trees chopped and seeds sown.

May 6–May 19   *Kethi* — dark clouds, frequent rains. Dried leaves are burnt and the ashes spread over the fields. Sowing continues.

May 20–Jun 2   *Roanu* — storms, strong winds and rough seas. Fields are sown on some islands during this period.

Jun 3–Jun 16   *Miyahelia* — storms, rough seas and strong westerly winds. Fields are sown and weeded.

Jun 17–Jun 30   *Adha* — south-westerly winds, light rain and schools of fish. Fields are weeded and transplanted.

Jul 1–Jul 14   *Funoas* — storms and rough seas with frequent sudden gales. Weeding and transplanting continues.

Jul 15–Jul 28   *Fus* — wet and overcast. Fishing is good.

Jul 29–Aug 10   *Ahuliha* — less frequent storms, calmer days. Grain harvests are reaped.

Aug 11–Aug 23   *Maa* — generally calm. Harvesting continues.

Aug 24–Sep 6   *Fura* — isolated showers, usually dry with light north-westerly winds. Harvesting continues.

Sep 7–Sep 20   *Uthura* — strong north-westerly winds, isolated showers.

Sep 21–Oct 3   *Atha* — generally clear and calm with isolated showers.

Oct 4–Oct 17   *Hitha* — light winds, isolated showers.

Oct 18–Oct 30   *Hey* — strong winds from all directions. Fishing is excellent and the markets are filled with large tuna.

Nov 1–Nov 13   *Viha* — calm days. Fishing is good.

Nov 14–Nov 26   *Nora* — light winds, some sun showers. Sea currents are unsettled as the north-east monsoon approaches.

Nov 27–Dec 9   *Dosha* — light north-easterly winds. Good fishing.

In tourist jargon, the seasons are described as 'high' and 'low'. From November through to April, tourists flock to the islands to enjoy clear blue skies and tropical sunshine. From May until October, the weather can be temperamental — a mixed bag of sunshine, showers and storms — and tourist prices are slashed to entice visitors in spite of the weather.

Year round, the temperature rarely falls below 25°C, most often settling around 30°C. Annual rainfall is approximately 1750 mm.

	Jan	Feb	Mar	Apr	May	Jun	Jul	Aug	Sep	Oct	Nov	Dec
Min Temp (°C)	25.7	25.8	26.1	26.8	26.3	25.6	25.6	25.2	25.5	25.5	25.2	25.4
Max Temp (°C)	30.4	30.9	31.6	31.8	31.3	30.6	30.5	30.2	30.3	30.2	30.2	30.0
Rainfall (mm)	89.9	19.4	57.8	103.5	192.6	212.8	145.8	185.5	160.3	174.6	217.9	185.6
Sunshine (hrs)	243.9	266.7	292.8	265.2	221.0	199.6	215.5	205.9	222.5	239.6	218.5	216.9

Vegetation and fauna

Plants

On most islands, the vegetation is, on a small scale, much like that of lowland Sri Lanka — tropical rainforest with banyan, bamboo, screwpine, vines, herbs, mangroves and, of course, the ubiquitous coconut palm.

'Sparse' is a word that leaps to mind when one refers to vegetation in the Maldives. The coral substance of the islands and the saline conditions make survival for plants extremely difficult. The extent of vegetation on any given island depends largely on the age and size of the island, and on the degree of human habitation.

There are five categories of native vegetation throughout the archipelago, including 20 different species of grass and sedge that grow along the shorelines of the islands. The most common is the *Launaea sarmentosa* (known locally as *kulhlhafilaa*) with its rosettes of edible leaf. Beyond this is an extensive spread of shrubs and small pandanus trees. In well-drained areas, some trees grow up to 5 m high, eg the *Hibiscus tiliaceus* (*dhiggaa*) and the *Cordian subcordata* (*kaani*). Many of the larger islands have thick forests where *Hernandia nymphaeifolia* (*kandoo*) and *Terminalia cattappa* (*midhili*) are common. Where there are inland depressions, rich soil and brackish water give rise to mangrove and swamp forests. Hereabouts, the *Morinda citrifolia* (*ahi*) thrive, and long-leaf herbs grow in open clusters.

Only about five per cent of the land surface of the islands is suitable for arable farming. The major crops are finger millet and Italian millet, and sorghum is grown on a few islands. Fibre crops include sweet potato and taro, and garden crops of chilli, small onion, marrow, watermelon, pineapple and betel leaf are grown. Breadfruit is widespread, many households grow their own bananas, limes and areca nut, and arrowroot grows in sandy thickets on many islands.

Wildlife

The Maldives is not noted for its abundant wildlife. Geckos are found in most homes, searching for prey with large unblinking eyes. A colourful species of garden lizard is common to most islands — the male has a reddish head and yellow tail while the female is dull in colour. Skinks are rare and only two types of snake are known to exist, neither of which is poisonous. There are more than 67 species of butterfly. Common to many islands are a small scorpion with a nasty sting and a large centipede that bites with its front claws. Paper wasps and large armoured rhinoceros beetles are abundant.

Birds

There are more than 100 species of bird that have been sighted around the islands. About 20 of them are permanent residents, the rest are migratory.

The Indian house crow and the koel bird are most common — the crow is a pest, stealing fish, poultry, fruits and vegetables, while the koel bird (a member of the cuckoo family) is a nuisance, screeching and hooting from treetops in the early hours of the morning.

Seen everywhere around Kaafu Atoll is the small kestrel (a bird of prey) and the long-tailed rose-ringed parakeet, with red beak and green feathers. On densely vegetated islands, white-breasted waterhens are frequently sighted.

There are 13 different types of heron sitting on the Maldive reefs, waiting to swoop down and capture fish in their long sharp bills. The most common is the grey heron.

At least 15 species of seabird are resident in the Maldives and terns are common. Down in Seenu Atoll, graceful, pure-white fairy terns are seen swooping through the air in their hundreds, attacking any birds that are dark in colour. Local lore has it that they were imported by a Muslim priest to drive away the crows. Along the shoreline of Seenu, you often find dark noddy terns, lying dead or with wings broken from an attack by white terns.

Also common to these parts of the archipelago are the greater and lesser frigatebirds. These large black birds with long forked tails attack and hassle the terns until they are forced to drop the fish they have caught. Then, in a masterful aerobic display, they spiral down to catch the fish before they hit the surface of the water.

Throughout the archipelago, far out to sea, common and lesser noddy terns are found. When they appear in flocks it is a sure sign that there is a school of tuna nearby. Fishermen are forever on the lookout for them.

The most stunning of the seabirds is the tropic bird with its long streaming tail feathers.

Mammals

The only mammals endemic to the Maldives are two types of bat. Flying foxes are often seen on the large uninhabited islands and, in the early evenings, they fly around the islands, ravaging fruit crops and coconut trees.

Only three other species of mammal exist, all of which were introduced to the islands during their early settlement. The black rat and house mouse are everywhere, and the Indian house shrew is a visitor to many households around Male'.

Under the water

Well-travelled diving enthusiasts will tell you that the Maldives has some of the most superb reef systems in the world. It is home to 200 species of coral, 2000 species of fish and 5000 species of shell.

Stone corals are the backbone of the reef system; in sheltered waters you find delicate leaflike corals; white fan-shape corals grow perpendicular to the reef; and whip corals grow up to several metres a day.

Besides a variety of coral formations, the reef system also houses a great diversity of other creatures. Sponges, sea-squirts, starfish and molluscs are commonplace. The most distinctive creature is the banded coral shrimp which lives with a partner inside small crevices.

Under the water, the most fascinating life forms are the fishes. Sharks and moray eels are the most feared creatures, although neither attacks unless provoked. On some islands, deep-sea divers have trained schools of shark to be fed by hand, and even mouth to mouth. Lion fish and scorpion fish are to be admired and avoided — each has a row of poisonous spines along its back.

Among the most beautiful of all the reef fish are the tiny angel fish. Blue-lined snapper are often seen in large schools and parrotfish are striking with their bright colours and strong jaws. A medium-size parrotfish chews coral, passing it out as sand at the rate of one tonne per year. Little wonder there are so many sandy shorelines in the Maldives!

These islands are an ideal refuge for turtles, the hawksbill turtle being the most common. Between June and November, it is typical for female turtles to scurry ashore three or four times in order to nestle among shrubs and lay as many as 1000 eggs at a time. Only a small portion of these eggs ever hatch (turtle-egg pancakes are a local delicacy). Those turtles that do hatch from their eggs are lucky if they are able to escape sweeping terns on their way to the water.

As you travel through the archipelago, schools of dolphin and flying fish are common sights.

▬ Coral

The gardens of coral that decorate these shallow tropical waters are not, as they appear, plants. They are built up by aggregations of tiny tentacled animals called polyps, which battle through life against a host of enemies, including crustaceans, protozoans, reef fish, starfish and the human species.

Polyps need only three things to survive: food, oxygen and warmth. They feed happily on plankton, receive oxygen (up to 50 m below the surface) from the sun, and thrive in clear salty water where the temperature is between 20°C and 30°C.

Like other animals, polyps secrete and have sex, and herein lies the secret of the reef. After extracting the soluble calcium ions from the ocean, a polyp excretes a cup-shaped limestone skeleton, in much the same way as an oyster secretes its protective shell. This miniscule cup, produced by billions of polyps, accounts for the rocklike texture of the reef.

It is the fascinating process by which polyps reproduce that explains the variety of shapes, sizes and colours along the reef. As the new moon arrives during the winter months, and the full moon during the summer months, the polyps engage in sexual and asexual encounters, producing planula, or offspring, by the billions. Although many of them die as they are born, enough survive to perpetuate the species — and the reef. The survivors are washed to and fro by the ocean currents, then attach themselves to a solid foundation — a submerged volcano or a coastline — and secrete and reproduce, eventually forming a colony of polyps. Over a millenium, the colony grows larger and more complex, until a thin ribbon of reef runs parallel to the foundation.

The reef, or colony of polyps if you will, survives best on the seaward side. Elsewhere, particularly between the reef and the shore, the colonies die off due to lack of food, or under attack from lifelong enemies, such as parrotfish.

Ironically, it is the people whose lives depend on the protection of the reef who are the polyp's number one enemy. The renowned explorer, Jacques Cousteau, was alarmed when he discovered what the Maldivians were doing to their coral reefs. In *The Ocean World of Jacques Cousteau* he writes:

> 'Traditionally, the islanders built their houses of thatch but, as the modern world began to catch up with the islands, large buildings and roads had to be built and the only construction material available was that from the coral reef. Now the Maldivians harvest

the coral year round, using large chunks of it as building blocks. By destroying the fringing coral reefs, the Maldive people are unknowingly dooming their islands, and without a protective ring to shield the atolls from the pounding trade-wind waves, the islands must themselves disappear.'

If you care to conserve what has taken billions of years to create, think twice before being tempted to take a piece of the reef, however small, home as a souvenir.

Environmental update

The threat of sea-level rise and the fragility of the Maldives' marine environment became national issues in 1987, when unusually high waves struck the entire Maldive archipelago. The government forged an environmental management plan, called the National Action Plan, with the following as its objectives.

- Continuous assessment of the state of the environment.
- Development and implementation of management methods suited to the country's natural and social environments.
- Legislation of comprehensive national regulations and participation in international agreements, regarding the environment.
- The strengthening of institutional frameworks within the country and financial support from international organisations.

In 1989, the government initiated a Small States Conference in Male'. Representatives from small island nations were invited to discuss the changing global environment and, in particular, the overwhelming threat posed by rising sea-levels.

The conference called upon all nations to take immediate action to reduce their emissions of greenhouse gases, to enhance energy efficiency, and to install energy sources which were less harmful to the environment. They also appealed to the international community to embark on intensive afforestation and revegetation programs.

The Intergovernmental Panel on Climatic Change published its first assessment in August 1990, indicating that global sea-levels would rise by 20 cm by the year 2030, and by 1 m by the year 2100. The panel concluded by saying that increased concentrations of chlorofluorocarbons, carbon dioxide and other greenhouse gases in the atmosphere would cause the polar icecaps to melt, leading in turn to greater rises in sea-levels.

HISTORY

Information about the origins of the Maldivian people, or *Dhivehin* (islanders) as they prefer to be called, is a curious mixture of myth and fact. According to some observers, the islands were discovered by travellers who explored the world in reed ships. Thor Heyerdahl, renowned *Kon Tiki* explorer, visited the southern atolls and discovered a set of coral slabs bearing images and scripts which, he says, closely resemble artefacts from the ancient Indus Valley civilisation that thrived between 2500 BC and 1500 BC in modern-day Pakistan.

According to folklore, the Maldives was first colonised by an Indo-Aryan race between the fourth and fifth centuries BC. The late historian and former archaeologist with the Ceylon Civil Service, HCP Bell, recounts the legend in his definitive work, *The Maldive Islands: Monograph on the History, Archaeology and Epigraphy:*

> 'Once upon a time, when the Maldives was sparsely inhabited, a prince of royal birth, named Koimala Kalo, made a voyage with his wife, the daughter of the King of Serendip [modern-day Sri Lanka]. On reaching the Maldives their vessel was becalmed, so they rested a while at Rasgetheemu Island in North Maalhosmadulu [Raa] Atoll.

> Learning that their two visitors were of royal descent, the islanders invited them to remain. Koimala was later proclaimed King of Rasgetheemu.
>
> In the 12th century AD, Koimala and his wife travelled to Male' and settled there with the consent of the Giraavaru, the most powerful aboriginal tribe of Kaafu [Male'] Atoll.
>
> To Koimala and his Queen was born a son called Kalaminja. He reigned as a Buddhist for 12 years, then converted to Islam and ruled for 13 more years before finally departing for Mecca. Kalaminja's daughter married the Chief Minister and reigned as nominal Sultana. She gave birth to a son also called Kalaminja, who in turn married a lady of the country.
>
> From them the subsequent rulers of the Maldives were descended.'

Whatever truth lies behind this legend, one thing is certain: early settlers came via Sri Lanka and practised age-old Buddhist customs. Testimony to this is the modern-day language Dhivehi, which is akin to Elu, an archaic form of Sinhala (spoken in Sri Lanka). As well as this, the ancient Maldivian scripts, Eveyla Akuru (written on copper plates) and Dhives Akuru (found on tombstones, documents and boards), bear strong resemblances to a mediaeval Sinhala alphabet. And the *foi kakkan* (rice cooking) festival once celebrated by Maldivians on a particular full moon, in celebration of the first time rice was brought to the islands, is similar to the Sri Lankan commemoration of the attainment of Nirvana by Buddha. Finally, on a few islands there are hemispherical mounds of coral stone (stupas) from which Buddhist relics have been unearthed. The remains resemble similar monuments and relics of Buddhist saints found in the ancient Buddhist capitals of Sri Lanka.

Age-old navigational charts and travellers' tales suggest that the present-day population is descendant not only from an ancient Buddhist culture, but from a potpourri of cultures. Arab travellers, Dravidians and Aryans from India and slaves from Africa were all, at one time or another, part of early Maldivian settlement. HCP Bell visited the islands in 1888, 1920 and 1940 and subsequently published a copy of the *Tarikh*, the major chronicle of Maldivian history. It offers a brief account of life and times in the Maldives between AD 1153 and 1821. We begin to get a clearer picture when this book is complemented by travelogues penned by Ibn Batuta, who lived in the islands during the mid-14th century, and François Pyrard, a French sailor who spent five years in Male' after his ship was wrecked in 1602. More recently, Young and Christopher, two British naval officers, published their memoirs, giving us an insight into Maldivian customs and manners during the 19th century.

Aborigines

Not much is known about the aborigines who met Koimala and his wife nearly 2000 years ago. The small surviving community of aboriginal people found in Male' Atoll today, known as the Giraavaru, claim they are the descendants of a South Indian Tamil tribe. They also say that they were once the most powerful community in the Maldives. To this day, they maintain a unique identity. A Giraavaru woman, for example, wears her hair in a bun on the left side of her head (other Maldivian women wear their buns on the right) and Giraavaru women wear dresses with distinctive, white, neck embroidery.

Arabs

The most profound impact on the history and culture of the Maldives came from Arab travellers. As early as the ninth century, Arabs had spread their influence and knowledge across the Asian mainland. The Maldives (or Dibajat as it was known to them) was a popular stopover en route to other ports of call. Here they replenished their water supplies, bought dried fish and coconuts, and even enjoyed 'temporary wives'. Ibn Batuta said it was the most agreeable society he had ever seen (and he had visited 92 countries). He wrote, 'Any newcomer could marry if he so desired, then on leaving simply repudiate his wife.' The Maldives' greatest attraction in those days was a small white mollusc, the cowrie shell, which clung to driftwood and lay along the island shores. Used as local currency, cowrie shells could also buy slaves in Africa and sacks of rice from India. Needless to say, the Arabs collected cowries by the boatloads.

An outstanding milestone in Arab–Maldivian relations occurred in AD 1153, when the Maldivian people converted to Islam. Legend tells us that Abu al-Barakat, a pious saint, arrived in the Maldives and discovered, '... a colony of ignorant idolaters ... ' At this time, the people believed there was a spirit in the sea which rose each month to molest and murder a virgin girl. On hearing this, al-Barakat proceeded to exorcise the spirit, thereby earning the confidence of the King. Thereafter, everyone was instructed to practise al-Barakat's faith — Islam. Maldivian doors were flung open, and Arabs from afar were welcomed with much pomp and esteem. Some were elected as sultans, many others became judges.

Ali Rajas and Portuguese

Until the turn of the 15th century, trade between the Maldives and the outside world rested solely with Muslim merchants on the south-west coast of India. They were known as the 'sea kings' — the Ali Rajas of Cannanore. So widespread was their influence that they became affectionately known as the 'lords of the Maldive Islands'.

During the early 16th century, powerful Portuguese forces began demanding shares in all the lucrative Indian Ocean trade routes. A successful coup d'etat, and the reinstatement of Kalu Mohammed to the throne, ensured the Portugese excessive liberties in the island kingdom. Mohammed, who quickly gained a reputation as a heartless and deceitful tyrant, permitted the Portuguese to build a factory and a fort in Male' Another sultan, Sultan Hasan IX, later invited the Portuguese to take complete control of the islands. The people revolted and fought vehemently for a number of years before succumbing to the Portuguese infidels in 1558. For the next 17 years, the sea grew red with Muslim blood as the Portugese enforced their Christian beliefs upon the islanders.

Each year, on the first day of the third month of the Islamic calendar, Maldivians commemorate the overthrow of the Portugese. In 1573, Mohammed Thakurufaanu, Chief of Utheemu, an island to the far north, led a small band of men into Male' harbour. In the pitch-black stillness of the night, they silently searched for and slaughtered their enemy. Following several aborted attempts to regain control, the Portuguese finally acquiesced and allowed the Maldivians their independence. They did insist, however, that they retain sole trading rights to and from the islands, and demanded an annual pension for Hasan IX, the so-called 'Christian King'. Thakurufaanu was made Sultan and reigned for the next 12 years. He remains a national hero to this day.

By the turn of the 16th century, the Portugese were no longer a feared adversary, so the Sultan ended their tributes and trade monopoly. He established diplomatic relations with the Dutch Governor in Sri Lanka and began trading cowrie shells for spices, areca nut and ammunition. Meanwhile, the Ali Rajas were reforming and still had a keen eye on the Maldives. In 1782, they attacked Male' in retaliation to the Sultan's takeover of Minicoy, part of modern-day Lakshadweep. The Ali Rajas succeeded in destroying the palace, kidnapping the Sultan and taking control of the government. But their victory was short-lived. Within months, a local uprising, aided by a fleet of French ships, ousted the Ali Rajas from power.

British and Borahs

In 1796, the Dutch ceded Sri Lanka to the British. A regular trade route was soon established between Colombo and Male', and the Maldives thrived. By the mid-1800s, however, the somnolent, spendthrift sultan of the time took the Maldives to the brink of bankruptcy. The government was forced, in 1860, to invite Borah merchants from India to set up godowns and shops in Male'. Almost overnight, these astute businessmen captured a monopoly on the import–export trade and before long became the financiers of many government projects.

Word spread far and wide that the Borahs would soon rule the islands. Demonstrations erupted and shops and warehouses were burnt to the ground. Sensing the danger, the British Governor signed a treaty ensuring the Maldivians their independence — for a price. In 1887, the Maldives became a British protectorate.

The Sultanate

Although the Maldives did not have a written constitution until 1932, it has always had a well-defined system of adminstration. Ancient documents refer to methods of taxation, national defence, the discharge of public duties and the administration of justice.

After conversion to Islam, the Sultanate lasted from 1153 to 1968, except for a 15-year interlude of Portuguese rule and a brief period of Presidential rule in 1953. It was more or less a constitutional monarchy, with its rulers adhering to and following the examples set by their predecessors (who always abided by a wide range of customs and conventions that had long been regarded as the unwritten laws of the land). Their actions were constantly reviewed by councils of advisors. There were 93 such rulers — 89 sultans and four sultanas.

The Raskamuge Is Majlis was the first advisory council. It included the Sultan/Sultana, their most trusted advisors (friends and immediate family) and the Chief Justice.

The second council was known as Raskamuge Dhevana Majlis and comprised the Chief Justice, trusted advisors, the leaders of the four Male' suburbs, and nine officials appointed personally by the Sultan/Sultana. The most influential official was the Hadhegiri, who was responsible for atoll administration.

Raskamuge Thinvana Majlis was the third council of the realm. It consisted of the members of the first and second councils and nine security guards known as Edhuru Beykalun, five of whom were exponents of martial arts and the rest being gunners.

During the course of the Sultanate there were six dynasties. The first was known as the Kalaminja Dynasty, but the longest reigning was the Theemuge Dynasty, which ruled for 169 years and three months under 16 sultans.

Ceremonial parades were commonplace and members of the royal entourage were resplendent in magnificent clothing, gold ornamentation, silk scarves and turbans. Wherever they went, they were preceded by elephants, banners and trumpets. The royal family lived in a beautiful two-storey teak palace which had a copper roof, two audience halls and an indoor swimming pool.

THE 20TH CENTURY

Twentieth-century Maldives has been battered, soothed and shaped by time and nature, coups and constitutions, sultans and presidents. The following occurrences were among the most significant to take place during this century.

1900 The Sultanate was in debt to Carimjee Jaferjee and Company, the most successful Borah merchants in the Maldives. Political factions emerged and Sultan Mohammed Imaduddeen VI sacked his Prime Minister, Ibrahim Didi.

1902 Imaduddeen left for Cairo in search of a wife (an Egyptian lady of high standing). Meanwhile, a revolution brewed at home.

1903 The British sent an envoy to investigate rumours of injustice, oppression, misanthropy and misrule levelled at Imaduddeen.

1904 The British Governor recognised Mohammed Shamshuddeen III as the new Sultan, despite protestations from Imaduddeen and his friends.

1905 Imaduddeen made several attempts to regain control of the Sultanate, with assistance from Indian pirates.
Also this year, Lloyds of London questioned the age-old Maldivian salvage law which claimed that the salvaged goods from any ship wrecked in the Maldives and left unmanned shall be the property of the government.

1906 Shamshuddeen opened the first post office and a regular mail service to Colombo began.

1917 A British seaplane crashed in the central atolls.
A German warship lurked in the southern atolls.

1920 Shamshuddeen was awarded the Most Distinguished Order of Saint Michael and Saint George.

1922 An epidemic swept through Male', causing over 300 deaths. It was known as 'Maldive fever' and was, in fact, cholera.

1923 A storm devastated many islands to the north of the archipelago.

1924 Imaduddeen's son, Abd-Allah, was soon deported when the Secret Service unearthed his plot to overthrow the government.

1932 Shamshuddeen was forced to accept a constitution that would limit his power. The first-ever written constitution in the Maldives was created.

1934 Shamshuddeen was sacked for attempting to sidestep the constitution. Nuruddeen took the throne.

1939 The constitution was discarded as being unsuited to local conditions.

1942 A second constitution was drawn up.

1943 Nuruddeen was forced to abdicate. He was considered to be incompatible with the constitution. Abdul Majeed Didi was elected Sultan number 93, but he was already old and soon retired. Mohammed Amin Didi, the Prime Minister, assumed control of the government. He was energetic and ambitious, banning smoking and introducing a modernisation program, a national security service and a government monopoly on the export of fish.

1948 A mutual defence pact was signed with the British.

'You sound like you're in the next room'

Telephone conversations as clear as a bell despite a 72,450-kilometre journey through space—that's the miracle of modern communications. And that's the business of Dhiraagu, the communications lifeline of the Maldives.

We provide telephone, telex and facsimile services to all parts of the world through the Maldives Earth Station. Global communication with international standards of service and quality.

Dhiraagu provides specialist services to improve and expand telecommunications of every kind: public and private, national and international, local and mobile.

DHIRAAGU
THE MALDIVES TELECOMS COMPANY

19 Medhuziyaaraiy Magu, Male' 20-03, Republic of Maldives.
Telephone: +960 322802 Facsimile: +960 322800 Telex: +896 77022

The easy pace of island life

Kaafu Atoll

Take home more than just a memory

For fine quality mementos of your stay, visit Najaah Artpalace, the largest one-stop centre for genuine, traditional and contemporary Maldivian handicrafts and souvenirs. All at one convenient location in Male'.

You'll be pleasantly surprised by our friendly and attentive service as you shop in the comfort of our fully air-conditioned showroom.

Najaah ARTPALACE

MHA Building
1st and Ground Floor,
Orchid Magu, Male'
Republic of Maldives
Telephone: (960)
322372/314171/322481
Facsimile: (960) 313035

1953 The Sultanate was abolished, the Maldives became a republic and Mohammed Amin Didi was elected President. Food shortages and the ban on smoking incurred the wrath of the people. Didi was attacked and arrested. He died on 7 March. The Republic was abolished and the constitution discarded.

1954 Mohammed Farid Didi, son of Abdul Majeed Didi (the 92nd sultan), was elected Sultan.

1955 On 9 January, a storm destroyed villages in the north.

1956 An agreement was drafted with the British, giving them a 100-year lease of Gan in the south, for £2000 a year. They began developing an RAF staging post and employed hundreds of locals as labourers, storekeepers and kitchen hands.

1957 Ibrahim Nasir was elected Prime Minister. He revoked the 1956 agreement with the British and insisted the lease be shortened, the rental increased and all local employees sacked.

1959 Inhabitants of the three southernmost atolls protested that the Male' government had reduced them to serfs. They formed the United Suvadive Islands. Abdulla Afif Didi was elected President, a people's council was formed, a trading corporation established and a bank founded. Their demands were published in the international press.

1960 Rumour spread that the British were behind this situation in the Maldives. To temper suspicion, the British formalised the lease of Gan. The new terms included a 30-year period of lease, £100,000 annual rental, a grant of £750,000 for general development and a new, fully equipped hospital in Male'. Nasir then sent armed men in launches to attack the southern atolls. Didi fled to the Seychelles, the United Suvadive Islands was leaderless and finally quashed.

1965 On 26 July, the British relinquished all protectorate status. The Maldives became independent and joined the United Nations.

1968 The Sultan was encouraged to retire to Colombo with a royal pension. On 11 November, Ibrahim Nasir was elected President of the Second Republic.

1972 The constitution was amended to give Nasir far-reaching powers. He opened his own hotel and travel agency, and the idea to promote the Maldives as a tropical paradise was launched. Nearly 1000 tourists arrived in this year.

1974 On Thursday 24 June, a large crowd gathered to protest about escalating food prices. Nasir retaliated by ordering the police to open fire. The revolt became known locally as 'Little Troubles Thursday' and represented the first popular uprising against Nasir's regime.

1975 Ahmed Zaki was elected to a second term as Prime Minister. Rumours spread that a no-confidence motion against Nasir was in the offing. Zaki was banished to a faraway island and the event became popularly known as 'Big Troubles Thursday'.

1978 Nasir retired, ostensibly for health reasons, and left the Maldives to live in Singapore. On 11 November, Maumoon Abdul Gayyoom, the third Maldivian ambassador to the United Nations, was elected President.

1979 Many people stood trial for corruption under the former regime. Some former ministers and affluent business people were placed under house arrest and others were banished to faraway islands.

1980 A coup against the government was aborted and two British mercenaries were deported. Many locals were arrested and some of them were banished.

1981 Gayyoom began a new style of government, broadening international contacts and introducing innovative development programs. The first regional hospital was opened on Kulhudhuffushi, in the northernmost atoll. An indoor sports stadium was built in Male', an international airport was opened on Hulhule, and domestic flights began to the southernmost atolls. The government also took control of the Japanese fish canning factory in Lhaviyani Atoll and invited foreign investors to open garment factories on Gan.

1982 By the end of 1982, the Maldives had extended its diplomatic ties to more than 50 countries and its membership to 22 international organisations. A cultural treaty was signed with Libya and a trade agreement with Sri Lanka, support was proclaimed for the Palestinian cause, and the Maldives was made a special member of the Commonwealth of Nations.

1983 In August, a feeble attempt was made to depose Gayyoom. In November, he was elected to a second term as President.

1984 The frequency of chartered and scheduled flights to the Maldives was increased to accommodate the ever increasing flow of tourists.

1985 On 1 October, delegates from nearly 50 countries attended the meeting of Commonwealth Finance Ministers at Club Med, on Farukolufushi.

1986 On 23 May, *Dheenuge Magu*, a weekly religious newspaper edited by Maumoon Abdul Gayyoom, was launched.
In August, a Taiwanese fishing boat was impounded and the owners fined $US1.25 million for illegally fishing in Maldivian territorial waters.
In September, Gayyoom opened the first national scouts' jamboree.

1987 A soap factory was installed in Male' and a school for hotel and catering services was declared open on 22 April.
Emirates Airlines began scheduled flights from Dubai to Male' on 27 June.
High waves devastated one-quarter of the capital island, Male', washing away nearly one-third of the reclaimed land. In April, the Maldives registered its highest-ever sea-level.

1988 The Speaker of the Citizen's Majlis, Ibrahim Shihab, died on 14 January.
On 4 May, heavy seas flooded parts of Male'. In June, strong winds destroyed houses in the southern atolls.
On 23 September, Maumoon Abdul Gayyoom was elected to his third consecutive term as President.
On 3 November, a group of 68 Sri Lankan mercenaries attempted to overthrow the government. They killed 19 people, took hostages and escaped aboard two vessels. With the assistance of Indian troops, the National Security Service apprehended the mercenaries two days later.

1989 In January, the Department of Women's Affairs was created and, for the first time in Maldivian history, women were recruited to the National Security Service.
The trial of the Sri Lankan mercenaries and Maldivians involved in the 1988 coup attempt began on 16 March. In August, four Maldivians and two Sri Lankans were sentenced to death (later commuted to life imprisonment), while others were extradited or sentenced to jail terms ranging from 11 years to 38 years.

1990 On 8 April, a cyclone destroyed homes and boats and injured four people on Iguraidhoo in Raa Atoll.

The fifth SAARC (South Asian Association for Regional Cooperation) summit was held in Male'.
The Maldivian people celebrated their 25th anniversary of independence with parades, singing, dancing and colourful festivities.

1991 On 9 January, the *Banglar Kakolhi*, a Bangladeshi cargo ship, ran aground off Male'.
During the last week of May, severe storms devastated the islands, leaving more than 20,000 people homeless.
In October, the Esjehi Gallery was opened in Male' to promote Maldivian art.

1992 The National Security Service celebrated its centenary.
Also this year, the Department of Women's Affairs established women's centres in the outer atolls, in order to improve the economic well-being of women.
In April, the government of Saudi Arabia presented 14,290 copies of the *Quran* to the Maldives Ministry of Education.

1993 Maldives celebrated the 25th anniversary of its Second Republic, formed on 11 November, 1968.
President Maumoon Abdul Gayyoom was elected for a fourth term of office as President of the Republic.
A fourth regional airport was opened at Kaadehdhoo in Gaafu Dhaalu Atoll.

1994 Police arrested Abdulla Rasheed, a Maldive national, when he was caught attempting to smuggle 289,800 counterfeit US dollars into the country.

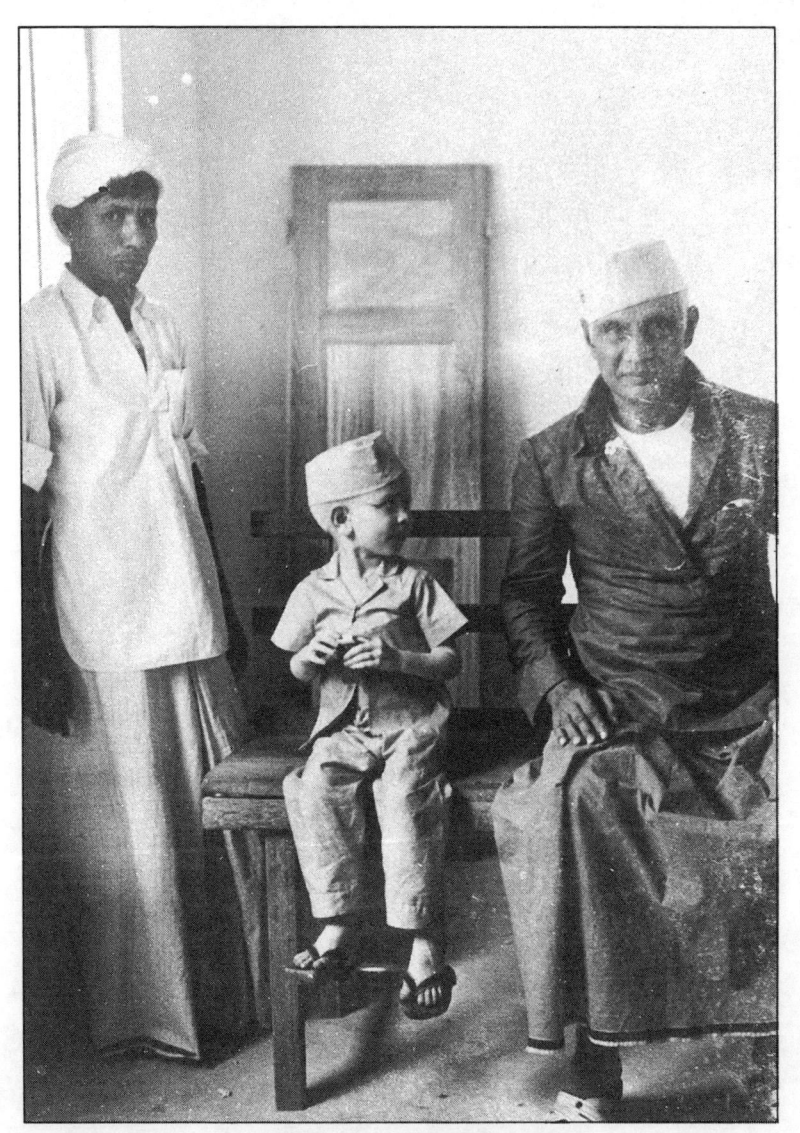

Sultan Mohammed Farid I and his son

Removing the husks from grain

ISLAND LIFE

People 42
Government 63
Economy 65
Food 67
Language 70

PEOPLE

Honest and pious, sincere and strong-willed.
Ibn Batuta

Quick and apprehensive, subtle and crafty.
François Pyrard

Sober, honest and cheerful.
C W Rosset

Constructive and ordered.
Dr Campbell

Quiet, peaceable, hospitable and kind, but suspicious of strangers.
Young and Christopher

With a total population of around 238,363, the Maldives is the smallest independent nation in Asia. An average per capita income of $US684 a year makes it one of the poorest nations in the world. Astonishingly, however, the grinding poverty found in other parts of Asia is rarely seen on these islands. Beggars are a rarity. According to HCP Bell, '… the people desire nothing so greatly as to be left by the outside world, as much as possible, alone and undisturbed in their sea-girt happy isolation …'

The majority of Maldivians live their lives on tiny islands where interaction is limited to a few hundred fellow islanders. To this day, the *dhon meehuu* (white person) is often regarded with fear and suspicion on the far-flung islands where tourists rarely go. So don't be surprised if you are met there by screeching children, women in flight, and cold, pensive stares from the menfolk. But human nature is paradoxical and the Maldivian people can be as bold as they are shy, as knowledgeable as they are naive, and as hospitable as they are hesitant. To accept and be accepted by this small, closely knit, rigidly structured and disciplined society demands a fundamental appreciation of the politics, beliefs and customs of its people.

Social classes

It was once considered dishonourable to eat with a member of an inferior class or to be seated physically higher than someone from a superior class. The superior class were the *beyfulhu*, made up of sultans and their relatives. They bore titles, such as 'Maniku' and 'Didi', and prohibited anyone without a permit to wear shoes, buy a flashlight, erect a fence around their house or study a foreign language. Nowadays, things are a lot different. 'More civilised,' Bell would say. Maniku and Didi are popular surnames and 'Kalegefaanu' is the most coveted title. Something of a knighthood, it is bestowed on only a handful of people, including the President and those who render outstanding services to the community.

While a caste system does not operate now, the texture of Maldivian society shows its effects. The most overt form of social distance today is found in the language. Different words and phrases are used according to whom one speaks. For example, if referring to yourself when speaking to a fisherman, you would say *aharen* (I), but to a government official you would say *alhugandu* (slave self).

Traditionally, the population is socially ranked according to job status. Fishermen occupy the largest peer group, making up almost 50 per cent of the total work force. The captain of a fishing crew, the *keyolhu*, earns one fifth of the catch and that may equate to 1000 fish on a good day. Carpenters are highly respected and the best carpenters are found in Raa Atoll, where they are renowned for their boat-building skills. On the same social rung are the *hakeem* (local medicine men and astrologers) who are held in high esteem. Throughout the country, there are many such men who are considered to possess mysterious powers. They combine traditional herbal remedies with Unani (Arabic) philosophy to treat their patients.

In a class of their own are the *raaveri*, the men who tap the coconut trees for sap. They cook the sap for several hours, until it forms a delicious creamy honey, and then sell it for a pittance.

Social status today is greatly influenced by wealth and education. Those with prominent government positions earn instant respect, as do those who run successful businesses and own multi-storey homes and offices.

Marriage and divorce

Years ago, it was a mark of pride and piety for a man to be married many times, especially if he had four wives at any one time. Few men today, however, are wealthy enough to support more than one wife. It is not uncommon to find that those who have been married 10 or 20 times have often divorced and remarried the same partners. There is a man in Male', for example, who has been married 89 times!

The Maldives has the highest divorce rate in the United Nations (eight out of 10 people have been divorced at least once). A man can divorce simply by saying, 'I divorce you' and then reporting the matter to a local judge. Women are more restricted and can initiate divorce only on the grounds of cruelty, desertion or adultery. If a husband refuses to divorce his wife, she must apply to the Ministry of Justice and Islamic Affairs to divorce him. For three months after a divorce, a woman cannot marry another man other than her immediate ex-husband. During this three-month period, the ex-husband must support his ex-wife and she must live somewhere agreeable to him.

It is hardly surprising, then, that a marriage ceremony is a simple affair. Officials from the Ministry of Justice and Islamic Affairs perform the marriage ceremony. In addition to the bride and groom, the fathers or guardians of the couple are present as well as two witnesses chosen by the groom.

Women

Since the Maldives became a Muslim nation, four queens have ruled, the last one in the early 16th century.

In Maldivian society, the woman has the greater influence on major family decisions, although the man is literally the head of the house and has the final voice. A woman maintains her maiden name after marriage and does not adopt her husband's name. A married woman can acquire land, property or business, manage it in her own name and dispose of it at will.

In the distribution of family property, women inherit smaller shares than their male counterparts. Under the existing system, a son receives half the property while a daughter inherits one-quarter. This is generally accepted because, according to Islamic law, men are responsible for supporting women and hence are entitled to a larger share.

After a divorce, however, a woman is given half of all the property jointly owned with her husband as well as any property acquired through her own efforts. After the death of her husband, a widow is entitled by law to one-eighth of his property.

Husking bimbi

Religion

For the past 800 years, Islam has been the backbone of Maldivian society. A non-Muslim is regarded as a non-believer and can never marry into Maldivian society nor become a Maldivian citizen.

From an early age, every child is taught the Arabic alphabet. By the age of five or six, most children are able to chant verses from the *Quran*. Until their mid-teens, children attend a local *makthab* (school), where they receive lessons on Arabic and Islam from an island chief. An affluent few attend an Atoll Community School or the English-medium schools in Male', where Islam is studied in depth.

The Maldivian people are moderate rather than fanatical Muslims. They belong to the largest Islamic sect, the Sunni sect, and practice the liberal Shafi'i rite. Unlike other Muslim communities, the women do not observe purdah and criminals are treated leniently (the most brutal form of punishment is a light flogging with a taut leather strap). For a brief period in the 1950s, thieves did have their hands cut off, but nowadays it is more common to be placed under house-arrest or to be banished to a faraway island, exiled from family and friends.

Everyone generally adheres to the basic obligations of Islam, namely:

- repeat the creed—*La ilaha illa Allah; Mohammed rasul Allah* (There is no God but Allah; Mohammed is the messenger of Allah)
- pray five times a day
- fast for a month every year
- give donations to the poor (*zakaath*)
- make the pilgrimage to Mecca at least once (if they can afford it).

Every village has at least two mosques, one for the men and one for the women. Some mosques are new while others are centuries old; some are made of coral, others of thatch. All are meticulously cleaned and cared for by the local muezzin, who summon the people to prayer at dawn, midday, mid-afternoon, sunset and nightfall. Attendances at the mosques are usually quite small as people often pray at home or on board their *dhoni* (fishing boats). Fridays are special days at all mosques— men and young boys in crisp white sarongs and shirts head off to their local mosques for the main midday prayer.

Most families conduct religious ceremonies, such as a *maaloodh* or *salavaath*, in their homes. When a child is born, 'prayer callers' are summoned to recite some lengthy *maaloodh* from Muslim lore; and many families employ those well versed in the Islamic scriptures to chant regular *salavaath* (religious lectures) to ensure their homes remain free of evil spirits.

Some outer islanders believe evil spirits inhabit the sea, the sky, the bushes, and the tops of houses and trees. They lock their doors and windows at night, and leave small kerosene lamps burning to keep out demons.

The everyday beliefs and ideals of the Maldivian people, however, are governed by the Islamic scriptures, whereas superstitions and extraordinary events tend to be explained and treated by *fanditha*, a type of religious magic which has evolved from an earlier culture. Most Maldivians don't regard *fanditha* as being contrary to Islam, preferring to believe that it is a blessing from Allah. When the fish are not biting or the crops won't grow, when someone is sick or they want a particular person to love them, they look to *fanditha*. Nearly every village has someone trained in the art and, while black magic is prohibited, there are *fanditha* men who have been banished or placed under house arrest for performing it.

Islam

Islam is the youngest, one of the largest and the fastest growing of the world's great religions. It has one-third of a billion adherents, called Muslims, who believe that there is only one God, Allah, whose final and most complete revelation was given to Prophet Mohammed.

Born around AD 570, Mohammed lived in the rich and pagan city of Mecca. He worked hard, was honest, and everyone trusted him. But Mohammed worried about the fate of his people as all around him he saw false gods being worshipped. He used to go up into the hills to a special cave where he prayed and meditated. One night he was in the cave, a voice spoke to him and asked him to read. Terrified, Mohammed revealed to the voice that he could not read. The voice then asked him to repeat the following words:

> *Proclaim, in the name of the Lord and cherisher,*
> *Who created man out of a clot of congealed blood.*
> *Proclaim, and thy Lord is most bountiful.*
> *He who taught how to use the pen,*
> *Taught man that which he did not know.*

The voice revealed itself as the Angel Gabriel, sent by God to give the world the *Quran*. Mohammed was to be the pen which wrote down the words of God for all to read.

When Mohammed came to the citizens of Mecca, telling them of all that the Angel Gabriel had told him, he found many people who believed him and many who opposed him. The aged and the rich made their livelihoods from the idols and images that decorated the Kaaba, the huge wall that had been built to protect the sacred black stone, believed to have fallen from heaven in the days of Adam and Eve. Nevertheless, Mohammed continued to spread the word, until he was forced to flee, in AD 622, to Medina.

When he arrived in Medina, Mohammed found a divided and feuding city. Slowly, he enhanced his wealth and influence and brought order to the city. In AD 630, he led 10,000 followers to Mecca, destroyed the idols and images on the Kaaba, abolished all pagan festivals and became the leader of the Arabian people. Following his death in AD 632, God's revelations to Mohammed became the scriptures of Islam, the *Quran*, and some of his notable sayings comprised the *hadith*.

As Islam spread across several nations, there developed variations in certain beliefs and practices. Broadly speaking, two sects evolved. Eighty-five per cent of all Muslims attempt to follow the path of their religion as laid down by the Prophet and his first four successors, the 'orthodox caliphs'. These Muslims are known as traditionalists, or Sunnis. A large minority of Muslims, however, maintain that the real leaders of Islam are the 12 descendants of Ali, the Prophet's son-in-law and the last of the orthodox caliphs. Ali disappeared in AD 878 and the 'partisans of Ali', the Shi'ites, believe that some day he will return to lead Islam into a golden age. Hence the popularity of such people as the late Ayatollah Komeini.

The Sunni sect, in turn, embraces four schools of thought. The most conservative are the Hanabalites of Saudi Arabia, who interpret the *Quran* literally. More tolerant are the Muslims in Upper Egypt and Syria, known widely as the Malikites. Those in the Maldives, India, Indonesia, Lower Egypt and Syria are called Shafi'ites. They believe that some form of judicial consideration is a necessary and valid addition to the *Quran*. The most liberal of all Muslims are found in parts of western Asia, India and Lower Egypt, and are known as Hanifites.

Arts and crafts

The historical and cultural links with both South Asian and Arabian countries is apparent in many aspects of Maldivian art. These influences have combined with the indigenous culture to make the sophisticated, distinctive and unique art and craft styles of the Maldives.

One of the most interesting features of traditional Maldivian society is the confinement of certain specialised skills to particular atolls or islands. As François Pyrard noted in his 17th century travelogue, 'The craftsmen are collected on different isles—the weavers on one, the goldsmiths, the blacksmiths, the locksmiths, the potters, the turners and the carpenters on others. In short, craftsmen do not mingle together. Each craft has a separate island.'

To some extent, Pyrard's observation holds true today, although an increasing number of artisans have been drawn to Male'. Jewellers, once confined to Dhaalu Atoll, are now found throughout the archipelago. Lacquer workers still ply their craft in Baa Atoll, although a handful have also been active in Male' for some time. Most weaving is still practised almost exclusively in Gaafu Dhaalu Atoll, largely because the rushes from which the mats are made thrive best there.

Some traditional skills, such as lace making and cloth weaving, have been unable to compete with imported mass-produced products and may soon disappear altogether. Others, such as stone carving and metal work, have declined but continue to survive. Still others, most notably lacquer work, have been given a new lease of life by the growing tourist trade. Even mat weaving in Gaafu Dhaalu Atoll, the most resilient and successful of the indigenous crafts, has been modified to some extent by the importation of chemical dyes and the impact of tourism.

Mats

The best mats have traditionally been made on Gadhdhoo, a small island in the south-east corner of Gaafu Dhaalu Atoll. The rush used to weave the fine mats is called *hau* and grows profusely on Fiyou, a nearby uninhabited island. The entire production process is carried out exclusively by women.

After the *hau* has been harvested, it is collected in small bundles and left to dry. It is then coloured (black, dark brown, yellow and cream), predominantly using natural dyes, then trimmed to the desired lengths (long strips for sleeping mats, short strips for prayer mats). The strips are tightly woven on a horizontal loom and the finished product, called a *thundu kunaa*, is beautifully smooth on the upper surface. They are decorated with geometrical designs of varying complexity, as Maldivians believe that angels will not enter a house which contains pictures.

Lacquer work

There are many skilled workers who produce superb lacquered wooden items. The craftsmen on Thulaadhoo, in Baa Atoll, are among the best lacquer workers in the country and they are able to command high prices for their most outstanding pots

Resort entertainment

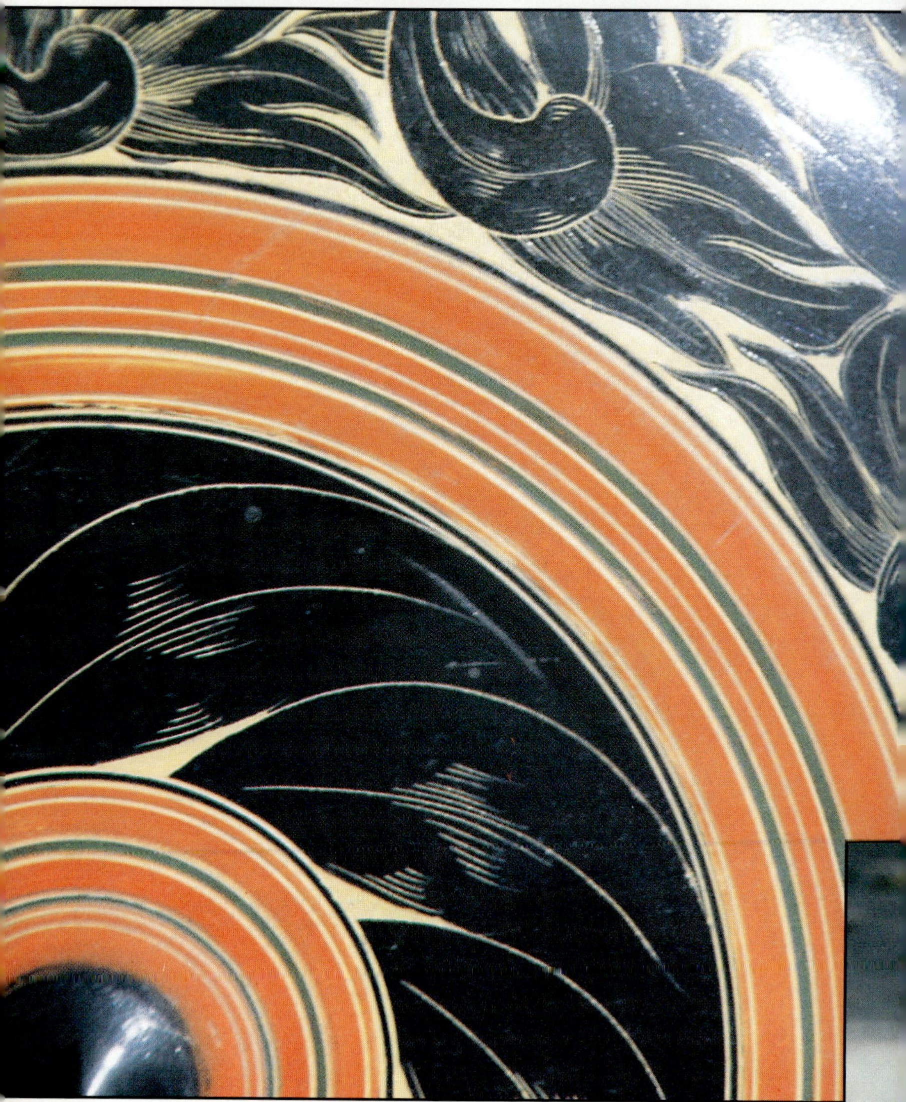

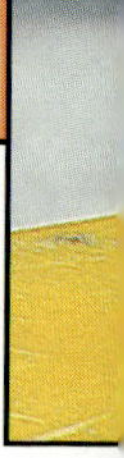

A HUGE RANGE OF DUTY-FREE, FREE OF HUSTLE AND BUSTLE

The very latest hi-fi systems, video cameras,
French perfumes, and exotic silks and cottons from India...
Tax Free Aero Boutique offers the same huge range of goods
you'll find in Singapore. But without the hassle.
And you won't find our exclusively packaged
Ceylon teas and souvenirs anywhere else.
So don't struggle with crowds when you can
shop in a tax-free paradise!

Tax Free Aero Boutique
Male' International Airport
Telephone: (960) 313187 Facsimile: (960) 323863

DIVE INTO THE ACTION!

*A*t *Kandooma Tourist Resort, the crystal clear lagoon is teeming with life. But diving and snorkeling amidst exotic marine life is only one way to enjoy our island retreat. You might also take pleasure from a touch of tennis, volleyball, windsurfing or waterskiing. And there's always the charm of our beach barbeques and cosmopolitan buffets. Bask in the comfort of your own beachfront air-conditioned chalet—tomorrow is another day!*

TALK TO YOUR TRAVEL AGENT.

Kandooma Tourist Resort

Telephone: (960) 444452/323360   Facsimile: (960) 445948/326880
Telex: (896) 77073 KANDOO MF

and boxes (some of their large wooden boxes sell for Rf1000 or more). Each piece is lacquered in strands of red, black and yellow, and abstract sketches are lightly carved into the black strands. Most Maldivian families own large *maaloodh foshi*, beautiful lacquer-work boxes used to store family feasts during religious ceremonies.

Jewellery

Since way back in the days of the early sultans, the Maldives has been known for its fine goldsmiths and silversmiths. Back then, jewellers used treasure from shipwrecks to make bracelets, armlets, belts and chains, mainly for the nobility. Today, the gold and silver is imported but the work remains as fine as it ever was, particularly among the handful of jewellers on Ribudhoo and Hulhudeli in Dhaalu Atoll. Not many valuable items of adornment are worn by the Maldivians themselves, although you occasionally see women with necklaces of gold coins, as were worn in Ibn Batuta's time, and there is a demand for finger rings, bangles, necklaces and *fanditha* cases.

Since the advent of tourism, the jewellery industry has grown. Young locals free dive to great depths in order to collect black coral, mother-of-pearl, sea-shells and turtles for the jewellery trade. The tourist shops in Male' are literally dripping with coral earrings, mother-of-pearl necklaces, turtle-shell bangles and the like. Women and young children are employed to grind down the shells and coral and then the men set them in silver or gold surrounds. The bejewelled daggers made from mother-of-pearl are superb, as are the miniature dhoni carved out of black coral.

The government is aware of the adverse effects on the environment if this cottage industry proceeds out of hand. It is now illegal to capture and kill turtles under a certain size. You only need to witness the tragic slaughter of one busy little bald-headed turtle to be turned off turtle-shell jewellery forever.

Music and dance

The most popular Maldivian dance involves the men swinging their arms and legs in gay abandon to the rhythmic beat of a *bodu beru*, a local drum. When the beat reaches a crescendo, the dancers fling themselves into a frenzy, some even going into a trance.

The *thaara* (Dhivehi for 'tambourine'), was introduced to the Maldives by Gulf Arabs in the 17th century. It is performed by about 22 people seated in two parallel rows, facing each other. It was originally played in the fulfillment of vows and was accompanied, on special occasions, by a pseudo act called *wajid*. At the height of their hysteria, dancers would poke their skulls repeatedly with iron spikes until blood ran. This part of the *thaara* is now banned but the singing and dancing are still popular forms of entertainment.

The most popular dance for women is the *bandiyaa jehun*. A small group of women swing their bodies in formation as they tap out a beat on their metal water pots. A similar dance is the *dhandi jehun*, in which either men or women move to a rhythm while tapping sticks.

Gaa odi lava is music and dance which expresses the satisfaction of a group of people on completion of a shared task which has involved strenuous manual labour.

The *langiri* is a dance accompanied by music and performed by young men as an evening stage show. Each dancer holds two sticks (*langiri dhandi*) decorated with colourful artificial flowers at one end. The performers sit in two rows of 12 or six and, as they sing, sway their bodies while tapping the *langiri dhandi* in different styles. Each dancer hits six *langiri dhandi* belonging to his three neighbours sitting in the front row. Dating back to the early 20th century, it is a modified version of the *thaara*.

Bolimalaafath neshun is a dance performed exclusively by women. It reflects the past tradition of women offering gifts to the sultans on special occasions. Around 24 women, dressed in colourful local dresses which have been fumigated by burning incense, sing songs to express sentiments or national themes.

The movements for *maafathi neshun* are similar to *langiri* but the performers are all women, dressed in national dress. It is a group dance performed in two rows of ten. Each woman dances with a piece of string to which artifical flowers have been attached. The women dance in small rows or groups of two or three, displaying different symbols. The dance is accompanied by drummers or taped music.

The *kadhaa maali* dates back centuries and today survives only on Kulhudhuffushi in Haa Dhaalu Atoll. The dance is initiated by the beating of drums and a *kadhaa*, an instrument made up of a copper plate and rod. About 30 men, dressed in costumes depicting different evil spirits and ghosts, usually take part in the dance. The *kadhaa maali* traditionally marked the end of a period of three nights in which island elders walked around their island to ward off evil spirits associated with sickness and epidemics.

Raivaru are often heard when sailing far out to sea or while sitting in someone's backyard under the moonlight in a far-flung village. They are a sort of poetic lament, dedicated to love or expressing happiness, loneliness or simply a philosophy of life. It is an extremely peaceful experience to lay back on the deck of a dhoni, listening to the old man at the helm chant his favourite selection of *raivaru*.

The national anthem is sung at public gatherings:

Qawmee mi ekuveri kan mathee thibegen kureeme salaam.
Qawmee bahun gina heyo dhua'a kuramun kureeme salaam.

Qawmee nishaan ah hurmathaa eku boa labaa thibegen
Audhaana kan libigen evaa dhidha ah kureeme salaam.

Nasraa naseebaa kaamiyaabu ge ramzakah himeney
Fessa rathaai hudhaa ekee fenumun kureeme salaam.

(In national unity we do salute our nation.
In the national language we do offer our prayers and salute our nation.

We bow in respect to the emblem of our nation
And salute the flag so exalted.

We salute the colours of our flag:
Green, red and white which symbolise victory, blessing and success.)

Festivals, holidays and commemorations

Most Asians celebrate auspicious occasions with colourful frivolity and fanfare. Maldivians celebrate theirs by feasting and fasting. Gastronomical feasts accompany all major religious festivals, and organised sports and speeches mark historical anniversaries.

Please note that the religious festivals covered in this section fall according to the Islamic calendar, which loses 10–11 days every year against the western calendar. As no extra month is added to the Islamic calendar, these festivals move backwards every year on the western calendar. Muslim dates begin from the time Prophet Mohammed went to Medina (the Hijra), and so dates on the Islamic calendar are labelled AH (After Hijra).

Religious
Ramadan
Ramadan is the ninth month in the Muslim calendar, the fasting month and the most outstanding national event. It commemorates the revelation of the *Quran* and is meant to

encourage Muslims to control themselves and to put Allah before all else. Everyone, except those pregnant, too young, too sick or travelling overseas, abstains from all food, water, cigarettes and sex during daylight hours for an entire lunar month. The days are slow and tempers short. By sunset each evening, the women and young girls have prepared wondrous spreads of food and drink and, at the sound of the sunset prayer call, the evenings become gay and gastronomical.

After initially quenching their thirst with either coconut or fruit juice, Maldivians sit down to light meals known as *tharaavees*, usually consisting of snacks. Around midnight, full meals (*haaru*) fill the tables with mounds of rice and relays of curries. The time between *tharaavees* and *haaru* is spent in various forms of entertainment. In addition to being a very religious time, the month of Ramadan is also an occasion when people socialise a great deal.

Kuda Eid

At the end of Ramadan, when the new moon is sighted, everyone rejoices with feasts of chicken curry and by wearing new clothes. It is Kuda Eid (Eid ul-Fitr). The day starts with dawn prayer at the mosque after which families give generously to charity. These offerings (*zakaath*) must be food or money and are one of the five duties of all Muslims. After the *zakaath* come the festival prayers—families go, if possible, to a cemetery to pray for the dead and to remember that they too will die one day. People then greet each other by saying, 'Eid Mubarak' ('Blessed Festival'). Kuda Eid celebrates the glory and triumph of Allah and stresses, through *zakaath*, the responsibilities attached to being a Muslim.

Bodu Eid

Bodu Eid (Eid ul-Al'h'aa), or the Festival of Sacrifice, falls exactly two Muslim months and 10 days after Ramadan. At this time, many Muslims go on pilgrimage (*hajj*) to the holy city of Mecca. Those Maldivians who can afford to go don't hesitate. Others stay home to celebrate by sacrificing a chicken and perhaps sending Eid cards to friends abroad.

This festival has its origins with the great Prophet Abraham, who knew and believed in the one God, Allah. Abraham had a son, Isma'ail, of whom he was very fond. Isma'ail was a quiet and helpful boy who also loved Allah. One day, Abraham had a strange and frightening dream in which he was commanded to take Isma'ail and sacrifice him as an offering to Allah. With great sadness, Abraham told his son what he had dreamt. Without hesitation, Isma'ail replied that if this was what Allah wanted then they must do it.

So Isma'ail lay down and Abraham, a sharp knife in his hand, prepared to do what Allah commanded. He was just about to sacrifice Isma'ail when the voice of Allah spoke, telling him not to harm the boy. Amazed and delighted, Abraham and Isma'ail realised that the dream had been a test to see how much they loved and trusted Allah. Abraham found that Allah had placed an animal nearby, which he killed in place of Isma'ail.

Pilgrims on *hajj* visit the site of this story each year and the Festival of Sacrifice serves as a powerful reminder of how Allah provides and cares for those who do his will.

Prophet Mohammed's birthday

The birthday of the Prophet is a highlight each year. Each family usually has a feast to which they might invite friends and relatives. I have fond memories of such a time in Shaviyani Atoll when I was invited to 'Ade kaan' ('Come and eat'). No matter how poor the family, I was offered an assortment of dishes, anything from *roshi* and *mas huni* (see 'Food') to breadfruit and banana chips.

Rites of passage
Birth

Traditionally, after a baby is born and has been washed, the father, or another man, writes the *Shahadat* ('I bear witness that there is no God but Allah and Mohammed is the Prophet of Allah') in honey, and then feeds the honey to the baby. A call to prayer is then made. The parents choose a name for their child which is bestowed on the seventh day and some parents shave the baby's head on this day in keeping with tradition. A small donation is then given to the poor, neighbouring men come to recite a *maaloodh*, and the ceremony concludes with a feast.

Circumcision

Boys are circumcised between six and eight years of age. The local *hakeem* takes each boy into a bathing room or behind the house (only the father or an uncle may be present), cuts the foreskin while reciting a *salavaath* and applies medicine. Several boys are usually circumcised on the same day and a joint celebration is held. The boys are put on camp beds in the same room and remain there for one week. A little tent of cloth, suspended by string from the ceiling, is placed over each boy's middle, visitors come and go, drummers and dancers may be hired (sometimes tapes and a loudspeaker) and feasts prepared.

Death

Muslims believe in life after death. As the *Quran* teaches that the dead will have their bodies restored on the Day of Judgment, cremation is forbidden. When someone dies, verses from the *Quran*, which answer basic questions about life after death and the Day of Judgment, are read. The body must be buried as soon as possible (usually within 24 hours). Ready-made coffins are available in Male', however, the normal practise is to make a coffin once someone dies.

The body is washed three times, using soap (first the ears, nose, mouth, head, feet, hands and forearms—those parts of the body washed before entering a mosque). The corpse is tied in five places (toes, ankles, knees, arms crossed, and hair), according to Islamic tradition, annointed with sandalwood powder and scents, and wrapped as a shroud in three pieces of white cotton. The body lies in state, face uncovered, as verses from the *Quran* are read.

The coffin is carried to the mosque by neighbouring men and further prayers are said (women do not attend the mosque or the funeral). A gravesite is then chosen and the body is buried facing Mecca. Prayers are said for a week or more beside the grave and at home. On the 40th day of mourning, a memorial service is conducted and a feast takes place. Families often hold such a service each year, sometimes over several generations.

Anniversaries

Independence Day is celebrated on 26 July. Men, women and children in various traditional costumes walk, in glittering parade, through the streets of Male'. In the National Stadium, military displays and traditional dances are performed. Crowds of people fill the stadium and line the fences and roof tops of the capital.

On 3 November, *Victory Day* commemorates victory over the Sri Lankan mercenaries who tried to overthrow the government in 1988.

The *Anniversary of the Second Republic* is celebrated on 11 November with special meetings and celebrations held throughout the Republic.

National Day commemorates the overthrow of the Portuguese in 1573. The celebration falls on the first day of the third month of the Islamic calendar. In 1944 it falls on 9 August and will move back 10–11 days each year.

Other celebrations include *Huravee Day*, which commemorates the overthrow of the Malabaris in 1752; *Martyr's Day*, honouring the death of Sultan Ali VI in 1558; *Fisherman's Day* on 10 December, celebrating the importance of the fishing industry.

GOVERNMENT

In the Maldives, there are three levels of governing. At the grassroots level is island administration. Every citizen is registered at one of the 199 inhabited islands and each family is given a plot of land. The inhabited islands are ruled by Chiefs (*Katheeb*) and Deputy Chiefs (*Kuda Katheeb*) who are responsible for controlling political factions, reporting extraordinary occurrences, and managing nearby uninhabited islands.

For administrative purposes, the islands are grouped into 20 'administrative atolls' (the administrative atolls differ completely to the geographical atolls), with Male' as the capital. These administrative atolls are ruled by Chiefs. The Chiefs are responsible for political and economic welfare while the Judges (*Gaazee*) attend to judicial matters and religious queries. Daily reports are sent via walkie-talkie from the island Chiefs to the Atoll Office. The Atoll Chiefs relay relevant details via radio-telephone to head office in Male'. And facsimile services are currently being installed in many Atoll Offices to enable faster and easier communications between the atolls. In this way, the national government is attuned to day-to-day affairs throughout the archipelago.

The basic law code of the Maldives is *Shari'ah* or Islamic law, handling criminal, civil, religious and political cases. The Attorney General's Office examines all cases sent in from the atolls before passing them on to the Ministry of Justice and Islamic Affairs. Banishment is the most common form of punishment.

At the apex of the political system is the President, elected every five years by national referendum after being nominated by the Citizens Majlis (Parliament). The Citizens Majlis is a body of 48 members, consisting of two representatives from each atoll, two representatives from Male', and eight Presidential nominees. A single candidate for President is nominated and the people simply vote 'yes' or 'no'. In the 1988 elections, Gayyoom was re-elected by a 96.37 per cent majority. The 1993 election saw him elected for a fourth term by a 92.76 per cent majority.

Maumoon Abdul Gayyoom

The national flag is a green rectangle with a white crescent in the centre, surrounded by a red border. The green rectangle denotes life, progress and prosperity. The crescent represents the Islamic faith of the nation. The red border symbolises the blood of the national heroes who sacrificed their lives for the independence and sovereignty of the nation.

The national emblem consists of a coconut palm, a crescent, a star, and two national flags, crisscrossed and bearing the traditional state title: *Ad-Dawlat Al-Mahaldheebiyya*. The coconut palm illustrates the nation's livelihood, while the crescent, star and flags embody the nation's Islamic faith.

National flag

ECONOMY

Fishing dominates the economy. It is traditionally the main occupation and employs about one-quarter of the country's total labour force. Almost two-thirds of the annual catch is exported and the rest is consumed locally. The fishing industry generates about 14 per cent of GDP (tourism, at 17.7 per cent, is now the biggest single contributor to GDP), accounting for 75 per cent of export products.

The predominant methods of fishing are pole and line for skipjack, and trolling for tuna, mackerel and wahoo. Maldivian fishing vessels are called dhoni and closely resemble Arab dhows. In the 1970s, the government launched a program of modernising and mechanising the fishing fleet, and recently embarked on a new design for a second-generation Mark II dhoni which is sleeker, faster and holds more fish than the older-style dhoni.

In the past, the bulk of the catch was exported to Sri Lanka in the form of dried and smoked tuna. In 1971, however, when the Sri Lankans reduced the quantity of Maldivian fish they wished to import, the need to find alternative markets and new processing methods became urgent. The government acted promptly, signing agreements to sell frozen fish to several foreign companies. In 1977, a small fish-canning factory was established, by Japanese investors, on Felivaru in Lhaviyani Atoll. Today, the factory is wholly owned and operated by the Maldives Industrial Fisheries Corporation, and has the capacity to produce 50 tonnes of canned tuna per day for exportation to the Far East and Europe.

The national shipping line, which is operated by Maldives National Ship Management Limited, handles 95 per cent of the country's imports. Since the mid-1960s, the shipping industry's profits have been an important source of foreign exchange. During the 1980s, however, a glut of shipping services sent freight prices crashing and, to make matters worse, the war between Iran and Iraq affected trade between the Maldives and the Middle East.

Tourism has been the most dynamic sector of the economy over the last two decades. Since the first resort was built in 1972, the number of tourist arrivals has risen from 1000 to 200,000 per year. Tourism contributes nearly 26.6 per cent of the national revenue and is the country's biggest earner of foreign exchange.

Agriculture is mostly a supplementary source of income. Coconut farming and the cultivation of cash crops, such as millet, areca nut, mangoes, bananas, onions and chillies, are widespread. The main markets for agricultural produce are Male' and the tourist resorts. Unfortunately, large quantities of fruits, vegetables and poultry products still need to be imported, but the government has implemented measures, such as coconut rehabilitation, pest control and the utilisation of more uninhabited islands, to help stimulate and improve agriculture in the Maldives.

Traditional cottage industries, such as boat building, mat weaving, rope making, ironmongery and handicrafts, have been strengthened by the growth in tourism. These industries account for nearly one-quarter of the workforce, predominantly women. Modern industries which have recently evolved include fish canning, garment manufacture, the production of PVC pipes and soaps and washing powders, and the bottling of soft drinks.

FOOD

Maldivian cuisine is tasty and particularly interesting considering so many dishes have similar ingredients yet taste unique. The staple diet is rice and *garudhiya*, a fish broth. It may appear bland and boring to the newcomer, but the taste is immediately enhanced with a dash of thick fish paste and a spicy side-dish of onion, lime and chilli. Another popular dish is *roshi* (unleavened bread) and *mas huni*, a mixture of grated coconut, fish, lime and chilli which is eaten as a snack or main meal. Mild creamy curries made from ground curry pastes, fish and locally grown vegetables, such as breadfruit, pumpkin, sweet potato and eggplant, are delicious.

Teashop temptations

For most visitors, the highlights of the local cuisine are the sweet and savoury snacks which are served in all the teashops in Male', cooked for special occasions on far-flung islands and occasionally served on the resorts. The savoury snacks are usually a mixture of smoked tuna, grated coconut, lime juice, onion and chilli, while the sweet snacks are concoctions of flour, sugar, eggs and a few generous slurps of coconut honey. It is quite amazing that they all look and taste so different. Here is a selection to whet the appetite.

Savouries

fihunu mas	fish brushed with chilli paste and cooked slowly over hot coals
gulha	fish mixture wrapped in a pastry ball and deep fried
kavaabu	deep-fried fish rissole
keemia	deep-fried fish roll, the local answer to a sausage roll

kulhi bis	fish mixture wrapped in egg-shaped pastry, steamed and then turned in a thick, creamy curry paste (eaten with a spoon)
kulhi borkibaa	mildly spiced fishcake
bajiya	slightly sweet fish mixture wrapped in triangular-shaped pastry and deep fried
theluli bambukeyo	strips of breadfruit, deep fried until golden brown on the outside and soft and mushy in the middle
theluli kavaabu	fish rissole dipped in bright yellow batter and deep fried
theluli mas	chunks of fish brushed with a chilli–onion garlic paste and fried

Sweets

banas	small sweet bread rolls
bondi	white, finger-long coconut sticks
bondi-baiy	sticky rice custard
foni borkibaa	glutinous cake
foni folhi	thick pikelets
keyku	fluffy plain cake
roas paan	slices of bread dipped in egg and sugar, then fried
suji	drink made with semolina, coconut milk, sultanas, nuts, sugar and a dash of cinnamon and cardamom

Recipes

Mas huni

Ingredients

1 onion, finely chopped
1 fresh chilli, finely chopped
juice of 1 lime
pinch of salt
2 cups freshly grated coconut
2 cups fish (flaked dry fish, tinned tuna, cold cooked fish)

Method
Combine onion, chilli and lime juice, then mix in the remaining ingredients. Serve with freshly cooked *roshi*.

Roshi

Ingredients

3 cups plain flour	pinch of salt
1½ cups freshly grated coconut	water

Method
Mix all ingredients in a bowl and make a well in the middle. Slowly knead in the water until the dough is firm and doesn't stick. Divide into balls and roll out into large, fairly thick circles. Cook each side on a hot metal surface (no oil). Serve immediately.

Fish and pumpkin curry

Ingredients

500 g pumpkin, chopped into large cubes
1 onion, chopped
4 cloves garlic, finely sliced
2 fresh chillies, chopped
2 tsp cinnamon
3 tsp cummin
2 tsp fennel
½ tsp turmeric
1 tbs fresh coriander, chopped
1 tsp ground coriander
good dash black pepper
salt to taste

1 pinch fresh chopped ginger
½ lime
3 tbs oil
250 g fish (flaked smoked fish, fresh tuna, tinned tuna)
enough coconut milk (preferably fresh or, if not fresh, powdered coconut milk to which you add water) to almost cover the ingredients

Method

Fry a small amount of the onion and garlic in the oil until soft. Fold in the pumpkin, along with the ginger and half the remaining onion and garlic. Cover the pan, lower the heat and cook until the pumpkin is a little soft, stirring occasionally. Pour in the coconut milk and add the remaining onion, chilli, ginger, cummin, fennel, ground coriander, turmeric, black pepper and fish. Add salt to taste. Simmer slowly until the pumpkin and fish are cooked, adding more coconut milk if necessary. Fold in the remaining garlic, fresh coriander, cinnamon and lime juice. Simmer a further three minutes with the lid on. Serve with boiled rice or *roshi*.

Fresh coconut milk

If you are a regular curry cooker, it is worth purchasing one of the excellent coconut scrapers available from the bazaar in Male'. There are two types: locally made *huni gondi*—low stools which you sit on to scrape coconuts; and coconut scrapers imported from Sri Lanka, which you attach to a bench or table.

Scrape the white meat from two coconuts. Just cover the scrapings with tepid water and squeeze the mixture with your hand until it forms a milk. Drain off the milk. Maldivians repeat this process twice more, but unless you're an expert you tend to end up with a tasteless watery liquid bound to spoil any creamy curry.

LANGUAGE

The language spoken almost uniformly throughout the Maldives is called Dhivehi. It is closely related to Elu, an ancient form of Sinhala (spoken in Sri Lanka), and contains a smattering of Arabic, Hindi and English words.

We know the Maldives

Allow us to share it with you

We know the Maldives because we've lived here all our lives. For a holiday you'll never forget, allow us to share the Maldive experience with you. See us first for:

- resort, hotel and guesthouse accommodation
- diving and surfing safaris
- fishing and sightseeing expeditions
- aerial tours
- inbound and outbound packages
- a meet-and-greet airport service
- flight confirmation.

SUN TRAVEL & TOURS PVT LTD

Manaage' Maveyo Magu, Machangolhi
Male' 20-03 PO Box 2083
Republic of Maldives
Telephone: (960) 325975/325976/325977
Facsimile: (960) 320419
Telex: (896) 66212 STT MF

Preparing tuna fillets for sale

Above: Male' transport
Below: Fruit and vegetable market, Male'

Peak hour on Thulhagiri

Imagine the classic deserted tropical island.
Intimate. Beautiful. And no crowds.
Thulhagiri has 58 comfortable rooms,
a restaurant, coffee shop, grill, bar and disco -
all in stunning natural surroundings.
Talk to your travel agent sooner than later.

Thulhagiri Resort
Telephone: (960) 445929 Facsimile: (960) 445939
Telex: (896) 77110 THULHA MF

Given the wide dispersion of islands, however, it is not surprising that vocabulary and pronunciation vary from atoll to atoll. As one moves south towards the equator, for example, the differences are significant. There are three distinct dialects of Dhivehi, each similar in stress and intonation but with quite different words and phrases. In the north, for example, 'rice' is *baiy*, but in the south it is *bateh* or *bai*.

Different words and phrases also appear within the various classes of society. In fact there are three 'levels' of Dhivehi. The highest, the *reethi bas* or 'nice language', is used in the company of the upper echelon and on national radio and television. The second level is used to show respect for elders or influential persons, and the lowest is used by the masses. Along the well-worn tourist tracks and deep down in the south, where the British once lived, you can get by quite easily using English. In other far-flung villages you will need at least a few Dhivehi phrases.

Reading and writing

Thaana, the local script, was invented during the 16th century, not long after the overthrow of the Portuguese and when the locals were determined to revive their Islamic faith. Unlike earlier scripts, it was written from right to left in order to accommodate Arabic phrases. Thaana is not difficult to learn and 98 per cent of locals are able to read and write. There are 24 letters in the alphabet, nine of which are Arabic numerals. Vowels are indicated by a dash above or below a letter.

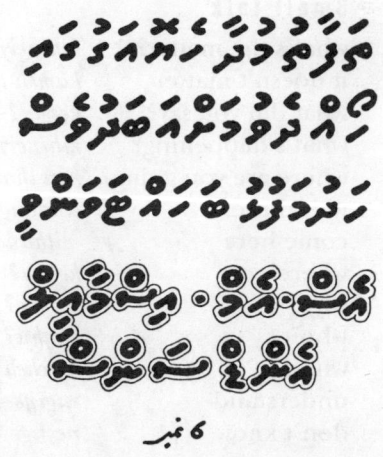

— 75 — *Island life*

Pronunciation

a	as in	c*u*t	ai	as in	*eye*
eh	as in	r*e*d	ee	as in	tr*ee*
i	as in	f*i*t	th	as in	*th*rough
o	as in	h*o*t	dh	as in	*th*e
u	as in	p*u*t	eiy	as in	ob*ey*
aa	as in	f*a*ther			

Greetings and civilities

hello!	*assalaam alaikum!*
how are you?	*kihineiy?*
not bad	*goaheh noon*
very well	*varah rangalhu*
good	*rangalhu*
I'm going	*aharen dhanee; aharen goslanee*
see you later	*fahun badhdhaluvaane*
thankyou	*shukriyya*

Small talk

what's the matter?	*kihineiy vee?*
it doesn't matter	*kameh nuvey*
what did you say?	*keekey?*
what's happening?	*kihineiy vanee?*
where are you going?	*kon thaakah dhanee?*
wait there	*ethaanga hurey*
come here	*mithanah aadhey*
where?	*kobaa?*
why?	*keevve?*
who?	*kaaku?*
what?	*korcheh?*
understand	*engijje*
don't know	*neynge*
yes	*aan*
no	*noon*

Personal talk

who is that?	*e-ee kaaku?*	mother	*mamma*
those people	*e meehun*	brother	*beybe*
who is this?	*mee kaaku?*	sister	*dhaththa*
I, me	*aharen, ma*	uncle	*bodu beybe*
you	*kaley*	aunt	*bodu dhaitha*
he, she	*eyna*	son/daughter	*dharifulhu*
man	*firiheneh*	friend	*rattehi*
woman	*anheneh*	close friend	*rahumaiytheri*
father	*bappa*		

Ge is also a useful term to know. It turns nouns into pronouns, eg *ma* (me) becomes *mage* (my).

Time

what time is it?	*gadin kihaireh?*	sunset	*iru ossenee*
Sunday	*Aadheeththa*	evening	*reygandu, haveeru*
Monday	*Horma*		
Tuesday	*Angaara*	two o'clock	*dheyh jehee*
Wednesday	*Budha*	quarter past three	*thin gadi fanara*
Thursday	*Buraasfathi*		
Friday	*Hukuru*	half past nine	*nuva gadi bai*
Saturday	*Honihiru*		
yesterday	*iyye*	before	*kurin*
today	*miadhu*	now	*mihaaru*
tonight	*mirey*	after	*fahun*
tomorrow	*maadhamaa*	in a little while	*thankolheh fahun*
dawn	*fathis*		
sunrise	*iru aranee*	day	*dhuvas*
morning	*hendhunu*	week	*hafthaa*
midday	*mendhuru*	month	*mas*
afternoon	*mendhuru fas*	year	*aharu*

Numbers

1	ekeh	11	egaara	30	thirees
2	dheyh	12	baara	40	saalhees
3	thineh	13	theyra	50	fansaas
4	hathareh	14	saadha	60	fasdholhas
5	faheh	15	funara	70	haiy-dhiha
6	haeh	16	soalha	80	ah-dhiha
7	hatheh	17	sathaara	90	nura-dhiha
8	asheh	18	ashaara	100	satheyka
9	nuvaeh	19	onavihi		
10	dhihaeh	20	vihi		

200	dhui-saththa	1000	eh-haas
300	thin-satheyka	10,000	dhiha-haas
400	hatharue-satheyka	100,000	eh-lakka
500	fas-satheyka	zero	sumeh

At the market

how much is this?	mee kihaa varakah?	papaya	falhoa
what is that?	e-ee korcheh?, thee korcheh?	breadfruit	bambukeyo
		pumpkin	barabor
		cabbage leaf	kopee faiy
expensive	agu bodu	chilli	mirus
cheap	agu heyo	lentils	mugu
fruit	meyvaa	rice (uncooked)	handoo
vegetables	tharukaaree	coconut (old)	kaashi
fish	mas	onions	fiyaa
banana	dhonkeyo	garlic	lonumedhu
mango	ambu		

Fish market, Male'

At the markets in Male' and on the far-flung islands, the most common unit of measurement for grains and liquids is the *laahi*. A 250-g aluminium container or a coconut shell is used to measure a *laahi*. Four *laahi* of rice is called a *naali*, and four *laahi* of honey is called an *adubaa*. Lengths of material are measured in *muh* and *rian*.

Two commonly used words are *tha* and *dhoa*. Both turn a statement into a question. For example: *ebahuri* means 'have'; *ebahuri tha?* means 'do you have?'; *ebahuri dhoa?* means 'you have it, don't you?'

Ingey is another term you will hear often. It is used at the end of a sentence, as if to ensure the other person is listening. *Aharen dhanee, ingey!* means 'I'm going, OK!' or 'I'm going, understand?'

Remember that the market in Male' is a place for bargaining. Confidently sprout a few exclamations. *Ekamakuvaa!* is a popular expression, loosely meaning 'good grief!' Use it if you think the price is too high.

In the restaurant

what is there to eat?	*kon kaa-echcheh huree?*
rice (cooked)	*baiy*
unleavened bread	*roshi*
curry	*riha*
tea (black)	*kalhu sai*
tea (white)	*kiru sai*
tea (no sugar)	*sai, hakuru naalhaa*
snacks	*hedhi-kaa*
knife	*valhi*
spoon	*samsaa*
fork	*oo*
that's enough	*dhen heyo*
a little bit more	*adhi kuda ethi kolheh*
not too much chilli	*kulhi madu*
tasty	*meeru*
bad taste	*nubai*
lentil curry	*mugu riha*
vegetable curry	*tharakaaree riha*
cold drink	*fini boa echcheh*
drinking water	*boa fen*
much too sweet	*maa foni gadha*
I'm hungry	*aharen banduhai vejje*
I'm thirsty	*aharen fen bovai janejje*
I'm full	*aharen bundu bodu vejje*
sit here!	*mithaa isheendhey!*
a good teashop	*rangalu hotaa*

Travelling around

when do you leave?	*furanee kon irakun?*
how long does it take?	*dheveynee kihaa irakun?*
will you take me?	*gengos dheynantha?*
good wind	*vai rangalhu*
bad current	*oi nubai*
I'm seasick	*aharen hodu lavanee*
what's that island?	*e-ee kon rasheh?*
how much is the fare?	*fee kihaavareh?*

is it time to go?	*furan vejje tha?*
bon voyage!	*hiyy heyo kuraathi!*
hoist the sail!	*riyaa nagoa!*

Place names

Visitors are often confused by the long tongue-twisting island names. When looked at syllable by syllable, they are not quite so indecipherable. For example, Meerufenfushi (*meeru-fen-fushi*) means 'sweet-water-island'; Hudhuveli (*hudhu-veli*) means 'white-sand'. Some islands have meanings closely tied to foreign languages. Maafilaafushi is derived from the Maappilas, a Muslim caste in India. Lankanfushi is borrowed from Sri Lanka.

Atoll names are also tongue twisters. In the 1940s, for ease of administration, traditional atoll names were renamed according to letters of the Dhivehi alphabet. Today it is common to use both the traditional and administrative nuances for the atolls. It is worth noting both. From north to south, they are:

Traditional	*Administrative*
North Thiladhunmathi	Haa Alifu
South Thiladhunmathi	Haa Dhaalu
North Miladhunmadulu	Shaviyani
South Miladhunmadulu	Noonu
North Maalhosmadulu	Raa
South Maalhosmadulu	Baa
Faadhippolhu	Lhaviyani
Male'	Kaafu
Ari	Alifu
Felidhe	Vaavu
Mulaku	Meemu
North Nilandhe	Faafu
South Nilandhe	Dhaalu
Kolhumadulu	Thaa
Hadhdhunmathi	Laamu
North Huvadhu	Gaafu Alifu
South Huvadhu	Gaafu Dhaalu
Foammulah	Gnyaviyani
Addu	Seenu

Island life

A boatful of tuna

FACTS FOR THE VISITOR

Getting there 84
At the airport 85
Formalities 86
Things to do 89
Places to stay 90
Getting around 97
General information 100

ESSENTIAL FACTS

Getting there

Despite its apparent isolation, the Maldives is easy to get to. Many airlines offer regular scheduled and chartered flights from Asia and Europe, and the islands are a popular entrepôt for world-cruising yachts.

By sea

Cargo boats ply regularly between Male' and Colombo, and Male' and Tuticorin, a small port on the south-west coast of India. The 60-hour voyage costs about $US35 one way, meals included. It is by no means comfortable, sleeping and eating on the deck and being tossed to and fro by the ocean swells. But if you don't mind roughing it to the extreme, it is an experience you will long remember.

By air

Airlines offering scheduled or chartered flights to the Maldives include Air Lanka, Alitalia, Austrian Airways, Condor, Impala Air, Indian Airlines, Lauda Air, Sterling Airways, Singapore Airlines, Pakistan International Airlines, Emirates Airways, Finnair, Balair, LTU, Romanian Air Systems, Caledonian Airways, and Zas Air.

From Asia There is a 4-hour direct flight from Singapore to Male', operated by Singapore Airlines. The return fare is around $U3500, provided you stay a minimum of five days or a maximum of 30 days. Air Lanka has regular flights from Colombo, and one-way fares for the 1-hour flight are $US72. Indian Airlines operates a daily scheduled service from Trivandrum ($US63 one way).

From Australia Singapore Airlines offers regular flights to Male', via Singapore, from all major cities. Despite the convenient connections, many passengers break their journeys, choosing to spend a day or two in Singapore before flying on to Male'. There are several 'Island Affair' packages on offer, ranging between $A1600 and $A2500 for seven days on a resort (all meals and return air fares included).

From Europe There are a number of alternatives. During the peak season there are frequent chartered flights: Sterling Airways operates from Stockholm, Copenhagen and Helsinki; LTU from Dusseldorf, Munich, Hamburg; Balair from Zurich; Condor from Frankfurt, Hamburg, Dusseldorf, and Munich; Alitalia from Rome; Lauda Air from Vienna; Finnair from Helsinki; Air Caledonia from London. There are scheduled services on offer with Singapore Airlines and Air Lanka from several major cities, including Zurich, Paris and Brussels. The return fare is around $US1600.

From the United Kingdom The most popular route is from London, via Colombo with Air Lanka, or via Dubai with Emirates Airways. Several companies offer attractive packages. A typical two-week holiday costs around £750, including return air fare and half-board rates. During the peak season, Monarch Airlines offers chartered flights. Discounted air tickets are always available from travel agents in London—just peruse the travel advertisements in *Time Out*.

From America There are no direct flights to the Maldives, so shop around for a flight to London or Singapore (around $US 1000 return) and continue on from there.

At the airport

In days gone by, the island of Hulhule was a royal retreat, reserved for sultans, their families and friends. Nowadays, Male' International Airport is located on Hulhule, a 10-minute Rf50 boat ride from Male'.

A single aeroplane load is all it takes to stretch the island's facilities to the limit. It generally takes the best part of an hour to clear immigration and customs. Just smile, and with a bit of luck you'll get through with a cursory wave rather than a comprehensive baggage search.

The foyer of the terminal has a bank, boutiques, coffee shop, tourist-information counter and the Satellite Restaurant. Once outside the terminal, you will be greeted by congregations of representatives from various resorts and travel agents. A short stroll along the coral walkway leads to a long row of dhoni and cabin cruisers, ready to whisk passengers away. Porters charge about Rf10 per bag to carry your luggage to the boat. Trolleys are also available.

Departing passengers should note that a $US10 departure tax applies. The departure lounge has a duty-free shop and a counter serving cold drinks.

Anyone wishing to visit Hulhule to meet or farewell someone should first obtain a Rf2 permit at the entrance to the airport.

Formalities

Visas

A valid passport is required for entrance to the Maldives. Italians, Indians, Pakistanis and Bangladeshis are automatically given 90-day visas and Sri Lankans 30-day visas on arrival. Everyone else—except Israelis who are not permitted to enter the Maldives—is given a 30-day visa on arrival. If you are arriving from a country known to be plagued with yellow fever you will be asked to show proof of vaccination. If you are not entering the Maldives through a tourist agency or on recruitment, you must be in possession of a minimum of $US25 for each day of stay and a return ticket.

If you wish to extend your visit, you should apply to the Department of Immigration and Emigration in Male'. On completing the necessary forms and presenting a passport photograph of yourself along with your passport, a one-, two- or three-month 'tourist visa', costing Rf300, may be granted the following day. Like many other Asian nations, the Maldives is somewhat cautious in granting these extensions. A neat appearance and patient pleasant manner, along with a justifiable reason as to why you want to extend your visit, will prove worthwhile.

Permits

In order to visit any of the inhabited islands beyond Male' you usually need to travel on an organised tour. All the resorts organise regular tours to nearby villages for their guests, and the travel agents in Male' offer island-hopping tours around some atolls (Alifu, Vaavu, Lhaviyani, Baa, Haa Dhaalu and Haa Alifu).

The days of hitching a ride on a dhoni and sailing off into the deep blue yonder to the far-flung islands are fast disappearing. Independent adventurous travellers now require Rf10 permits from the Ministry of Atolls Administration before staying at any island village. And to get the permit you need a written invitation from a local resident.

Customs

An article in *Time* magazine once described the Maldives as '... a land of leisurely customs as unchanging as the sea ...' In the late 1970s, before tourism became significant, you were welcomed to the Maldives with no more formality than a handshake, and you could stay as long as you liked. Some people are still there, married with children, managing resorts and guesthouses, or sailing around the atolls.

Times have changed, however. The queues at the airport grow longer each year. Passports are now checked, visas issued and luggage searched. It generally takes about 1 hour to complete the formalities.

Visitors should remember that this is a strictly Muslim nation. You are prohibited to import guns, dogs, liquor, drugs, pork products and pornographic literature without a license. There is not a single dog in the Maldives; liquor is available only at the resorts; any unusual pill or potion should be accompanied with a prescription; and make sure you leave your *Playboy* and *Penthouse* at home.

A visit to any country is always more enjoyable if you honour local customs. Nudity in public is forbidden and it is a mark of respect to dress more conservatively when visiting Male' or any of the villages. Women should refrain from wearing see-through or skimpy garments and walking barefoot; men should resist walking about bare chested or without shoes.

If you are fortunate enough to share a meal with a local family, there are certain table manners you should note. Most Maldivians eat with their right hands. Under no circumstance should you ever eat with your left hand. If you use your right hand to eat then you handle serving cutlery with your left hand and wash both your hands when you have finished eating. Maldivians actually find it quite strange to see white people using their hands to eat as overseas-educated, middle-class and upper-class Maldivians tend to eat with spoons and forks these days.

Currency

Foreign currency can be exchanged for local currency—rufiyaa and laari—only through authorised moneychangers, such as banks, resorts and some private shops. The rates vary and are generally higher around the Ahmedi Bazaar in Male'.

The rufiyaa is the paper currency and appears in denominations of 2, 5, 10, 50 and 100. There is now also a Rf1 coin. All other coinage are laari, worth 1, 2, 5, 10, 25 and 50 laari. One rufiyaa is equivalent to 100 laari and the rates of exchange are closely linked to the American dollar, the most widely accepted foreign currency. Prices quoted in this book, therefore, are in American dollars unless specified otherwise. Some popular rates, effective at time of writing, are:

$US	Rf11.06	£E	Rf15.89
$C	Rf0.07	Fr Franc	Rf1.789
$A	Rf7.40	DM	Rf6.06
$S	Rf6.61	Yen	Rf0.10
Sw Franc	Rf7.22	Austrian Sch	Rf0.86
It Lira	Rf0.01	Neth Gui	Rf5.42

There are no regulations regarding the import or export of foreign or local currency, and 'plastic money' is accepted on most of the resorts (see the 'Travel directory'). If you are visiting any of the villages, make sure to stock up on Rf1 coins and Rf2 and Rf5 notes as it is often difficult to find someone who is able to give change of Rf10 and over.

▭ Things to do

The Ministry of Tourism uses the following slogan to advertise the Maldives: 'The art of doing nothing'. A large proportion of visitors are attracted to the Maldives simply because it is idyllic for doing absolutely nothing other than lazing in the sun, eating and sleeping. You can do it in style at one of the resorts, or in true Robinson Crusoe fashion on one of the many uninhabited islands.

Not everyone, of course, is content to spend their entire time in the Maldives doing nothing. And nor should they—the islands have much to offer. All the resorts offer a variety of activities for their guests. Typical water sports (and their average costs) include: scuba diving—Rf240 per dive; windsurfing—Rf60 per hour; game fishing—Rf140 per person per hour; night fishing—Rf110 per person.

Excursions to nearby villages are also popular with resort guests. It usually costs around Rf200 per person for the day's outing and a barbeque lunch on the beach, with perhaps a game of volleyball or soccer with the village children. A visit to the capital island is a must. Male' is the hub of the nation and even a short visit will give you an insight into many facets of Maldivian life.

Prices on the resorts are subject to change so it is advisable to check with the resort of your choice for the latest prices.

An alternative to staying on a resort is to arrange an island-hopping safari (see 'Getting around—By organised tour/By hitching'). These safaris appeal to those who easily dismiss modern comforts for a closer view of this intriguing seafaring culture.

Places to stay

The government requests that every visitor to the Maldives stay at a registered resort, tourist hotel, vessel or guesthouse, where facilities are periodically checked to ensure they meet government-approved standards. A daily tourism tax of $US6 is levied on each guest.

Most accommodation is a matter of minutes or, at most, a few hours from the airport. Unless otherwise stated, the rates quoted in this book include the government tax. Anyone arriving independently should first enquire at the airport tourist-information counter where lists of guesthouses, hotels and resorts, and their rates, locations and facilities, are available on request.

The majority of visitors to the Maldives stay on the resort islands. Anyone arriving on a package tour with their accommodation prearranged will be met at the airport by a tour guide, then whisked away in a motorised dhoni, cabin cruiser or helicopter to their resort. Some resorts have reservation booths outside the main airport terminal and, failing that, all the resorts can be contacted by telephone. Transport is soon arranged and one-way fares vary between $US12 and $US300, depending on the distance and whether you are travelling by air or sea. Those who arrive late at night and are destined for the faraway resorts might need to spend their first night in one of the capital's tourist hotels. Budget-conscious travellers usually stay in the guesthouses scattered around Male'.

Resort islands

More than 60 resort islands are scattered around Kaafu Atoll and the neighbouring atolls. Room rates (single/double) vary from $US50/70 upwards, meals included.

The facilities are somewhat similar from resort to resort, although standards, service and ambience vary. Thankfully, the Ministry of Tourism makes regular inspections and those resorts that don't meet the required standards are instantly closed until they do. It is wise to enquire about the clientele

Bandos Island Resort

If it were any more exclusive,

you wouldn't be allowed
on the island.

If it were any more exclusive, the Nika Hotel would be a private island resort. Spacious bungalows lie right on the edge of secluded pristine beaches and crystal clear waters. This is absolute luxury in the heart of the Maldives. Book now!

Nika Hotel

PO Box 2076, 10 Fareedhee Magu, Male' 20-02 Republic of Maldives
Tel: (960) 325087 Fax: (960) 325097 Tlx: (896) 66124 NIKA MF

Resort souvenir shop

before you make a booking—a few resorts are geared almost exclusively for Italian or German guests, some have mixed guest lists, and others refuse children.

The catchcry is 'peace and tranquility' and the general setting is small bungalow-style individual rooms around the fringe of the island, a restaurant, bar and boutique centrally located, and a diving school which provides facilities for various types of water sport. Most resorts have desalinised hot and cold water.

Rooms may be fan-cooled or air-conditioned. The restaurants range from offering à la carte, lavish buffets and beach barbeques to dishing out the same tiresome rice dishes night after night. The bars stock a variety of imported beers, whiskies and wines, and the boutiques sell local souvenirs, imported Asian handicrafts and clothes, Kodak and Agfa film at good prices, cosmetics, posters and postcards.

During the sunny and dry north-east monsoon, from November to April, the resorts are bursting with tourists, usually escaping the European winter, and so reservations need to be made well in advance. During the south-west monsoon, from May to October, when the skies may pour out sunshine, showers or squalls, tourists are few and far between, some resorts close down and others slash their rates (up to 25 per cent off) to attract a trickle of visitors.

Some resorts enjoy long-term leases on their islands and are thus encouraged to reinvest in and continually upgrade their facilities. Those with short-term leases will, by necessity, allow their resorts to deteriorate towards the end of their leases, renovating and refurbishing when the contracts are renewed, or selling out if they are not. As is the case wherever you go, there are good and bad places to stay. There are also great places—some resorts have received international awards for their standards of service, and each year there are Maldivian resorts included in someone's list of the top 300 hotels in the world.

Tourist hotels

There are three tourist hotels in Male' (see 'Male'—Places to stay'). They are the capital's answer to star-class comfort but 'comfortable' is perhaps a better description.

Each of the hotels has an à la carte restaurant and rates for singles/doubles vary from $US25/$US40 upward.

Guesthouses

Anyone travelling on a shoestring budget should perhaps think twice before visiting the Maldives. Whereas once the villages around Kaafu Atoll were teeming with guesthouses, nowadays visitors are prohibited from staying overnight in a village (other than Male', the capital) unless they know someone willing to sponsor them. So if you wish to stay overnight on Gulhi, for example, you must have written permission from a resident of Kaafu Atoll, and if you wish to stay on Mahibadhoo, you would need a sponsor who is a resident of Alifu Atoll. Written permission enables you to then obtain a permit from the Ministry of Atolls Administration which in turn allows you to stay anywhere within the atoll for which it has been issued.

Frankly speaking, your chances of finding a sponsor are slim but if you do the effort will be well worth it. The government forbids any payment to change hands for such accommodation. Repay the hospitality in kind (stock the kitchen with a few imported delights), however, and your stay will be appreciated and memorable.

More often than not, visitors on tight travel budgets spend most of their time in Male', where a sparsely furnished fan-cooled room costs from $US15 upward per day (per person).

Vessels

A wide range of seafaring craft, including local dhoni as well as imported schooners, ketches and cabin cruisers, are available for hire and have been approved by the government as suitable for accommodating tourists. Most of them provide cabins or bunks for groups of eight to 10 passengers, come with a crew of two or three local sailors, and have cooking and toilet facilities on board. The usual charge, including meals, varies upwards of $US30 per person per day. An additional charge is levied for the hire of scuba-diving equipment. You can arrange a short- or long-distance island-hopping tour on a registered vessel through the resorts or any of the travel agents in Male'.

Getting around

Five hundred years ago, according to Joao de Barros, 'You could hop from island to island by swinging from the branches of trees.' Today, you island hop by chartering a seaplane, planning an organised boat tour or, most adventurous of all, hitching a ride on any one of the thousands of dhoni that are forever criss-crossing the archipelago.

By flying

Air Maldives (tel: 322436) is the domestic airline. It operates daily flights between Male' and Gan (Seenu Atoll); flies every day except Friday between Male' and Hanimaadhoo (Haa Dhaalu Atoll); operates four times a week (Sunday, Monday, Wednesday and Friday) between Male' and Kahdhoo (Laamu Atoll); and three times a week (Monday, Wednesday and Thursday) between Male' and Kaadehdhoo (Gaafu Dhaalu Atoll).

Approximate return fares (visitors pay Rf200 more than locals):

Male'–Gan	Rf1600
Male'–Kahdhoo	Rf900
Male'–Hanimaadhoo	Rf900
Male'–Kaadehdhoo	Rf1300.

Air Maldives also offers charter services. It costs Rf40,000 per person to fly to Gan and spend 3 hours looking around, returning to Male' in the afternoon. A similar excursion to Kahdhoo or Hanimaadhoo costs Rf20,000 per person, and Rf30,000 to Kaadehdhoo. If you wish to charter the plane for an hour-long photo shoot it costs $US1400.

Hummingbird Helicopters (tel: 325708) and *Seagull Airways* (tel: 315234) operate helicopter services between Male' and the helipads in Kaafu and Alifu Atolls. The 15-minute flight from Male' to Rasdhoo costs $US100 one way, and from there it's a short 5-minute boat ride to Kuramathi, a huge island(by Maldivian standards), boasting three separate resorts. A word of advice: en route to Alifu, sit on the right-hand side for breathtaking aerial views.

Maldivian Air Taxi (tel: 315201) has a small fleet of seaplanes based at the international airport. Regular services operate from there to most resorts.

By organised tour

Speedboats, cabin cruisers or engine dhoni are the most popular forms of transport for island hopping. Most of the resorts have a fleet of boats and offer tours to nearby villages for hourly rentals. A full-day excursion might include visits to a number of resorts, fishing villages and uninhabited islands, and generally costs around $US25 per person.

There are many travel agents to choose from in Male', some specialising in resort tours, others in island-hopping excursions to far-flung atolls.

MTCC (tel: 325321) and *ZSS* (tel: 322505) are the best contacts for speedboats. Rates vary from $US8 an hour to $US300 a day, not including petrol.

Voyages Maldives (tel: 322019) owns a fleet of dhoni that motor and sail on extended tours to the northern and southern atolls. It costs between $US30 and $US40 a day per person, including meals. Scuba diving is available at extra charge (about $US17 a dive). The dhoni range in size from 13 m to 19 m and accommodate up to 12 people.

Galena Maldives (tel: 324743) offers similar tours aboard their 30-m diesel-powered cabin cruiser, *MSY Nora*. It has eight cabins, a master bedroom, two spacious sundecks and a comfortable saloon with video and stereo systems. Tours cost around $US35 per person per day, including meals, and are usually two to three weeks in duration.

Beach Travel and Tours (tel: 324572) is a reliable and efficient organisation that specialises in island-hopping safaris, boat hire and resort accommodation. They also operate two popular guesthouses in Male'.

Sunland Travel (tel: 323467) and *Sun Travel and Tours* (tel: 325975) are highly recommended and both offer a range of services from accommodation to aerial tours.

By hitching

The entire north-eastern shoreline of Male' is dotted with dhoni, most of them available for day hire or for short trips. Be sure to haggle, the price is negotiable and it's not uncommon for tourists to pay twice the local fare. Normally these dhoni can be hired for around Rf1200 a day; Rf50 gets you to the airport; and Rf100 gets you to Kurumba. Wooden benches and plastic awnings to shield passengers from the sun and rain are the only comforts.

If you are keen enough (and lucky enough) to obtain a permit to visit the far-flung villages, chances are you will travel on the traditional sail dhoni. Hundreds of them are anchored near the markets in Male', plying to and fro between the capital and outlying islands, and filled with all manner of cargo (fish, wood, rice, sugar, flour and vegetables). This is how to get right to the heart of Maldivian life and it is an experience you are bound to remember for years (and one your body will ache over for days). In other words, you rough it! Be sure to stock up on a few snacks and canned foods as you may be in for a lengthy voyage if the wind and weather are not favourable.

To ensure that you are on the right dhoni, check the registration on the bow. The letter indicates the atoll from which the dhoni has come.

A–Haa Alifu	G–Lhaviyani	M–Dhaalu	S–Seenu
B–Haa Dhaalu	H–Kaafu	N–Thaa	T–Male'
C–Shaviyani	I–Alifu	O–Laamu	
D–Noonu	J–Vaavu	P–Gaafu Alifu	
E–Raa	K–Meemu	Q–Gaafu Dhaalu	
F–Baa	L–Faafu	R–Gnyaviyani	

General information
Consulates, embassies and information offices

Countries which have diplomatic relations with the Maldives operate their offices, on the whole, from Colombo in Sri Lanka. Some have offices in Male'. The Maldives, in turn, has a consular office, or at least a consultant, in several countries. Tourist information is available at most of these offices.

Austria
Honorary Consul,
Weimarerstrasse 104,
A 1190 Wien
(tel: [1] 345273)

Belgium
Honorary Consul,
Rue de Vignes 16,
1020 Brussels
(tel: [2] 4781426)

Egypt
Honorary Consul,
16 Ahmed Omar Road,
4th Floor, Flat 7,
El-Helmeya-El Adida,
Cairo (tel: [2] 391052)

France
Honorary Consul,
Zone Artisanale,
5 Rue de Lafontaine,
21560 Arc sur Tille
(tel: 80372660)

Germany
Honorary Consul,
Immanuel-Kant Strasse 16,
D-6380 Bad Hamburg
(tel: 69066789)

Hong Kong
Honorary Consul,
201-5 Kowloon Centre,
29-39 Ashley Road,
Kowloon
(tel: [852] 3762114)

India
Honorary Consul,
202 Sethi Bhavan,
7 Rajendra Place,
New Delhi 110000
(tel: [11] 5718590)
Nathan Road,
Vidyavihar,
Bombay 400086
(tel: [22] 515111)

Japan
Honorary Consul,
Chiyoda Building 1-2,
2 Chome Marunochi,
Chiyodaku,
Tokyo (tel: [3] 2115463)
Tourism Representative,
Takekazu Asakura,
3-32-13 Horikiri,
Katsushika-ku,
Tokyo (tel: [3] 6924455)

Malaysia
Honorary Consul,
15A Jalan Jelawatiga,
Bangsaru Baru,
59100 Kuala Lumpur
(tel: [3] 2540941)

Norway
Tourism Representative,
Stubbratan 20, 1352 Kolsas,
Oslo (tel: [2] 137221)

Pakistan
Honorary Consul,
PO Box 51, Campbell Street,
Karachi (tel: [21] 737945)

Saudi Arabia
Honorary Consul,
PO Box 404,
Jeddah 21411
(tel: [2] 6423666)

Singapore
Trade Representative,
10 Anson Road,
18–20 International Plaza
(tel: 2258955)

Sri Lanka
High Commission,
25 Melbourne Avenue,
Colombo 4 (tel: [1] 586762)

Switzerland
Honorary Consul,
Gerechtigkeitsgasse,
238002 Zurich
(tel: [1] 2028448)

UK
Tourism Representative,
Esher House,
11 Edith Terrace,
London SW1OH
(tel: [01] 3522246)
Trade Representative,
Unit 9, Printing House Yard,
15A Hackney Road,
London E27PR
(tel: [01] 7295721)

USA
Permanent Mission to
the United Nations,
820 Second Avenue,
Suite 800C,
New York NY 10017
(tel: [212] 5996195).

The Ministry of Tourism has a counter at the airport and its headquarters in the Ghaazee Building in Male'. Brochures, leaflets, booklets and maps are available. The Ministry of Information and Culture in Buruzu Magu, Male', and the Department of Linguistics and Historical Research, also in Male', are good reference sources for academic works. There are also a couple of good libraries in Male' which stock a range of publications relating to the Maldivian environment, history and culture.

Health

There is an Atoll Health Centre on the capital island of each atoll. In Male', there is a new government hospital, the Indira Gandhi Memorial Hospital (built with aid from the Indian Government), a smaller private hospital, many pharmacies, and a number of good doctors both in private practices and at the hospitals.

In the past, a great many travellers succumbed to the infamous 'Maldive fever'. While malaria is not widespread today, many people still believe it is better to be safe than sorry, and so malaria tablets are recommended (they should be taken two weeks before you arrive and several weeks after you leave). Others simply suggest you carry a reliable mosquito repellant, some citronella oil or *madhiri dhundhandi* (mosquito coils).

A certificate of vaccination against yellow fever is required for anyone arriving from an infected area. Many people think it is wise to have precautionary vaccinations for typhoid, tetanus, hepatitis, polio and cholera when travelling anywhere in Asia for an extended period of time, and certainly if you like to go to out-of-the-way places.

The average life span in the Maldives is 67 years, due mainly to intestinal diseases and poor diet (those on the poverty line often exist on rice, fish and sugar, and Maldivians eat few vegetables). To prevent stomach complaints, avoid drinking water from island wells—ask for boiled water, rainwater, a *kurumba* (drinking coconut) or the deliciously sweet *raa* (coconut toddy). A slight stomach upset is to be expected when adjusting to a new environment. Should you develop a fever as well, however, it would be wise to consult a doctor.

Sunburn is by far the most common health problem for travellers to the Maldives. Some form of protection is essential, even for bronzed sunworshippers. Don't underestimate the strength of those equatorial rays (even when it's overcast), particularly when travelling by boat when you can so easily be fooled by the soft sea breezes. There is not a wide range of sun creams available locally so it is wise to bring your own.

Sunglasses, too, are a must for protection against the blinding glare that bounces off the white sand and whitewashed buildings. Make sure you drink plenty of fluids and keep your salt intake up if you perspire excessively.

If you cut yourself at all in a tropical climate such as this, it is wise to treat the wound carefully. Keep it clean and dry at all times, avoid bandages unless absolutely necessary and apply an antibiotic powder.

Last, but not least—if you are prone to seasickness, bring along the necessary medication.

Time and business hours

The Maldives is 5 hours ahead of Greenwich Mean Time. When it is 12 noon locally, it is: 12.30 pm in India and Sri Lanka; 5 pm in Sydney; 2 am in New York; 7 am in London; and 11 pm the previous day in San Francisco.

As with all Islamic nations, every Friday is a holiday. Government offices are closed all day, restaurants and shops shut around 11 am and open again at 2 pm. On every other day, government offices open from 7.30 am to 1.30 pm, while shops and restaurants open from 8 am to 11 pm (except the bazaar that closes at 6 pm), closing for 15 minutes four times a day for prayers.

The post office is open every day except Friday from 7.30 am to 1.30 pm, and again from 3 pm to 5 pm. Banks open from Sunday to Thursday, 9 am to 1 pm, and on Saturday from 9 am to 11 am.

During the fasting month of Ramadan, commercial working hours may be staggered or shortened, and even non-existent in some places.

Post and telecommunications

Mail to and from anywhere in the world takes up to 10 days. Parcels sent by surface mail may take six months or more. In fact, sending a parcel of gifts or souvenirs out of the country is a somewhat laborious affair. Custom officers are obliged to check the goods being sent and they are invariably confronted by a sea of Indian businessmen, all pleading for attention. Set aside, therefore, at least half a day if you want to send a parcel overseas. Should your parcel contain any local handicrafts or objects made of gold, silver or brass, then it must first be checked at the Customs Office.

Philatelists will love the colour and variety of Maldivian stamps and, if you are truly interested, a fine old collection can be viewed in Male' at Raiyvilaa, 10 Fareedhee Magu.

Telephone calls are easily made and telex or facsimile messages can be sent to anywhere in the world from Dhiraagu, the telecommunications company in Male', or from any of the resorts. From the island villages, neighbouring islands are contacted by walkie-talkie and distant islands by radio-telephone.

Electricity

On the resorts and in Male', plug fittings are of the square-pin variety and power is 240 volts, alternating currents and five cycles. The small generator plant that supplies electricity to Male' is more often than not stretched to its limits. There are occasional blackouts and the air-conditioning in your Male' tourist hotel may sometimes be out of order during the midday heatwaves.

Those travelling to the fishing villages and far-flung islands will not be relying on electrical appliances—kerosene is used for lamps and stoves, although most islanders cook over wood-fuelled stoves and ovens made of coral. Limited supplies of electricity from generators are available for official use on some islands.

Photography

Professional photographers will tell you one thing about the tropics—it ruins your film. It is best to keep any film in a cool, dry place. The best time to take photographs is before 10 am and after 3 pm and you usually need a polarising filter to combat the glare.

Most locals are only too eager to be photographed (they'd love you to send them a copy) and it doesn't take a group of 10 or so children more than a few seconds to gather before your lens. Some of the older folk may be a little more reticent and it is only polite to ask first for their permission.

There are certain situations where photographs should not be taken. It is understandably frowned upon to take close-up shots of people praying; it is forbidden to take photographs of Theemuge, the President's residence, and of the National Security Service headquarters, and it's wise not to photograph airports and military equipment or property.

Film can be processed in Male' at *Reethi Foto* and *Fotogenic* on Majeedi Magu, and *Fototeknik*, which has several branches. Print and slide film is available in Male' and on the resorts at reasonable prices.

Anyone wishing to shoot documentary, publicity or feature film must apply to the Ministry of Information and Culture for permission to do so. They charge $US50 per day for documentary films and $100 per day for publicity and feature films.

Tipping

Tipping is not the norm for local people, although it has become generally accepted by waiters and domestic staff on the resorts. Needless to say, a tip now and then always brings a little extra effort with the service. Restaurants add a 10 per cent service charge to the bill whereas teashops do not.

Investments

Since the birth of tourism in the Maldives, more and more foreign investors are keen to lease islands and construct resorts in order to reap the benefits of tax-free profits and duty-free imports. Of course there are certain guidelines to adhere to, and there are as many failures as there are success stories. Information on foreign investment is available from the Ministry of Trade and Industries in Male'.

Media

There are a few local newspapers, including the daily *Aa Fathis* and *Haveeru*, which contain a few paragraphs of English news. The Ministry of Information and Culture publishes a weekly news bulletin in English, and the international magazines *Time* and *Newsweek* are available each week.

The prime media outlets are radio and television and both are government-controlled. *The Voice of Maldives* broadcasts from 5.30 am until 10.45 pm every day. While the bulk of the programs are in Dhivehi, there is the occasional pop song in English, an abundance of Hindi love songs, and an English news bulletin at 6.00 pm each day. *TV Maldives* provides a mixture of recitals from the *Quran*, local plays, Hindi and English movies, news in Dhivehi and English, and a variety of English programs including sports, entertainment and documentaries. *CNN* is also available via satellite to those resorts, hotels and private homes that have installed dish antennas.

There are also a small number of privately owned cinemas in Male' which predominantly show the action-packed Hindi adventure (or was it a musical?) style of movie. The locals love them and, if you've never seen one, here's your chance!

Shopping

Occasionally, a large craft exhibition is held in Male'. The best work from all over the archipelago is on show and up for sale. The finest pieces are usually sold to government dignitaries before the exhibition opens, but these remain on show and there is still plenty for everyone. The prices are not negotiable, each item having a price-tag attached.

It is always cheaper, of course, to buy direct from the source. Unless you are planning an extensive trip through the islands, however, this just isn't possible. You should still be able to bargain for some good prices in the tourist shops around Male' and on the nearby fishing villages. Some of the articles you are likely to come across include the following.

Jewellery Brittle branches of black coral are plucked from the deep by young island divers. You can't export the black coral in its natural state but the veinlike branches are cut and polished, then set into rings, earrings, pendants, bangles and jewellery boxes.

In the central atolls, there are a few jewellers who specialise in gold and silver. None of it, however, seems quite as beautiful as the jewellery made by their ancestors, which is still readily available today—intricately carved, heavy silver bracelets and armlets; thin, meshed silver belts that wrap several times around your waist; silver charm boxes; and gold chains and necklaces.

Turtle shell The government now prohibits the capture of smaller-sized turtles. Although there are stuffed turtles on display in Male', they cannot be taken out of the country.

Turtles' shells are made into all sorts of decorative item, but there is nothing more delightful than seeing those beautiful shells float past you under the water and on the backs of busy bald-headed turtles where they belong.

Sea-shells There are thousands of sea-shells along the island shores. Cowries and nautilus shells are abundant. Conch, pearl, and trident shells are rare. All can be bought from tourist shops, either in their raw state or beautifully polished.

Wooden boxes Among the most popular purchases are the carved and lacquered wooden boxes from Baa Atoll. They range in size from pillboxes to the boxes used to carry family feasts to the mosques. All are lacquered in strands of red, black and yellow and have finely etched abstract designs.

Mats Women from villages in the northern and southern atolls weave fine reed mats. The most outstanding are the *thundu kunaa*, ranging in size from tablemats to 2-m-long prayer mats. The best *thundu kunaa* traditionally come from Gadhdhoo in Gaafu Dhaalu Atoll. They are woven on handlooms, using a locally grown reed which is dried then dyed various shades of cream, caramel, yellow, brown and black.

They sell for around Rf60 from the source, or up to $US60, depending on how intricate the Islamic design is, from shops and touts in Male'.

Drums   The *bodu beru* (local drum) is made from a hollowed piece of coconut wood with dried stingray hides enclosing each end. They are available from a few tourist shops or can be bought from the villages for around $US10 to $US15.

Materials   The Maldivians have their own fashions: the *mundu* (sarong) and *gamis* (shirt) for men; and the *faaskuri hedhun* (long-sleeved dress with wide scalloped collar, which reaches to the ankles) or *Dhivehi libaas* (long-sleeved dress of bright tropical colour which reaches to just below the knees, the neck of which is usually embroidered with fine lines of golden thread in symmetrical design) and *kandiki* (black sarong tucked around the waist) for women.

Most Maldivians, especially the young, seem to prefer bright polyesters, regardless of the heat. Some members of the older generation still wear the brown and cream, locally woven *feyli* cloth made in Baa Atoll. And the material shops in Male' sell a wide range of materials imported from India and Singapore. There are tailors along virtually every street in Male', some of them dabbling in safari-suit creations and *fatuloonu* (trousers), and others appealing directly to tourists with cheap cotton travel gear.

Hiki mas   The rock-hard fish which you see and smell everywhere in Male' is *hiki mas*, more popularly referred to as 'Maldive fish'. It is made by boiling and smoking fillets of tuna, then drying them under the sun over several days. They are regarded locally as a source of nourishment and are considered somewhat of a delicacy in neighbouring countries. The Sri Lankan merchants in the Colombo markets are known to pay up to four times the cost price for 1 kg of 'Maldive fish'. Tourists are permitted to export up to 5 kg each. You can buy *hiki mas* from the bazaar in Male', or from someone's kitchen in any of the villages, for around Rf10 per kilogram.

Ambergris For hundreds of years, the Maldives has been famous for ambergris, the opaque ash-coloured substance secreted from the gut of the sperm whale and usually found floating on the ocean or cast ashore. Fragrant when heated, ambergris is an important ingredient in the manufacture of expensive cosmetics and perfumes. One kilogram fetches around $US1000 on the local market and about 10 times that overseas. There is a 50-per-cent custom tax on its export.

Local oddities If you're a collector of knick-knacks then you will love the backstreets of the Male' bazaar, where you can scout around the small and unassuming 'junk shops'. There are many of them, and inside you will discover a conglomeration of local inventions made from recycled materials. Each one is useful in some way, be it for a sojourn in the outer atolls or as a decoration for the mantelpiece back home.

Imported wares You will find an assortment of imported cosmetics, cassettes, calculators, watches and the like around the Male' bazaar, but the prices are nothing to write home about.

Lace making in the southern atolls

Traditional ceremony in Male'

Start your perfect holiday long before you get there

When it comes to discussing the finest and most reputable travel company in the Maldives, only one name is mentioned — **VOYAGES MALDIVES**. We'll arrange the perfect holiday for you and your budget, before you even get there. From deluxe resort accommodation to simple beach huts, flight reservations to island hopping — all you do is sit back and enjoy the holiday of a lifetime. Allow our professional and expert team at **VOYAGES MALDIVES** to take care of the arrangements for you.

Voyages Maldives (Pvt) Ltd.

2 Fareedhee Magu, 20-02 Male' Republic of Maldives
Tel: (960) 322019 Fax: (960) 325336 Tlx: (896) 66063 VOYAGES MF

Fareedhee Magu, Male'

Male' fashion

The best of both worlds

Of the many fine resorts in the Maldives, Safari Tours owns and operates five of the best. From the carefree holiday style preferred by the 18–35s, to idyllic picture-postcard hideaways for honeymooners and first-class retreats for those who demand luxurious solitude. ***We have it all!***

And only Safari Tours, together with Blue Water Safaris, can offer you the exhilaration of serious gamefishing. Come catch a sailfish or do battle with a blue marlin onboard our 10-metre, fully equipped *Prowler*.

safari tours

Telephone: (960) 323524 • Facsimile: (960) 322516
Telex: (896) 66030 • Cable: SAFARI

KAAFU

Male' 116
Male' Atoll 137

MALE'

Male' (pronounced mar-leh) is the capital island, the business and political centre of the nation. For many visitors, particularly those bound for the outer atolls, Male' is the crossroad. For others, it is at least worth a visit.

Since Koimala Kalo first settled on the island nearly 2000 years ago, until sultanates were finally abolished in 1968, Male' was affectionately known as the 'isle of sultans'. It was the home of intellectuals and the elite and noble class, the *beyfulhu*.

According to the notable academic HCP Bell, 'Male', in its own quaint self-centred ways, is in certain respects an oriental utopia.' It is also, he added, '... an architectural eyesore ... a hideous medley of smugness and utilitarianism ... and teeming with a population of 5200 ...' One wonders what Bell would think of Male' today, some 70 years after his *Report on a Visit to Male'*.

On arrival, you no longer gain the impression, as Bell did, of '... a typical Asian village disclosing a long line of thatched dwellings and tropical vegetation ...' Since the 1950s, following Amin Didi's headlong program to modernise the island, what you now see is a maze of paved, immaculate coral streets, a profusion of whitewashed coral houses, shops, offices and mosques with corrugated-iron roofing, and a smattering of multi-storey office blocks. Dominating the skyline is the magnificent Grand Mosque, with its golden dome and towering minaret.

A village atmosphere still exists on the outskirts of the island, where women collect water from communal wells and gossip with their neighbours over palm-latticed fences. Men bring home fish from the bazaar and everyone calls out, 'Kihaa varakah?' ('How much?'). People living in the more sophisticated sections of Male' understandably enjoy their privacy and build their houses behind high coral walls. There are some beautiful old rambling houses with cool dark gardens and verandas found in many parts of the island but, in his enthusiasm to build wonderfully wide streets, Didi thought nothing of destroying most of the tropical vegetation in Male'. If you don't want to suffer sunstroke and sore eyes, make sure you wear a hat and sunglasses when exploring the island.

Bell would probably spin like a top in his grave if he knew that modern-day Male' housed a population of some 60,000, not to mention the regular 10,000 or so casual visitors who arrive from the nearby and far-flung villages to trade at the only produce market in the country. In order to keep pace with the mounting population, years of dredging, draining and filling of the lagoon have joined the two islands of Athamana Hura and Kuda Male' which now constitute Male', measuring nearly two square kilometres.

Surprisingly, visitors are not likely to view Male' as grossly overpopulated. The people are excessively clean and tidy (all rubbish is dumped on the outskirts of the island and used for reclamation work or, unfortunately, ends up floating out to sea).

For ease of orientation, and traditionally for administrative purposes, Male' is best viewed in terms of suburbs. *Henveiru* takes in the two-storey government offices along the Boduthakurufaanu Magu waterfront and some beautiful well-established homes along Ameer Ahmed Magu.

Galolhu embraces the small, congested residential pocket near the south-east corner of the island. To explore this suburb is like wandering through a maze of warrens. *Maafanu* extends from the bazaar and market to the western end of the island. It houses Theemuge, the President's private residence, several embassies and many thatch dwellings. The fourth suburb is *Machchangolhi*, with its boutiques and teashops dotted along Majeedi Magu, the largest and widest street on the island.

Places of interest

The showpiece is the golden-domed **Grand Friday Mosque**, or Masjid-al-Sultan Mohammed Thakurufaanu-al-A'z'am, built in honour of the national hero, Mohammed Thakurufaanu. This impressive building was erected in 1984 with substantial financial assistance from the Gulf States. Inside, the prayer hall accommodates up to 6000 worshippers and there is a conference hall, library and classroom. Beautifully carved wooden panels and doors enhance the decor. It is more commonly known as the Islamic Centre.

Visitors are welcome. Before entering, you are requested to remove your shoes and to wash your feet in the huge ablution blocks. Ensure you are well dressed; shorts and mini dresses are unacceptable. Before noon and around 2 pm are the best times to visit. You should avoid going during prayer times.

Close by, on the waterfront, is the **Jumhooree Maidan**, the public square which is the favourite meeting place in Male'. It leads to the jetty of officialdom, where the national flag is hoisted and the President and his ministers, VIPs and visiting dignitaries are often seen.

For many visitors, the capital's most outstanding attraction is the hustle and bustle of the **Ahmedi Bazaar**, market streets and harbour. Tonnes of local produce, such as rope, cadjan and fish, and imported provisions such as rice, flour and sugar, are loaded and unloaded from dhoni to dock, amidst boisterous good-natured bickering and bargaining. Island men recount tales and call out as you pass.

Close by, around Chandani Magu, is the bazaar which was once referred to as the **Singapore Bazaar** because of the large number of goods imported from Singapore and sold there. A score or more shops, with names like DIK, SEK and MAD, sell imported synthetics, cosmetics, cigarettes and electrical wares, and a small number of travel agents offer dhoni safaris and accommodation on nearby resorts.

For an historical appreciation of the island, stroll along Meduziyaaraiy Magu, behind the Singapore Bazaar. Here you will see the remains of the former Sultan's Palace, now called **Sultan Park**. Admission to the park is free, but it is only open on Fridays, from 4 pm until 6 pm. Hundreds of locals arrive during these hours to pose for family photographs and to while away the hours.

The quaint two-storey **National Museum**. is within the park grounds. It houses a scant albeit interesting collection of artefacts, regal costumery, weapons, antique furniture and archaeological finds. There are no tour guides to inform you about the exhibits, but it is well worth a browse. Admission is Rf5, and the museum is open every day from 9 am to noon and from 3 pm to 6 pm.

Just up the road is the centuries-old **Hukuru Miskiiy** (literally meaning Friday Mosque), adorned, sadly, with a corrugated iron roof. It was built in 1656 and inside are some ancient and incredibly intricate engravings. Before entering, non-Muslims should seek permission from the Ministry of Justice and Islamic Affairs. In 1667, a huge cylindrical tower was built close by and, until recently, the island muezzin would scurry to the top in order to summon the people to come to the mosque to pray. Nowadays he uses a loudspeaker, as do the other muezzin who cry out from each of the 28 mosques scattered around Male'.

Some of the mosques have meticulously preserved graveyards and the ancient tombstones of national heroes. Around the Hukuru Miskiiy are a number of gold-plated tombstones, honouring former sultans and members of the noble class. Opposite, behind the high whitewashed coral wall, is the **Tomb of Abu al-Barakat**, festooned with medieval-like white flags. Beside the **Bihuros Kamana Mosque** is the gravestone of the great Mohammed Thakurufaanu, and in the grounds of the **Ali Rasgefaanu Ziyaaraiy** lies the remains of the heroic Sultan Ali VI.

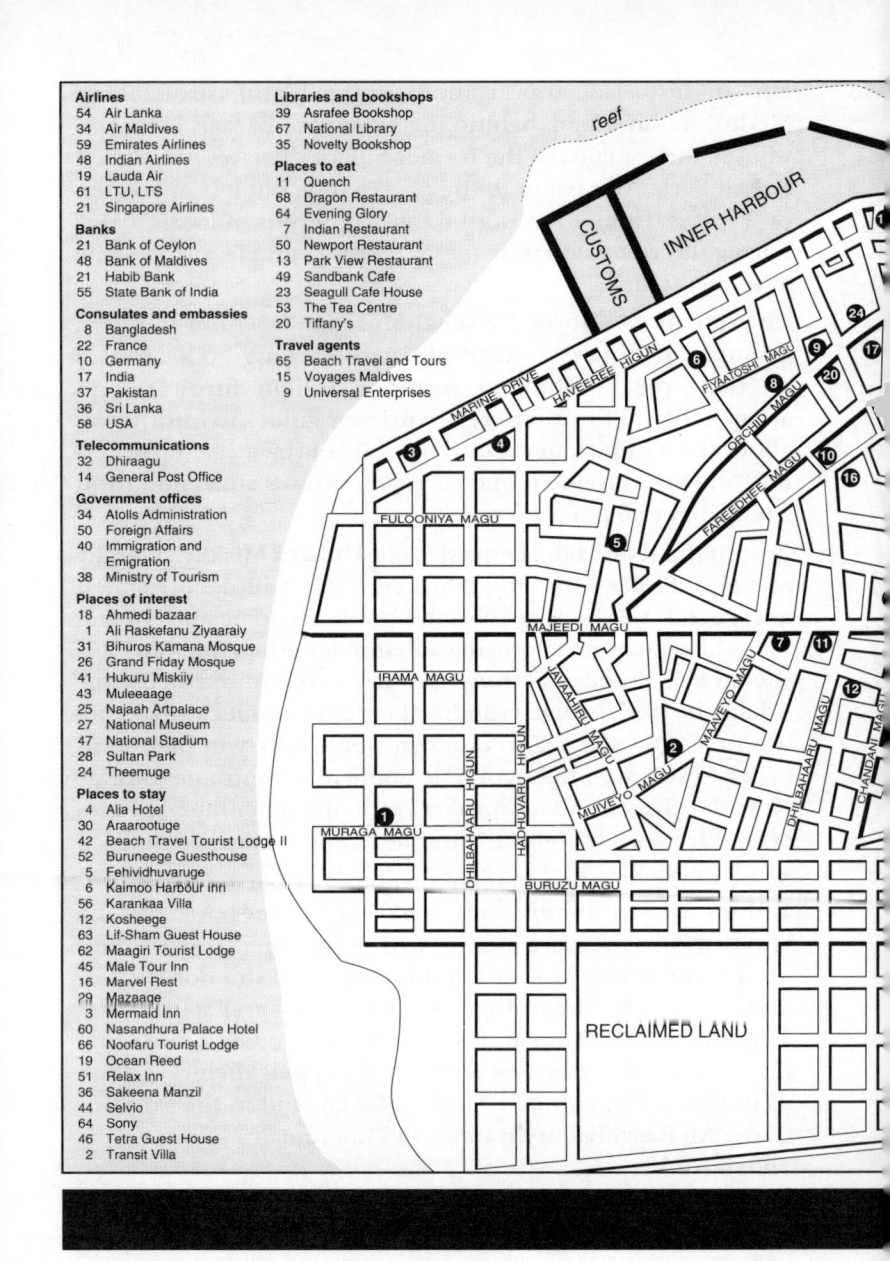

Airlines
54 Air Lanka
34 Air Maldives
59 Emirates Airlines
48 Indian Airlines
19 Lauda Air
61 LTU, LTS
21 Singapore Airlines

Banks
21 Bank of Ceylon
48 Bank of Maldives
21 Habib Bank
55 State Bank of India

Consulates and embassies
8 Bangladesh
22 France
10 Germany
17 India
37 Pakistan
36 Sri Lanka
58 USA

Telecommunications
32 Dhiraagu
14 General Post Office

Government offices
34 Atolls Administration
50 Foreign Affairs
40 Immigration and Emigration
38 Ministry of Tourism

Places of interest
18 Ahmedi bazaar
1 Ali Raskefanu Ziyaaraiy
31 Bihuros Kamana Mosque
26 Grand Friday Mosque
41 Hukuru Miskiiy
43 Muleeaage
25 Najaah Artpalace
27 National Museum
47 National Stadium
28 Sultan Park
24 Theemuge

Places to stay
4 Alia Hotel
30 Araarootuge
42 Beach Travel Tourist Lodge II
52 Buruneege Guesthouse
5 Fehividhuvaruge
6 Kaimoo Harbour Inn
56 Karankaa Villa
12 Kosheege
63 Lif-Sham Guest House
62 Maagiri Tourist Lodge
45 Male Tour Inn
16 Marvel Rest
29 Mazaage
3 Mermaid Inn
60 Nasandhura Palace Hotel
66 Noofaru Tourist Lodge
19 Ocean Reed
51 Relax Inn
36 Sakeena Manzil
44 Selvio
64 Sony
46 Tetra Guest House
2 Transit Villa

Libraries and bookshops
39 Asrafee Bookshop
67 National Library
35 Novelty Bookshop

Places to eat
11 Quench
68 Dragon Restaurant
64 Evening Glory
7 Indian Restaurant
50 Newport Restaurant
13 Park View Restaurant
49 Sandbank Cafe
23 Seagull Cafe House
53 The Tea Centre
20 Tiffany's

Travel agents
65 Beach Travel and Tours
15 Voyages Maldives
9 Universal Enterprises

Maldives — 120 —

MALE'

Emergency services
57 Hospital
33 Police

Getting around

Male' is easily explored on foot. In fact, you can walk the length of the island in about 20 minutes. For locals, the most popular form of transport is a bicycle. There are more than 5000 of them. Remember to lock your bicycle when you are not using it, or it's bound to go missing by mistake. Use a light after 6 pm, or the police will insist that you get off and walk. A bicycle light can be bought for Rf16 from many shops. Male', with its flat streets and various nooks and crannies to explore, seems ideal for cycling. However, evening throngs of shoppers and the growing number of motorised vehicles on the island have ensured it is no longer the pleasurable experience it once was.

Despite the innumerable potholes and the rare chance of ever using top gear, it is becoming more popular to import motorbikes and cars. There are 3500 registered motorcycles and autocycles, almost 650 cars and taxis, another 700-odd lorries, vans and pickup trucks, and many heavy vehicles, such as cranes, forklifts and tractors. Taxi license plates are yellow and their registration numbers begin with '9' or '1'. Fares are generally fixed at Rf10 per trip, regardless of distance. For a tour of the island, taxis can be hired at Rf60 an hour. Choose one that is air-conditioned. Contact *Fine Taxi* (tel: 328998), *Express Taxi* (tel: 323132), *Khaleej Taxi* (tel: 325060), *Kulee Dhuveli* (tel: 322122) or *New Taxi Service* (tel: 322454, 325757).

Places to stay

Accommodation is easily found in Male'. There are three tourist hotels and more than 40 guesthouses. (Alcohol is not available anywhere on Male' these days.) Room rates range from $US10 per night for a bed in a crowded dormitory, to $US60 per night for a comfortable air-conditioned room. Taxi drivers know the locations of all the guesthouses and hotels, but telephone first to ensure there are vacancies.

Up-market

Nasandhura Palace Hotel (tel: 323380) is hidden behind a high coral wall in Henveiru, right on the waterfront. It's in an excellent location. The rooms upstairs look over the wall and out to the fleet of dhoni on the harbour and to the islands beyond. There are 31 rooms and a restaurant. Flight crews often stay here during their stopovers. Room rates are $US55 single, $US75 double.

The *Alia Hotel* (tel: 322080) is at the western end of Male', on Haveeree Higun. The two-storey complex has 18 rooms and a restaurant. Room rates are $US40 single, $US55 double. Air-conditioned rooms are $US12 per day extra. Guests can enjoy three meals a day for less than $US20. The small garden area is a popular meeting place for the Sri Lankan teachers who work in Male'. They banter for hours on end each night.

Relax Inn (tel: 314531) is a six-storey hotel in Ameer Ahmed Magu. It has an excellent restaurant on the top floor, 13 comfortable air-conditioned rooms (some with balconies overlooking the harbour) and an elevator service to all floors.

Moderate

Kaimoo Harbour Inn (tel: 323241) is a stone's throw from the hustle and bustle of the markets. It is one of the best places to stay in Male' and excellent value at $US36 single, $42 double, including breakfast. There are only four rooms, each spacious and fan-cooled. Unlike most other places, it has a reasonable freshwater supply. Another big drawcard at Kaimoo is the open-air restaurant which specialises in French seafood cuisine. It is one of the best restaurants in town. The style and ambience of Kaimoo Harbour Inn is the work of Philippe Laurella, a Frenchman who has lived in the Maldives for more than 10 years. His Maldivian wife and child live in Noonu Atoll, and Philippe often escapes Male' for the peace of the far-flung islands.

Karankaa Villa (tel: 328544) sits atop an office block overlooking the waterfront, not far from Nasandhura Palace. Entry to the guesthouse is via a side door on Kurangi Goalhi. You go up a staircase and come to a large reception area with spectacular water views through sliding-glass windows. Up another spiralling staircase and you find three clean, comfortable and fan-cooled rooms. Room rates are $US35 single, $US45 double.

Noofaru Tourist Lodge (tel: 322731), on Boduthakurufaanu Magu in Henveiru, has four spick-and-span rooms and an adjoining restaurant. Room rates are $US38 single and $US52 double, including breakfast. All the rooms are fan-cooled, and air-conditioning is available for an extra $US10 a day.

Buruneege Guesthouse (tel: 322870) is hidden in the backstreets of Galolhu, on Hithaffiniva Magu. It is a rambling two-storey house with four rooms upstairs, three rooms downstairs, and another three rooms in the garden. Although the rooms are quite small, they each have an attached bathroom. The rooms are serviced and cleaned daily. Meals are provided in the spacious dining room which opens onto a veranda, overlooking a beautiful shady garden. Room rates are $US35 single and $US50 double, including breakfast. One of the rooms is air-conditioned and costs $US60 per day.

Tetra Guest House (tel: 322207) is a two-storey house on Hadheebee Higun in Galolhu, not far from the Male' Fitness Centre. It has four rooms with attached bathrooms, and a communal sitting room with television and video. Room rates are $US35 single, $US50 double.

Araarootuge (tel: 322661) is in Machchangolhi. A large two-storey house, it has six rooms upstairs and three rooms downstairs. All the rooms are small and fan-cooled, some have attached bathrooms and others share communal facilities. Room rates are $US25 single, $US42 double.

Maagiri Tourist Lodge (tel: 322576) is on Boduthakurufaanu Magu in Henveiru and has six rooms. Two of the rooms have attached bathrooms, and verandas with water views. The other rooms share communal facilities. Room 5, upstairs, is the most spacious and comfortable of the rooms. Downstairs is a large sitting room with television and video, and guests are welcome to use the well-equipped kitchen. Room rates are $US35 single and $US45 double, including breakfast.

Sunrise Lodge (tel: 321501), on Lonuziyaaraiy Magu in Galolhu, is managed by Naseer, a young, friendly Maldivian who will advise guests on resort accommodation and accompany them on night-fishing outings. There are nine clean, cosy rooms for $US25 single, $US40 double.

Lif-Sham Guest House (tel: 325386) is on Gulisthaanu Goalhi in Henveiru. It has three rooms with attached bathrooms and fans. Room rates are $US30 single and $US40 double, including breakfast.

Sony (tel: 325360) sits above a general store on Janavaree Magu in Henveiru. Once a small guesthouse, it now has 11 rooms costing $US35 single and $US45 double.

Beach Travel Tourist Lodge (tel: 320092), on Seesan Magu in Henveiru, is very popular with independent travellers. As the name suggests, it is owned by Beach Travel and Tours, so guests can expect to be well looked after. The lodge has six rooms, all with air-conditioning and freshwater showers. Room rates are $US30 single, $US50 double.

Rates and facilties are similar at *Beach Travel Tourist Lodge II* (tel: 325966) on Neelafaru Magu in Galolhu. It has seven rooms. The rates at both guesthouses include breakfast.

Inexpensive

Fehividhuvaruge (tel: 324470) is smack bang in the middle of town. It is invariably occupied by Indians in Male' on business, and Sri Lankan teachers who forgo comfort for less cost. There are four rooms and communal bathroom facilities. Room rates are $US10 single, $US15 double.

Male' Tour Inn (tel: 326220) is in Maafanu, on Shaheed Ali Higun, close to the Star Cinema. The four rooms are quite spacious and clean, and relatively well-priced at $US15 single and $US25 double, including breakfast.

Kosheege (tel: 323585), in Machchangolhi, has seven rooms with attached bathrooms. More often than not, they are permanently occupied by Sri Lankan teachers. There may be vacancies during the school holidays in December and January. Room rates are $US18 single, $US25 double.

Mermaid Inn (tel: 323329) is a two-storey building on Boduthakurufaanu Magu in Maafanu. Upstairs are seven small fan-cooled rooms with attached bathrooms. Downstairs is a restaurant, and a communal sitting room with television and video. Room rates are $US20 per person. Three meals a day costs $US14.

Sakeena Manzil (tel: 323281), on Medhuziyaaraiy Magu, is a large two-storey house close to the bazaar. It is extremely popular with the Indian clientele so, if you are able to get a room, prepare yourself for the loud and jolly atmosphere. There are several dormitory rooms with beds costing $US10 per day, meals included. A double room with attached bathroom costs $US30 per day, including meals. The family also manages Asgar Tours, a small travel agency specialising in day excursions to nearby resorts.

Ocean Reed (tel: 323311) is on Fareedhee Magu, near the KLM office. It provides cheap dormitory accommodation for $US8 per person, including meals. A large double room costs $US20 per day, including meals.

Selvio (tel: 324671), on Kalutukkala Magu, has five spacious rooms, each with an attached bathroom, and charges $US15 per person per day (or $US10 during the low season).

Mazaage (tel: 324669) is on Nikagas Magu, a short walk from some good restaurants. It has three rooms with rates around $US7 per person, or $US10 including breakfast.

Nivico (tel: 322942), on Chandani Magu, has seven rooms for $US10 single and $US15 double.

Green Lin (tel: 320750), on Neelafaru Magu, has six rooms with rates around $US7 per person, or $US10 including breakfast. It is usually occupied by Indian tourists and Sri Lankan teachers.

Places to eat

There is a restaurant on almost every street corner, along nearly every little *goalhi* and in the nooks and crannies of Male'. No matter where you are on the island, you can always find somewhere to eat!

The local restaurants are small and often crowded. Long tables are decorated with bowls of curries and plates of tasty tidbits. Diners wander in, sit anywhere, choose whatever they fancy, and then pay as they leave. You might have a bowl of rice, a selection of curries, a piece of spicy fried fish and a hot sweet cup of tea for around Rf15 (less than $US2). Half that amount buys you a variety of snacks, or *hedhi-kaa*, to enjoy with your cup of tea. The savoury ones, made with fish, coconut and spices, cost 50 laari or Rf 1 each, depending on size, and the sweet snacks are Rf1 each. While these eating houses are strictly a male domain for Maldivians, foreign women are admitted with a minimum of fuss.

Apart from these local restaurants-cum-teashops, there are a handful of European-style cafes and hotel restaurants.

Up-market

Both the Alia Hotel and Nasandhura Palace have air-conditioned restaurants, offering similarly priced, à la carte, Western-syle menus. Be aware that a 10-per-cent service charge is usually levied by the à la carte restaurants.

Moderate

On Chandani Magu, you will find *Park View Restaurant*. Specialties of the house come from the tandoor oven. Chicken immersed in a mildly spiced yoghurt sauce and grilled in the clay oven is a popular dish. The menu is dotted with a variety of curries that range from Rf35 to Rf70. It also includes western and Chinese dishes, such as grilled fillet steak, banana split and chicken chow mein. Not mentioned on the menu is the special three-course meal with coffee for $US10 per person. You can choose to dine in air-conditioned comfort inside or on the patio outside. Park View is open every day from 11 am until midnight.

Ground Six is on the top floor of Relax Inn. There are terrific views of Male' harbour from this restaurant. The service is pleasant and the menu reasonably priced. Curries and Chinese dishes are the specialty.

Slice is an air-conditioned restaurant on Faamudheyri Magu in Maafanu. Pasta and seafood prevail.

Twin Peaks, on Orchid Magu, is popular with young locals and business people. The menu includes curries, pasta dishes, seafood, ice-cream and coffee.

Intimate Restaurant on Sheerazi Magu, Galolhu, has snappy service and good food.

Quench has indoor and outdoor tables, and serves sandwiches, hamburgers, fish and chips and a few Indian-style meals.

Cheers and *Intime*, both on the waterfront in Henveiru, are the capital's answer to fast food. Fried foods, hamburgers and mildly spiced short-eats are popular offerings.

Dragon Restaurant is on Boduthakurufaanu Magu near Voice of Maldives. A potpourri of Thai dishes is moderately spiced and reasonably priced.

Shanghai Restaurant is clean, cosy and popular. Seafood stir-fries are a feature of the extensive menu.

Popular with tourists is the *Seagull Cafe House*. Located right in the heart of town, at the intersection of Chandani Magu and Fareedhee Magu, it is an ideal place to relax, sitting in the thatch-covered courtyard and enjoying one of the mouth-watering ice-cream concoctions. If in season, order the papaya filled with ice-cream and mixed fruits (it costs Rf95) and you won't be disappointed. The menu also includes a variety of sandwiches, burgers, and hot and cold drinks.

Another popular retreat is the *Newport Restaurant*, on the waterfront near the Bank of Maldives. This cosy little air-conditioned eatery offers a four-page menu that runs from cheese sandwiches and grilled chicken with salad to steamed macaroni with meat balls, fruit salad and milkshakes. It is open Thursday to Saturday from 10 am to 3 pm and from 6 pm to 11.30 pm, and on Friday from 6.30 pm to 11.30 pm.

Inexpensive

The *Evening Glory* on Janavaree Magu, near the football field in Henveiru, is a top place for short-eats. The sweets drip with coconut honey, the *bondi* (white coconut sticks) are simply the best, and the savouries are big and packed full with freshly smoked fish.

On Majeedi Magu, opposite the multi-storey health centre in Henveiru, is the *Iruvai Cafe*—another good place for short-eats and a cup of tea.

The *Tea Centre* is hidden away in the backstreets of Galolhu (around the corner from Buruneege Guesthouse). It is well worth the trouble to find it. In the evenings they specialise in Sri Lankan dishes. Try the egg hoppers.

A local favourite is the *Handhuvaru Hotel*, opposite the National Stadium on Majeedi Magu.

Camy Cool Spot, near the junction of Majeedi Magu and Sosun Magu, has some of the best short-eats in town.

Fish Market Hotel is, appropriately, smack bang in the middle of Ahmedi Bazaar. Don't miss it! The atmosphere is lively and loud, the curries rich and spicy.

If you can do without frills and air-conditioning, try the elbow-nudging *Indian Restaurant* on Majeedi Magu. Hordes of Indians flock here during their lightning shopping sprees in Male'.

There are many more local restaurants to choose from. They include the *Sandbank Cafe, Moon Cafe, Dawn Cafe, Queen of the Night* and *Junction Hotel*.

Night-life

Male' night-life is testimony to the fact that you don't need booze and rock 'n roll to have a good time. There are a small number of cinemas showing Hindi movies, and locals go shopping or visit friends and relatives. Majeedi Magu comes alive after dark when men, women and children walk up and down the street, stopping to talk to friends and relatives, sharing gossip and window shopping. In stark comparison to the hot daylight hours, it is a pleasant experience to join the throng, caressed by the soft sea breezes and enveloped by the carnival atmosphere. Away from the lights of Majeedi Magu, the houses radiate a general aura of frivolity.

Censored videos can be hired but if discotheques and live bands are more your style, then head for the resorts.

Useful addresses

Airlines

Air Lanka
Athireege Annex 2,
Ameer Ahmed Magu,
Henveiru (tel: 323459)

Air Maldives
Faashanaa Building,
Henveiru (tel: 322438)

Emirates Airlines
Boduthakurufaanu Magu,
Henveiru (tel: 325675)

Indian Airlines
Sifaa,
Boduthakurufaanu Magu,
Henveiru (tel: 323003)

LTU
Maleythila, Meheli Goalhi,
Henveiru (tel: 323202)

Pakistan Airlines
Luxwood No 4,
Boduthakurufaanu Magu,
Henveiru (tel: 323532)

Singapore Airlines
MHA Building
(tel: 320777)

Bakeries

Alcyon Bakery
Fulooniya Magu, Maafanu
(tel: 322627)

Bake House
Sosun Magu (tel: 322858)

KUM Bakery
Kashimaa Store,
Fenfiyaazu Goalhi,
Maafanu (tel: 322547)

Maafanu Aage Bakery
Shabnamee Higun

Veyoge Bakery
Husnuheena Magu,
Galolhu (tel: 327914)

Banks

Bank of Ceylon
1st Floor, Alia Building,
Orchid Magu, Maafanu
(tel: 323046)

Bank of Maldives
Head Office—
Boduthakurufaanu Magu,
Henveiru (tel: 323043)

KURUMBA VILLAGE.
THE LUXURY LEISURE ISLAND
IN THE MAGICAL MALDIVES.

Picture a whole island of unforgettable fun in the heart of the Maldives. Endless stretches of soft white sand. Azure blue waters. Lush greenery. 5-star luxury living. This is Kurumba Village.

Go atoll-hopping. Visit fishing villages. Windsurf. Water ski. Swim. Sail. Scuba-dive. Kurumba Village has it all and much more.

Rooms/Suites
• 156 rooms, 8 suites • Air-con • Piped-in music • Minibar • Hot and cold water • Hair dryer

Business/Convention
• Convention hall • IDD • Fax • Telex • Speedboat ferry service.

Food/Recreation
• Coffee shop • 2 bars • 3 restaurants serving International, Western and and Oriental cuisines • Nightly entertainment programmes • Barbeque terrace • Health centre/gym • Whirlpool bath • Sauna • Tennis • Billiards • 2 fresh water swimming pools • Sailing • Scuba-diving • Snorkelling • Windsurfing.

KURUMBA VILLAGE
MALDIVES
Universal Hotel Group

For more information, contact 38, Orchid Magu, Male 20-02, Republic of Maldives. Telephone: 343081, 343084, 342324, 323080, 322971. Telex: 77083, Kurumba MF, 66024 Unient MF. Telefax: 343885, 322678. Or call your travel agent.

Kurumba Village

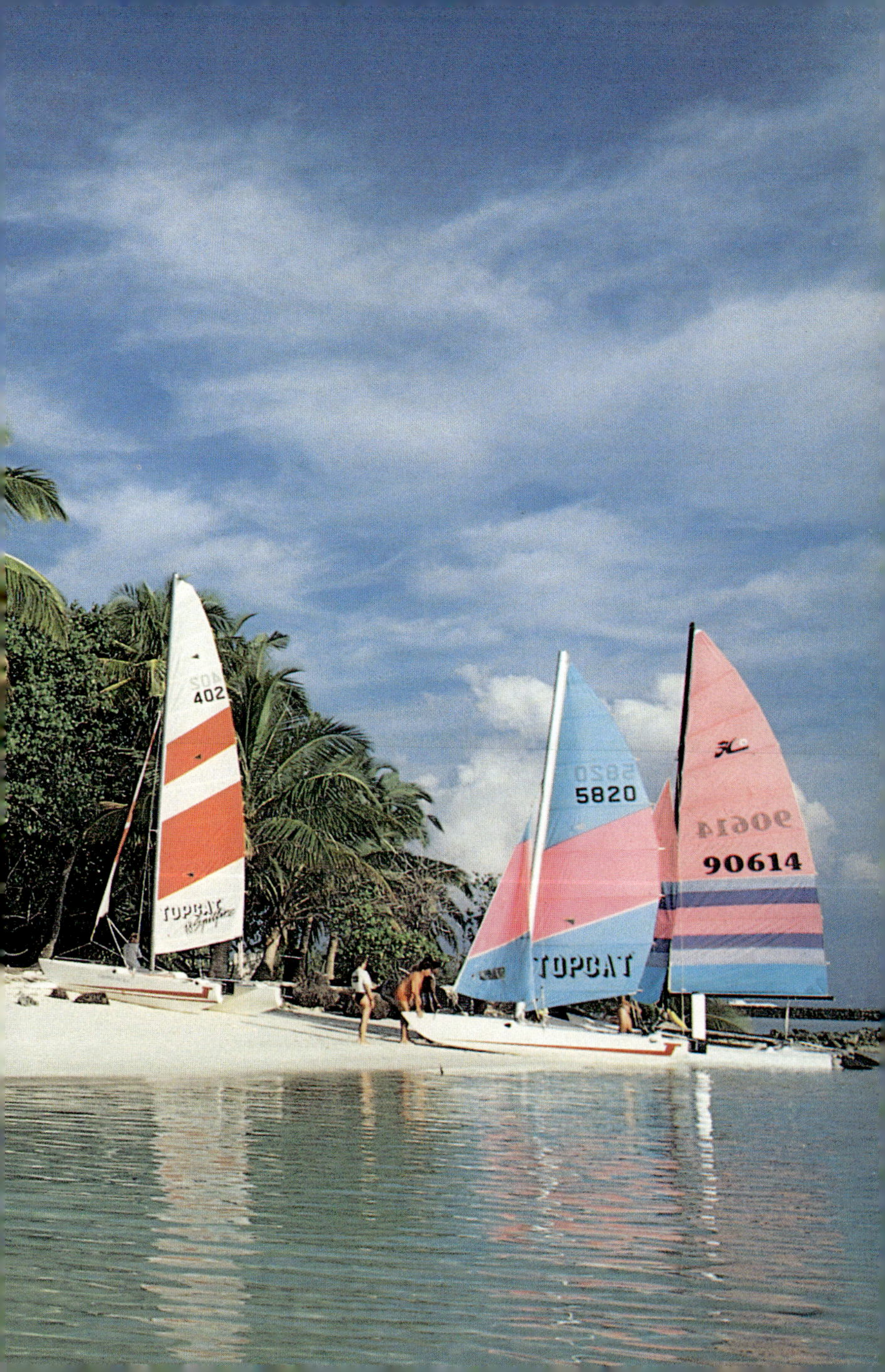
402
TOPCAT
5820
TOPCAT
90614

Grand Friday Mosque, Male'

Bazaar branch—
Boduthakurufaanu Magu,
Henveiru (tel: 322941)
Majeedi Magu branch—
Asrafee Building,
Machchangolhi
(tel: 326800)

Habib Bank
Ship Plaza, Orchid Magu,
Maafanu (tel: 322051)

State Bank of India
Zoneyria,
Boduthakurufaanu Magu,
Henveiru (tel: 323052)

Bookshops
Asrafee Bookshop
Asrafee Building,
Chandani Magu,
Machchangolhi
(tel: 323424)
Orchid Magu,
Maafanu (tel: 323464)

Novelty Bookshop
Fareedhee Magu, Maafanu
(tel: 322564)

Cinemas
Bukhaaree Cinema
Haveeree Higun, Maafanu
(tel: 326531)

Olympus
Majeedi Magu, Galolhu
(tel: 322497)

Star Cinema
Majeedi Magu, Maafanu
(tel: 322913)

Courier services
DHL International
25 Boduthakurufaanu Magu,
Henveiru (tel: 322451)

TNT Skypak
Boduthakurufaanu Magu,
Henveiru (tel: 327451)

Consulates and embassies
Bangladesh
Consulate
Universal Enterprises Ltd,
38 Orchid Magu,
Maafanu (tel: 323080)

Denmark/Norway/Sweden
Consulate
25 Boduthakurufaanu Magu,
Henveiru (tel: 322451)

France
Consular Agency
26 Chandani Magu,
Maafanu (tel: 320258)

India
High Commission
Orchid Magu,
Maafanu (tel: 323015)

Pakistan
High Commission
2 Moonimaage, Galolhu
(tel: 323005)

Palestine
Embassy
Moorithige, Maafanu
(tel: 323304)

Sri Lanka
High Commission
Sakeena Manzil, Henveiru
(tel: 322845)

United Kingdom
Consular Agency
Dhiraagu
(tel: 322802)

USA
Consular Agency
Mandhuedhuruge,
Henveiru (tel: 321981)

Emergency services

Ambulance (tel: 102)

Dental Clinic (tel: 323024)

Electricity (tel: 104)

Fire (tel: 118)

Hospital (tel: 322401)

Police (tel: 119)

Government offices

Customs
Customs Building,
Boduthakurufaanu Magu,
Maafanu
(tel: 325563/fax: 322633)

*Department of Emigration
and Immigration*
Huravee Building, Henveiru
(tel: 323913/fax: 320011)

General Post Office
Semi Deal Building,
Machchangolhi
(tel: 322255/fax: 320374)

Maldives Airport Authority
Male' International Airport
(tel: 323508/fax: 320957)

*Ministry of Atolls
  Administration*
Faashanaa Building,
Henveiru
(tel: 324418/fax: 327750)

Ministry of Education
Ghaazee Building, Henveiru
(tel: 323262/fax: 321201)

Ministry of Environment
Ghaazee Building, Henveiru
(tel: 323919)

Ministry of Foreign Affairs
Boduthakurufaanu Magu
(tel: 323401/fax: 323841)

Ministry of Health and Welfare
Ghaazee Building, Henveiru
(tel: 325768/fax: 328889)

Ministry of Home Affairs
Huravee Building, Henveiru
(tel: 323820/fax: 324739)

*Ministry of Information
  and Culture*
Buruzu Magu, Henveiru
(tel: 323837/fax: 326211)

*Ministry of Justice
  and Islamic Affairs*
Justice Building (tel: 322303)

Ministry of Tourism
Ghaazee Building, Henveiru
(tel: 323228/fax: 322512)

*Ministry of Trade
and Industries*
Ghaazee Building, Henveiru
(tel: 323668/fax: 323756)

*Ministry of Transport
and Communication*
Huravee Building, Henveiru
(tel: 323991/fax: 323994)

Office of the President
Boduthakurufaanu Magu,
Henveiru
(tel: 323701/fax: 325500)

Libraries
National Library
Billoorijehige,
Majeedi Magu, Galolhu
(tel: 323485)

MALE' ATOLL

*Population: 10,133 (plus Male': 60,105)
Inhabited islands: 10
Uninhabited islands: 95
Capital: Thulusdhoo*

Geographically, Male' is a mere link in a double chain of islands known traditionally as Male' Atoll, but referred to as Kaafu for administrative purposes. An agglomeration of islands and sandbanks spreads from the north to the south of the chain for more than 100 km, and only 10 islands, including Male', are inhabited. The remainder are predominantly tourist resorts and a few are reserved for government purposes.

Resort islands
North Male'
Resorts are scattered the length and breadth of Kaafu. Some are but a few minutes by boat from the airport, others are 1 or 2 hours away. If you are bound for the far north of the atoll, prepare yourself for a 4-hour journey and a stopover in Male' if the seas are rough or if your flight arrives at night. There is a

helipad on Madivaru, about midway along the western fringe of North Male' Atoll. It's a 10-minute flight from the international airport on Hulhule and another 10–20-minute dhoni ride to any one of a dozen or so resorts. The one-way fare to Madivaru is $US69.

Giraavaru was once home to the most powerful aboriginal tribe in the Maldives. Only a few kilometres from the airport, it now has a two-storey hotel with 48 air-conditioned rooms. Daily rates are $US110 single, $US190 double. There are some spectacular deep-sea caverns and caves nearby and schools of basking shark are often found in the area.

Farukolufushi is the home of *Club Med*. Located just 3 km from the airport, it has 52 rooms in blocks of Spanish-style two-storey bungalows. The large central complex hosts evening cabarets and buffet-style meals. Guests are offered a range of water sports free of charge. The all-inclusive rates at Club Med are $US130 per person per day.

Thulhagiri is a 2-hour boat ride from the airport. The resort has 58 tastefully furnished rooms, a pleasant restaurant and coffee shop, and an outdoor grill. Room rates are $US144 single, $US178 double.

Bandos is no more than 30 minutes by boat from the airport. Its convenient location makes Bandos popular with visiting diplomats, VIPs, business travellers and airline crews. The high-standard facilities and the spread-out resort grounds also attract families, young couples and a multinational clientele. Apart from being the biggest resort in the Maldives with 205 rooms, Bandos also has a 24-hour coffee shop, Italian and char-grill restaurants, a bar, disco, beauty salon, gym, tennis and squash courts, spa bath and swimming pool, and even a football field. Room rates are $US162 single, $192 double.

Hudhuveli is a pencil-thin sandy strip surrounded by a tremendous crystal-clear lagoon. Run by the same people who operate Bandos, Hudhuveli has 44 rooms, with fans and freshwater showers, which stretch along the length of the island. A restaurant, coffee shop and bar overlook the lagoon. At high

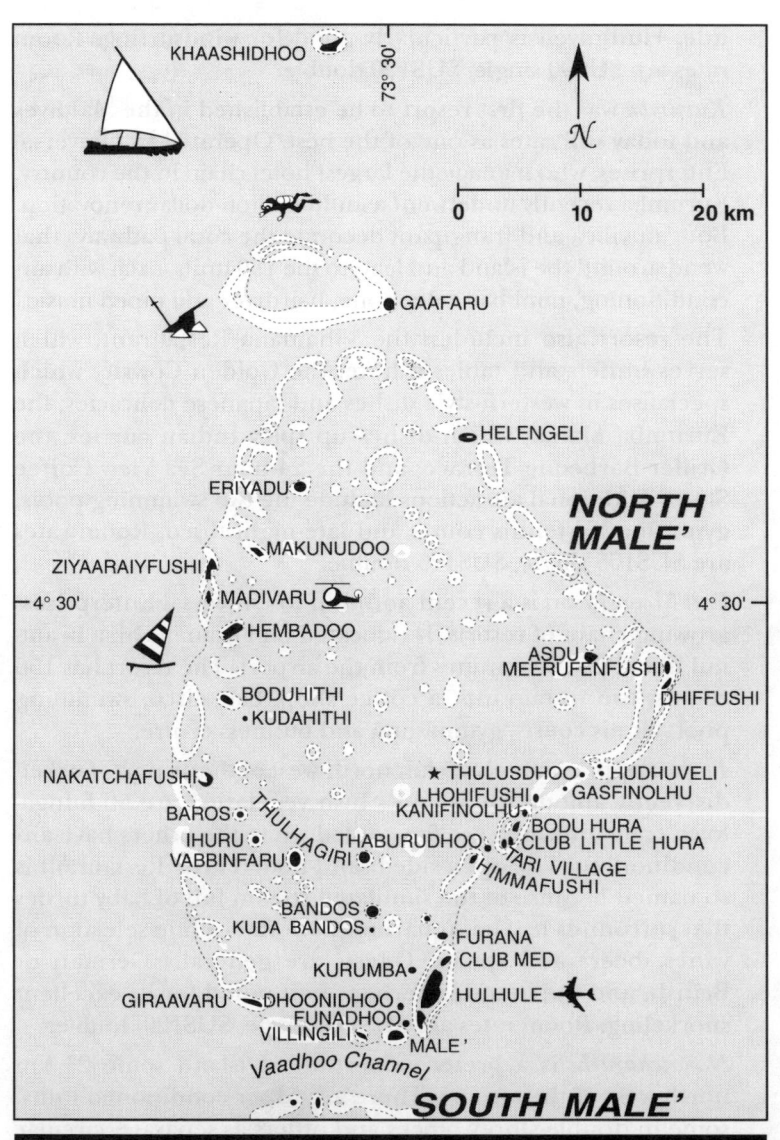

KAAFU: NORTH MALE'

tide, Hudhuveli is particularly good for windsurfing. Room rates are $US90 single, $US120 double.

Kurumba was the first resort to be established in the Maldives and today still rates as one of the best. Operated by Universal Enterprises, who manage the largest hotel chain in the country, Kurumba recently underwent a multi-million-dollar renovation. Bougainvillea and frangipani decorate the coral pathways that wend around the island and lead to the 150 units, each with air-conditioning, mini bar, telephone, hairdryer and piped music.

The resort also includes: the Vihamana Restaurant, which serves buffets and tables d'hôte; the Golden Cowrie, which specialises in western-style dishes and Japanese delicacies; the Kurumba Mahal, which dishes up spicy Indian curries; the Griller Barbeque Terrace; and the 24-hour Sea View Coffee Shop. Additional attractions include the two swimming pools, gym, floodlit tennis courts and late-night disco. Room rates are $US165 single, $US175 double.

Full Moon Resort is a recent addition to Universal Enterprises' growing chain of resorts. It is located on Furanafushi, a beautiful island just 20 minutes from the airport. The resort has 156 rooms, two restaurants, a coffee shop, bar, disco, swimming pool, tennis courts, gymnasium and business centre.

Baros is approximately 15 km north-west of the airport. Tucked discreetly among the island's lush vegetation are 56 bungalows, some of which are fan-cooled while the others have air-conditioning. The open-sided sand-floor Turtle Restaurant is so named because of the simulated stream full of baby turtles that surrounds it. The Aquarium Bar offers a fine selection of wines, beers and spirits. Guests are generally German or British, and the island is perhaps best noted for its excellent snorkeling. Room rates are $US110 single, $US120 double.

Nakatchafushi is a pretty palm-studded island some 25 km north-west of the airport. There are 51 air-conditioned units, some in double-storey blocks and others as separate, circular thatch-roof bungalows. The open-sided restaurant and coffee shop spill out onto a white sandy beach, while the bar extends onto a wooden deck perched over the water's edge. Room rates are $US120 single, $US130 double.

Tari Village is on a tiny island called Kana Oiy Hura. Each of the 24 air-conditioned units are in double-storey blocks. There are bedrooms upstairs and downstairs, and all the units come with fresh hot and cold water. The island's beach frontage is somewhat rugged, having more rocks than actual sand. The resort is best known for its excellent Italian-style cuisine and room rates are $US120 single, $US160 double.

Kanifinolhu is a large beautiful island with 113 comfortably furnished rooms scattered among the palm trees and thick foliage on both sides of the island. A large, centrally located thatch-roof complex houses the reception area, restaurant, bar, coffee shop and boutique. One of the resort's greatest assets is its professional management team. High standards of service are insisted upon and regular improvements are made to all the bungalows and sporting equipment and facilities. Room rates at 'Kani' are $US130 single, $US141 double.

Lohifushi is a spacious island with beautiful gardens and a big lagoon. It is ideal for windsurfing and snorkeling. The resort has four types of bungalow, ranging from deluxe to standard, two restaurants, a swimming pool and a small gymnasium. When compared with other resorts of a similar style, Lohifushi is good value for money. Room rates begin at $US100 single, $US120 double.

Ihuru is picture-postcard-pretty, small, almost perfectly oval-shaped, thickly vegetated, and wrapped neatly in a coral-fringed turquoise lagoon. It adorns much of the glossy tourist literature used to promote the Maldives. Alas, Ihuru has year-round bookings with a major European tour wholesaler. The island has room enough for only 40 bungalows and daily rates are $US100 single, $US160 double.

Boduhithi belongs to the chain of hotels managed by Safari Tours, one of the largest tour operators in the Maldives. As with the majority of their resorts, Italians form the body of their clientele. Pasta and bolognaise sauce is the order of the day, every day. The resort caters to 176 guests in 88 bungalows at a daily rate of $US110 single, $US165 double.

Kudahithi is the jewel in the Safari Tours' crown. Originally a sandy dot in the ocean, coconut palms were brought from other islands and planted. There are six exquisite bungalows, each with its own unique charm. Choose between the Room of the Sheik, King's Room, Rehendi, Safari Room and Captain's Cabin. Or try the Maldivian Room, with its private courtyard which encloses an outdoor bathroom. You can live close to nature with all the mod cons—air-conditioning, ceiling fans, and hot and cold purified water. Room rates are $US255 for two.

Club Little Hura is 16 km from the airport. The 43 rooms line the waterfront of this long narrow island. A thatch-roof sand-floor restaurant sits at the northern end of the island and looks out to the jetty and a wide lagoon. Room rates are $US77 single, $US118 double. From here, you can wade across to Bodu Hura, one of the largest inhabited islands in Kaafu Atoll.

Ziyaaraiyfushi is part of the Phoenix Travel hotel chain which also includes Giraavaru and Bolifushi. The resort has 79 rooms, a restaurant and a bar. Room rates are $US70 single, $US85 double. It is one of the cheapest resorts in the Maldives.

South Male'

South of the airport, beyond Male' and the 5-km-wide Vaadhoo Channel, is a 30-km-long chain of islands known traditionally as South Male' Atoll. It can take up to 4 hours by engine dhoni to get from the international airport to the resorts way down the bottom of South Male' Atoll. To save time, take a helicopter to Guraidhoo and continue by speedboat or dhoni from there. The one-way flight costs $US69.

Embudu Village is best known for the glorious reef which surrounds it. A small oval-shaped island, it has 106 air-conditioned rooms, each with hot and cold water. Rates are $US85 single, $US110 double.

Cocoa Island is better known to local fishermen as Makunufushi. The resort is managed by Eric Klemm, a former fashion photographer with *Playboy* magazine. The eight thatch-roof bungalows are tastefully decorated with local artefacts. Each has a bedroom upstairs and a spacious sitting room and bathroom downstairs. Guests are encouraged to dine together in the intimate open-air restaurant, while Eric entertains with stories about his most memorable fashion shoots. Room rates at Cocoa are $US390 a day, single or double.

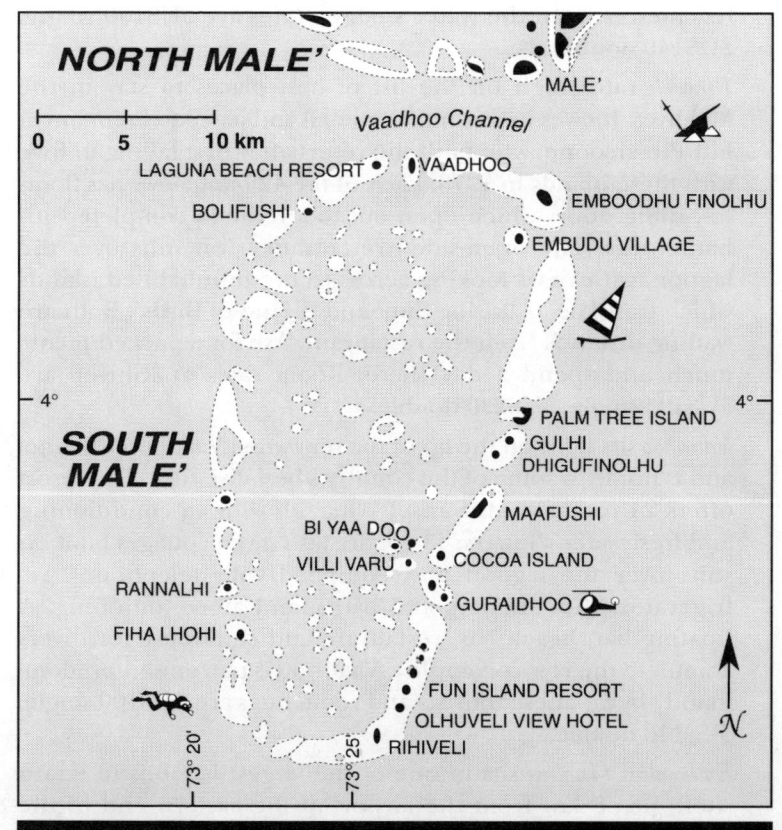

KAAFU: SOUTH MALE'

Bi Ya Doo is a two-storey complex of 96 air-conditioned rooms with hot and cold water and mini refrigerators. There is an air-conditioned restaurant and bar, another bar in the clubhouse, and beach barbeques and discos are held weekly. There is also a small hydroponics factory to ensure regular supplies of fresh fruit and vegetables. Room rates are $US130 single, $US140 double.

Villi Varu is a stone's throw away from Bi Ya Doo. It has 60 fan-cooled rooms with mini refrigerators and private verandas a few metres from the water's edge. Rates are $US130 single, $US140 double.

Rihiveli rates high on the list of best places to stay in the Maldives. It owes its warm continental ambience to Frenchman Pitt Pietersoone, who built the resort after first falling in love with these islands in 1978. Each of the 42 bungalows has floor-to-ceiling doors which open out to a veranda complete with hammocks. The open-sided restaurant is on stilts over the lagoon, with views looking across to two uninhabited islands which translate as 'Rising Sun' and 'Island of Birds'. Both are wading distance from the restaurant. Ask for a packed picnic lunch and spend a day there. Room rates at Rihiveli are $US195 single, $US230 double.

Vaadhoo sits right on the lip of the renowned Vaadhoo Channel and is home to some of the country's best dive sites. The resort offers 24 rooms in its Sunset Wing, all with air-conditioning and freshwater showers. There are also seven cottages built on stilts over the lagoon and equipped with telephones, refrigerators, hot showers and baths, and air-conditioning. A floating bar, beach bar, restaurant and clubhouse for divers complete the resort complex. Vaadhoo is patronised predominantly by Japanese tourists and room rates are $US100 single, $US140 double.

Emboodhu Finolhu sits in one of the largest lagoons in Kaafu Atoll, just 8 km from the airport at the eastern end of the Vaadhoo Channel. There are 24 spacious rooms with private balconies in 12 duplex cottages built on stilts over the lagoon.

And there are another 16 rooms along the beach. The rooms have thatch roofs, air-conditioning, mini refrigerators and hot and cold freshwater showers. A central dining room, well-stocked bar, coffee shop and boutique are located close to the entrance jetty. Emboodhu Finolhu is renowned for its diving, both in the world-famous Vaadhoo Channel and on its very own shipwreck. It has a peaceful, easy-going atmosphere and cosmopolitan clientele. Room rates are $100 single and $120 double.

Laguna Beach Resort is another recent addition to the ever-expanding chain of hotels under the Universal Enterprises' banner, and is typically one of the best-value resorts in the Maldives. It is ideally located on the beautiful island of Velassaru, 1 hour by boat from the airport. The resort complex has 104 air-conditioned rooms—some are split-level bungalows while others are two-storey units. They come with telephones, mini bars, piped music, hairdryers, and verandas or balconies with water views. There are three superb restaurants, a coffee shop, bar, swimming pool and, of course, incredible diving just metres offshore in the spectacular Vaadhoo Channel. Room rates are $US165 single, $US175 double.

Bolifushi is a small island with 32 rooms in a two-storey complex. It is part of the growing chain of hotels operated by Phoenix Travels. Room rates are $US65 single, $US90 double.

Palm Tree Island, on Veligandu Hura, has 60 bungalows complete with air-conditioning and hot and cold freshwater showers. A long wooden walkway spans the lagoon to neighbouring Dhigufinolhu. Room rates are $US150 single, $US190 double.

Dhigufinolhu is a long narrow island with 60 bungalows dotting the periphery. The rooms have air-conditioning, refrigerators and telephones. The spacious restaurant specialises in seafood dishes, and the coffee shop serves snacks and light meals. Daily rates are $US120 single, $US160 double.

Fun Island Resort on Bodufinolhu is located on the eastern reef of South Male' Atoll, some 40 km from the airport. There are

88 rooms with hot and cold freshwater showers, air-conditioning, telephones, and mini bars. There is also an intimate à la carte restaurant, three bars, and a dining room which serves buffets for breakfast and lunch. Room rates are $US135 single, $US145 double.

Kandooma is 30 km south of Male', or 2 hours by engine dhoni. It has 60 air-conditioned rooms. Excursions to the nearby village of Guraidhoo and lively beach barbeques are features at this popular resort. Room rates are $65 single, $85 double.

Olhuveli View Hotel is owned by a Japanese company called Emerald Resort. They have invested $US17 million to construct this sprawling 125-room resort, including 13 luxury suites on stilts over the water. The rooms have videos, mini bars, air-conditioning, and freshwater showers and baths. Room rates are $US275 single, $US300 double.

Fishing villages

According to travel brochures, the nine villages around Kaafu (excluding Male') are 'typical Maldivian fishing villages'. True or false, one thing is certain: these villages have reaped the rewards of being close to Male' and the bulk of the tourist traffic.

Almost every day these so-called 'fishing villages' welcome boatloads of tourists from the nearby resorts. The visits are well-planned: a quick tour of the island, some bargaining over the prices of shells, homemade jewellery and the like, and then a game of soccer or volleyball with the local kids. Unlike the far-flung villages, the people here are no longer afraid or suspicious of *dhon meehun* (white people). Indeed, tourists are now an integral part of the Kaafu economy.

Traditional occupations, such as fishing and weaving, no longer hold pride of place in these villages. It is easier and more profitable to make and sell local souvenirs. Even the general stores on these islands have expanded—alongside the sacks of rice, flour, sugar and spices you now find canned foods, biscuits, Coca Cola and toothpaste.

Himmafushi is the closest village to Male'. It takes 1 hour by engine dhoni or 2 hours by sail dhoni (wind permitting) to get there from Male'. Large and densely vegetated, it houses less than 400 people. Most of them are involved, in one way or another, in the tourist trade. A long row of small thatch-roof souvenir stalls, with their signboards in misspelt German, Italian, French and English, line the jetty. A few small coral houses have been converted into teashops, serving local snacks, soft drinks and tea.

Hura is a few kilometres north of Himmafushi. In its heyday it was the home of Hassan Izzuddeen, a popular 18th century sultan. Today the island Chief and his family are renowned throughout Kaafu for their immense wealth and influence. They own the largest tourist shop and teashop on the island, the biggest dhoni, and the generator which provides electricity to the homes of their friends and relatives on Hura.

Thulusdhoo is about 3 hours' cruising from Male'. Ringed by sandy coves, locals tell you it's the most beautiful village in Kaafu. Close by is a long deserted island. Traders from the neighbouring Raa and Baa Atolls often sail to Thulusdhoo to sell their salted fish at the government warehouse. On the outskirts of the village is a large garment factory where local women make T-shirts for export. And Thulusdhoo now has a boat yard, employing both locals and foreigners, where fibreglass vessels are constructed and engine-repair services rendered.

Dhiffushi is one of six islands floating in a wide expanse of shallow turquoise water which spreads for several kilometres across the eastern fringe of Kaafu. The village, with a population of around 500, is still renowned for its fishing. You regularly see dhoni from Diffushi bound for Male', laden with tonnes of tuna. During the tourist season, young boys from the village pluck lobsters from the caverns on the nearby reef with their bare hands. They are happy to sell them to anyone who is interested.

Gaafaru borrowed its name from the longest reef in the Maldives, measuring approximately 10 km long and 8 km wide. Isolated, the island is a popular destination with diving enthusiasts as Gaafaru Reef is the graveyard for many cargo ships.

Kaashidhoo, with over 1000 inhabitants, is the largest village in Kaafu. It lies isolated at the centre of the infamous Kaashidhoo Kandu, the massive channel that separates the northern atolls from the rest of the archipelago. The large sheltered lagoon that surrounds Kaashidhoo provides safe anchorage for passing boats and is a favourite entrepôt for dhoni heading north. The island is renowned among locals for producing the sweetest *raa* (toddy) in the country.

Gulhi is a small pretty island about 20 km south of Male'. It houses around 300 people, some of whom recall the day when a fire razed the island and left not a single house standing. The mosque here was built during the reign of Sultan Mohammed Shamshuddeen III (AD 1904–1934).

Maafushi is a long and narrow island slightly south of Gulhi. In one corner of the island is a reformatory school for orphaned and wayward children. There is also a government warehouse that buys salted fish from the nearby atolls. Almost every day, dhoni arrive from Alifu and Laamu Atolls, the crews unloading bundles of salted fish before setting sail for home.

Guraidhoo was once a holiday resort for locals. Nowadays it has a resident community of 400 people, some of whom have leprosy. HCP Bell visited the island in 1922 to see the grave of Sultan Hussain Faamuladeyri Kilagefaanu. The mosque here was built during the reign of Sultan Mohammed Shamshuddeen III (AD 1904–1934).

Other Islands

Dhoonidhoo, just north of Male', was the former residence of the British Governor. The large coral bungalow he once occupied still stands on this small oval-shaped island. Nowadays, it is often used to house political prisoners.

Nearby is **Kuda Bandos**, a small, densely vegetated island with a magnificent beach and lagoon. Several companies have offered astronomical amounts to lease the island in order to build a resort, but to no avail. The government reserves the island for locals and, on Fridays, boatloads of men, women and children motor across to enjoy a picnic lunch under the palms and to swim in the lagoon. On other days, anyone can visit provided they pay an entry fee (children Rf2, adults Rf5, tourists Rf10). As there is no ferry service other than on public holdays, when a ferry departs Male' at 7 am and returns between 4.30 pm and 5.00 pm, you will probably need to hire a boat. Guests from neighbouring Bandos Island Resort often visit Kuda Bandos.

Villingili was, until recently, a 128-room resort with all the dolce far niente trappings. It is now home to a few British expatriates who man the Earth Station and control telecommunications. Accommodation for approximately 10,000 people is presently under construction and is sure to ease the strain on overpopulated Male' once it is completed.

Funadhoo once housed a coconut-fibre mill and, later, a poultry farm. It is now reserved for the government employees who staff the oil-storage tanks.

To the north is **Thaburudhoo**, an island prison. Access is prohibited, although some surfers have been known to frequent the nearby reef, reputedly the best surfing spot in Kaafu Atoll.

Feydhoo was once a fairly large island but erosion and the removal of sand for building and other purposes washed the island away. In 1973, reclamation from the lagoon was started by Ibrahim Nasir, who considered Feydhoo to be his private property.

Beyond Kaafu

There are unique villages, deserted islands, unpolluted water, abundant sea life and some outstanding resorts beyond Kaafu.

The government has attempted to curb the threat tourism may pose to the traditional and sheltered lives of many Maldivians by introducing a travel-permit system. Tourists need to apply in writing at least one day in advance for a Rf10 travel permit from the Ministry of Atolls Administration. Tourists can go on excursions to inhabited islands of the atoll in which their resorts are situated, but a permit is needed to visit inhabited islands in all other atolls.

Each day in these far-flung villages brings a new experience to be savoured. On the beach, a local medicine man might be practising one of his rituals to bless a new boat before it is launched. Elsewhere, you might stumble across a reception for a newly married couple; a recital for a young boy who has just been circumcised; or a gathering of *raiathun*, when the whole village congregates to perform a community service, such as sweeping the streets or building a new wharf.

It is a nice idea to take a small gift when you visit any of these villages. A can of condensed milk will most likely earn you an invitation to share a cup of tea. The people are naturally inquisitive about the outside world and once they have overcome their initial shyness and suspicion, they will welcome you with endless banter. Attempt a few words of Dhivehi and you will delight and amuse all and sundry. Make sure you are dressed conservatively at all times and, as a courtesy, inform the island Chief of your arrival before you go traipsing all over his island.

A great way to see the Maldives is by cruising around the atolls. There are several local agents in Male' who offer island-hopping tours on board dhoni and cabin cruisers. Some of their itineraries take passengers to a number of villages and include camping overnight on uninhabited islands. Most of these islands have at least one freshwater well and a small thatch hut where the *ruuverl* lives. Ask him to tap you some *raa* from the coconut trees.

If you can weather the sometimes temperamental seas, a voyage beyond Kaafu will bring you nearer to the heart of the Maldives.

Traditional dress

Himmafushi, Kaafu Atoll

A day's catch

To get the best of Hudhuveli, most people get off the island

Hudhuveli is a lot like many resorts in the sensational Maldives. To find out what makes it so special, however, you need only step off the island and into its massive lagoon. Whether you want to windsurf, snorkel, or just paddle about, Hudhuveli's lagoon is better than perfect. Yes there's a restaurant, coffee shop, bar, and no more than 44 rooms. Talk to your travel agent now about the best waters in the world.

HUDHUVELI RESORT
Telephone: (960) 443396 Facsimile: (960) 443849 Telex: (896) 77035 HUDVELI MF

CENTRAL ATOLLS

Alifu 156
Vaavu 161
Meemu 164
Faafu 165
Dhaalu 166
Thaa 167
Laamu 170

ALIFU

Population: 4630
Inhabited islands: 10
Uninhabited islands: 64
Capital: Mahibadhoo

Getting there

It takes about 3 hours to motor across the Ariadhoo Channel, and another 3 hours to reach the southern tip of Ari Atoll. A speedboat does the trip in half the time and costs twice as much.

The quickest way to Ari is by helicopter. There are regular flights to the helipads on Guraidhoo, Rasdhoo, Kandholhudhoo, Bodufolhudhoo, Embudhoo, Ari Beach, Rangali and Maafushivaru. A one-way fare is around $US100 and the flights take between 25 and 35 minutes. Hang the expense—the aerial view is spectacular.

Places of interest

The region embracing Rasdhoo, Thoddoo and Ari is collectively known as Alifu. More than 20 islands have been developed as tourist resorts.

Sailing due west of Male', across the 40-km-wide Ariadhoo Channel, you come to a small group of islands and sandbanks known traditionally as Rasdhoo Atoll. Isolated and 10 km to the north is **Thoddoo**, with its vineyards of watermelon and the remains of an ancient Buddhist temple which was excavated in June, 1958. The island's Friday Mosque was built by Sultan Mohammed Ibn Al-Haj Ali (AD 1692–1701) and has since been renovated.

South-west is Ari Atoll, a perfect chain of islands extending 80 km from north to south and 30 km from east to west. For hundreds of years, the people here were skilled at catching turtles and weaving sails out of palm leaves. Now they are more noted for their fishing and carpentry skills, and a small cottage industry of sculptors specialising in coral tombstones. **Fenfushi**, in particular, is recognised for its coral carvings and its mosque (the larger of the two on the island) which was built by Sultan Mohammed Ibn Al-Haj Ali (AD 1692–1701).

Maamigili has a village of around 800 people. A large number of the menfolk earn their livings making limestone for building blocks. There is an old mosque on the island that dates back to the late 17th century.

Mahibadhoo is the site of the Atoll Office, a fish-processing centre and a cold-storage complex. It is a great place to witness fishing skills at their best.

Mathiveri is home to a restored 17th-century mosque built in the days when Sultan Ibrahim Iskandar I ruled.

In 1959, a number of objects, including a phallus measuring 38 cm in length and 30 cm in circumference at the base, were discovered on uninhabited **Eriyadhoo**.

The island of **Hangnaameedhoo**, which has a population of around 250, was inundated by high waves in December, 1964. It houses the tomb of Sultan Ibrahim Kalaafaanu who ruled from AD 1585 to AD 1609.

Resort islands

Kuramathi is the first island you sight en route west from Male'. It is long and covered with coconut trees. Universal Enterprises has discreetly erected three seperate resorts on the island. *Kuramathi Village* is the largest, with 90 terraced apartments and 22 thatch-roof circular houses. The *Blue Lagoon Club* has 20 bungalows built on stilts by the water's edge, and another 30 more conventional units amidst the trees. The *Cottage Club* is the smallest of the resorts with 30 bungalows. The great attraction with Kuramathi is that guests are able to use the facilites at any of the three resorts and enjoy a selection of restaurants. The Clubhouse at the Cottage Club hosts some wonderful buffets and the Lagoon Restaurant serves à la carte. Most guests spend at least one night in Kuramathi Village,

ALIFU

Maldives — 158 —

sipping cocktails at the large palm-frond bar which spills onto the beach. Room rates range from $US80–140 single, $US90–150 double.

The *Nika Hotel* is managed by the diminutive and affable Abdullah Rasheed. It is owned by the dynamic and affluent Giampiero Bellazzi who jets in now and again with a number of celebrities. This resort is for the well-heeled who like to 'get away from it all'. Room rates during the peak season go as high as $US285 single, $US440 double. The 25 bungalows, each with their own private beach, are airy, spacious and comfortably furnished. Young Italian yuppies rave about it and the word has spread. It is generally full all year round so you need to book well in advance. Facilities on this small oval-shaped island (called Kudafolhudhoo) include a diving school, synthetic-grass tennis court and bowling green, a large boutique brimful of Asian clothes, and a first-class restaurant. About 1 km offshore is a small secluded uninhabited island also leased by Bellazzi. Honeymoon couples go there regularly with their picnic baskets, champagne and chauffer-driven speedboats, courtesy of the management. The Nika Hotel just oozes style.

Fesdu sits at the centre of Alifu Atoll, some 3 hours' cruising from the airport. The managers of the resort, Universal Enterprises, have affectionately coined Fesdu 'the fun island' in order to attract a young-at-heart spirited clientele. Accommodation is in 55 thatch-roof circular houses a few metres from the shore. A 15-minute boat ride offshore brings you to the tiny uninhabited island of Gamatafushi. Ask the chef to prepare you a picnic lunch before you go. Room rates on Fesdu are $US90 single, $US100 double.

Moofushi is operated by a young and carefree group of Italians who will go to any lengths to ensure that their guests are satisfied. There are 60 bungalows and, of course, pasta is big on the menu. Room rates are $US140 single, $US210 double. The return fare, per person, from the airport is $US150 by sea, $US350 by air.

Gangehi is operated by Club Vacanze, a large Italian tour wholesaler. With a generous budget with which to work, the manager has designed an attractive resort. Wooden walkways wend from bungalow to bungalow through shady tropical vegetation. Some walkways extend over the lagoon to spacious well-furnished bungalows with floor-to-ceiling glass doors that open out to balconies with steps leading down to the water. The restaurant is open to the horizon beyond and has a large glass panel in the floor, looking down into the lagoon. Brush up on a few Italian phrases and anyone will enjoy the comforts of Gangehi. Room rates are $US130 single, $US190 double.

Ellaidhoo is 55 km from the airport. The 50 rooms are built from coral and have thatch roofs and Italian-tile bathrooms set in charming outdoor rock gardens. Room rates are $US70 single, $US100 double.

Halaveli is a large island with 40 fan-cooled bungalows positioned under the palm trees at one end. The clientele is predominantly Italian. Room rates are $US110 single, $US150 double.

Maayafushi appeals to a younger clientele who prefer to forgo plush comforts for a more casual ambience. There are 60 fan-cooled rooms with cold showers, a sand-floor restaurant and coffee shop, and an open-air bar. Room rates at this simple resort complex are $US75 single, $US110 double.

Bathala is, on the whole, patronised by scuba-diving enthusiasts. This tiny oval-shaped island is neatly enveloped in a coral reef with a 40-m vertical drop-off. The resort offers 37 fan-cooled bungalows, each with its own outdoor garden shower. There is also a small bar and restaurant. Room rates are $US85 single, $US90 double.

Veligandu is a small island with 63 comfortably furnished air-conditioned bungalows. Room rates are $US100 single, $US140 double.

Angaga has 50 bungalows overlooking a powder-soft sandy shoreline and an incredibly clear turquoise lagoon. Each bungalow is air-conditioned and features a delightful garden bathroom and an *undhoali* on the veranda. Room rates are $US100 single, $US120 double. These rates are shaved by 25 per cent during the low season.

Twin Island is another stylish resort operated by Universal Enterprises. Located deep down in the south of the atoll, on an island named Maafushivaru, the resort has 32 bungalows. Room rates are $US165 single, $US175 double. Guests are flown to the helipad on Dhigurah, from where it is a short boat trip to the resort. Return air fares are $US240 per person.

Kuda Rah appeals to those who are able to demand comfort and privacy, regardless of cost. Each of the 30 spacious bungalows has its own private veranda spilling out to its own private beach. The nearby reefs are among the best dive spots in Ari Atoll. Room rates are $US150 single, $US225 double.

VAAVU

Population: 5163
Inhabited islands: 5
Uninhabited islands: 14
Capital: Felidhoo

Vaavu is the administrative name given to the most irregularly shaped group of islands in the Maldives known traditionally as Felidhe Atoll. On a map, the reef looks boot-shaped, with a smattering of islands along the shin.

Leaving South Male' Atoll and crossing the deep 11-km-wide Fulidhoo Channel, you arrive at some of the best dive spots in the Maldives. Few underwater landscapes are more spectacular than the caves and caverns around Vattaru Reef.

Places of interest

Felidhoo, the atoll capital, is a small village of some 250 people who reap their rewards from fishing. They played host to HCP Bell when he visited the island in 1922. An island hop takes you across to **Keyodhoo**, the largest village in Vaavu with just 329 inhabitants. Not far from here, on the tip of the reef, is **Fotheyobodufushi**, the easternmost island in the Maldive archipelago. It was formally two islands, Fotheyo and Bodufushi, which merged naturally to form Fotheyobodufushi.

A ship named *Pioneer* ran aground on the reef off the uninhabited island of **Higaakulhi**, in May 1958. The ship was on its way from Colombo to Male' with general cargo, and has not since been refloated.

Along the southern rim of the atoll is **Rakeedhoo**. If you stand on the sandbar at the western tip of the island, you will see the effects of years of tropical monsoons. The island is, ever so slowly, eroding away. Against the horizon on a clear day, you might also see, about 3 km in the distance, several new islands being born along Vattaru Reef. The reef has already grown to about 6 km in length, bracing several small sandbanks. It is home to a multitude of multicoloured reef fish.

Resort islands

Alimatha and *Dhiggiri* are the only resorts in Vaavu. Both are operated by Safari Tours and enjoy almost exclusive Italian patronage. Diggiri is slightly smaller and cheaper with 30 bungalows and room rates at $US105 a double. Alimatha, just 2 km south, has 70 bungalows and room rates go as high as $US145 a double. It has an underwater-photography school which processes and assesses your work.

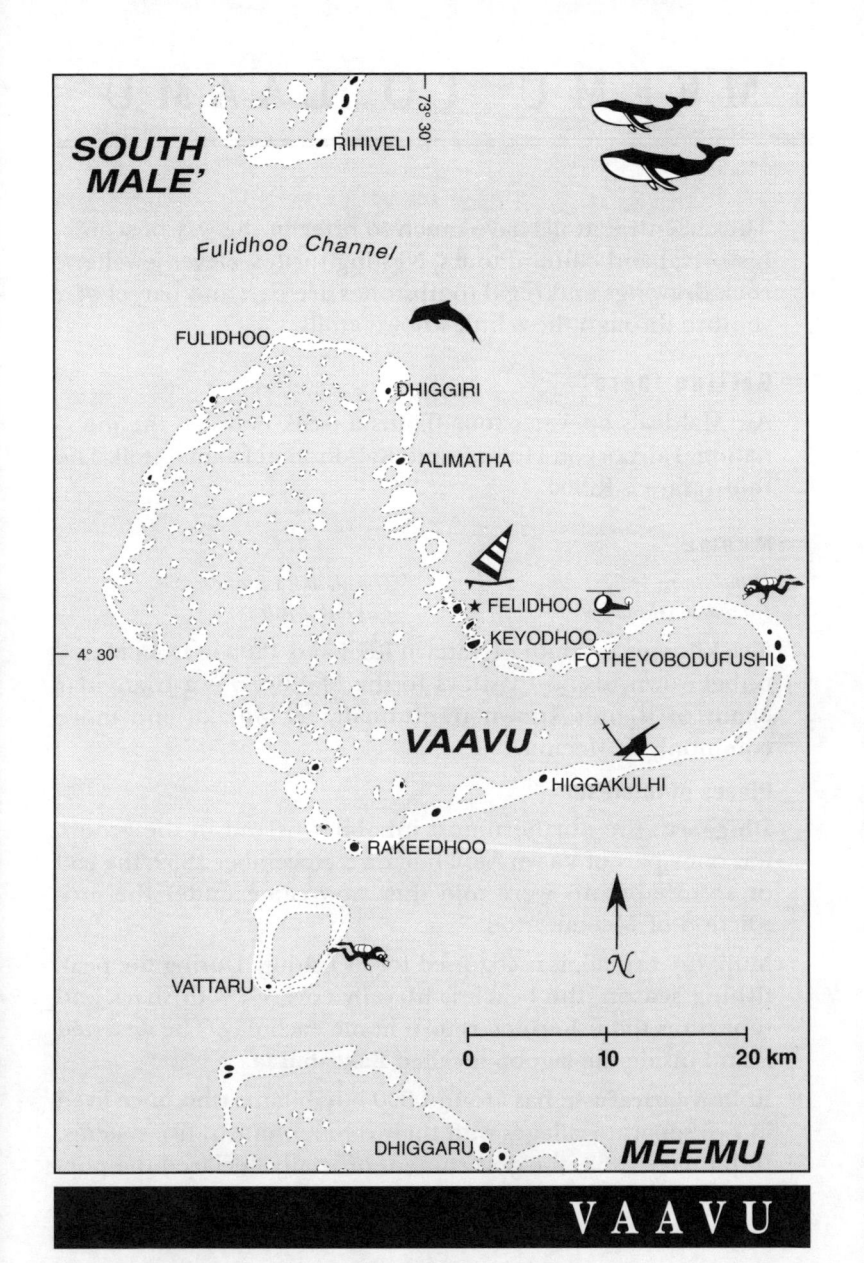

VAAVU

Central atolls

MEEMU TO LAAMU

These central atolls have much to offer in the way of scenic, historical and cultural tours. Nesting turtles, clever jewellers, rock drawings and regal tombstones are part and parcel of a venture through these little-known atolls.

Getting there

Air Maldives operates four flights a week between the international airport on Hulhule and Kahdhoo in Laamu Atoll. The return fare is Rf900.

Meemu

Population: 1697 *Uninhabited islands: 23*
Inhabited islands: 9 *Capital: Muli*

Five kilometres south of Vattaru Reef and 120 km from Male', unbeknown to most visitors to the Maldives, is a triangular chain of islands known traditionally as Mulaku and more commonly as Meemu.

Places of interest

Dhiggaru, the northernmost inhabited island in the group, was once part of Vaavu Atoll but, on 3 November 1959, the 650 or so inhabitants were told they now came under the jurisdiction of Meemu Atoll.

Muli, the capital, is recognised for its fishing. During the peak fishing season, the beach is literally covered with shark and tuna after the fishermen return home each day. The deserted island inside the lagoon is called **Kakaahuraa**.

Kolhuvaariyafushi has around 600 inhabitants who once lived in two separate villages with their own administrative systems. In January 1962, the government officially declared the population to be one village. The island is best known for its fishing and yams.

Maalhaveli is deserted. In 1844, its surrounding reef was the site of a shipwreck when the *Prazere Algeria* went down, taking 11 crewmen to their deaths.

Raiymandhoo has a population of little more than 100 people. Many of them recall, with vivid emotion, having to pack all their worldly possessions after the government declared the island uninhabitable in January 1969. It was to be more than six years before they returned.

Veyvah abounds with history, its name having been recorded in many ancient documents as Ve-oh, as it was once known. The old mosque in the village was built by Sultan Mohammed Ibn Al-Haj Ali in the late 17th century.

Mulah was once the capital of Meemu. It is now best known for its top-quality *hiki mas* and profusion of yams.

Faafu

Population: 4186 *Uninhabited islands: 18*
Inhabited islands: 5 *Capital: Magoodhoo*

South of Alifu, beyond a 15-km-wide, 420-m-deep channel, is a small oval-shaped chain of islands called Faafu (traditionally known as North Nilandhe Atoll).

Places of interest

Dharanboodhoo is outstanding: during the south-west monsoon, between April and October, you are bound to come across footprints along the beach and mounds of sand hidden beneath the bushes—the telltale signs that turtles have laid their eggs. Sadly, a great number of the eggs end up in island kitchens and the turtles in tourist shops, stuffed or their shells in pieces. Many of the inhabitants of this island claim to be descendants of Mohammed Muhiddeen, a beloved 17th-century sultan.

Nilandhoo is an inhabited island on which some fascinating discoveries have taken place. East of the centre of the island, there is a ruin measuring 44.5 m in circumference and 1.2 m high. The mosque was built by Sultan Mohammed Ibn

Abdullah (AD 1153–1166) and near the mosque are seven tombs. About 76 m from the shore on the eastern side of the island, a stone box, containing a gold statue and a bright red powder, was unearthed. When Thor Heyerdahl visited the island, he uncovered five phallic lingams and ruins which he believes were part of a prehistoric cult centre.

Bileiydhoo is home to almost 500 people. Walk into anyone's kitchen and you are bound to find racks of smoked tuna above the stove.

Felalee, with a 420-strong population, has also earned a reputation for its thriving fishing industry.

Himithi, now deserted, once housed 48 people but they were evacuated, on 26 March 1988, when the island began eroding. These islanders were known throughout the archipelago for their navigational skills.

Dhaalu

Population: 2614   *Uninhabited islands: 49*
Inhabited islands: 8   *Capital: Kudahuvadhoo*

South Nilandhe Atoll, as it is referred to traditionally, is the administrative atoll of Dhaalu. Larger than its northern neighbour, it stretches some 35 km from north to south, and 20 km from east to west.

Places of interest

The small village of **Hulhudheli** is famous for jewellery making. The craftsmen make silver amulets, chains and bracelets, using age-old techniques. Approximately 90 m from the shore, on the north-west side of the island, are the ruins of an old mosque.

On the uninhabited island of **Maadheli**, there are the foundations of what appears to have been dwellings. Their origins are unknown.

The people of **Ribudhoo** are famous for making gold jewellery and weaving the finest *ras roanu* ('king rope' used to hoist dhoni) in the country.

The mosque on the capital island, **Kudahuvadhoo**, has some fine examples of ancient stone masonry. The island's reef has also been the graveyard for a number of ships, notably the 1339-tonne cargo boat *Liffey* which ran aground in 1879, and the more recent sinking of *Utheem*, in 1960.

For some strange reason, the 300 or so people on **Badidhoo** were once included under the administrative banner of Faafu Atoll. On 18 July 1958, however, they were correctly incorporated under Dhaalu's administration. The same event happened to the 460-odd people on **Meedhoo**.

Thaa

Population: 4199   *Uninhabited islands: 53*
Inhabited islands: 13   *Capital: Veymandoo*

South across the Kudahuvadhoo Channel, or the Maa Channel as some locals call it, is a massive, almost unbroken, circular reef, embracing 700 sq km of ocean. Maldivians sail cautiously in these waters. The atoll, known traditionally as Kolhumadulu and more simply as Thaa, permits entry and exit only through a few narrow channels. The eastern rim of the reef is dotted with many deserted islands, sandbanks and villages, some separated only by knee-deep turquoise lagoons.

Places of interest

Fahala is one of the largest islands in the archipelago. It is 6 km long, densely vegetated and uninhabited. A mere island hop away is **Dhiyamigili**, once the home of Mohammed Imaduddeen, the 18th-century sultan (AD 1704–1721) who founded the Dhiyamigili Dynasty which ruled the nation for 200 years. The remains of his palace can be seen on the outskirts of the village.

Beyond a deep narrow channel and kilometre upon kilometre of protruding reef, is the island of **Guraidhoo**. A 14th-century sultan, Sultan Usman I, is buried here but hardly revered (he was banished to the island after reigning for less than two months and died not long after). The mosque on this island

Maldives — 168 —

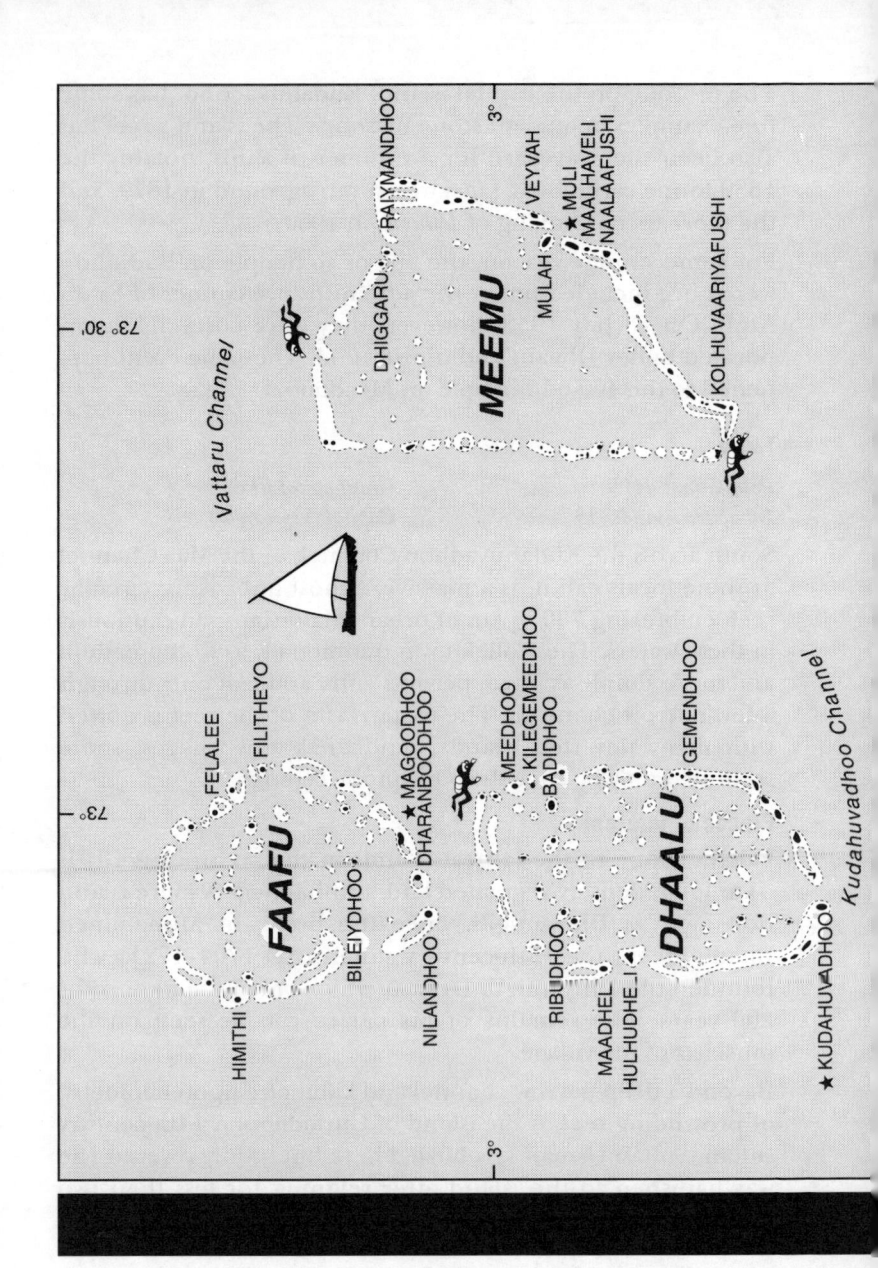

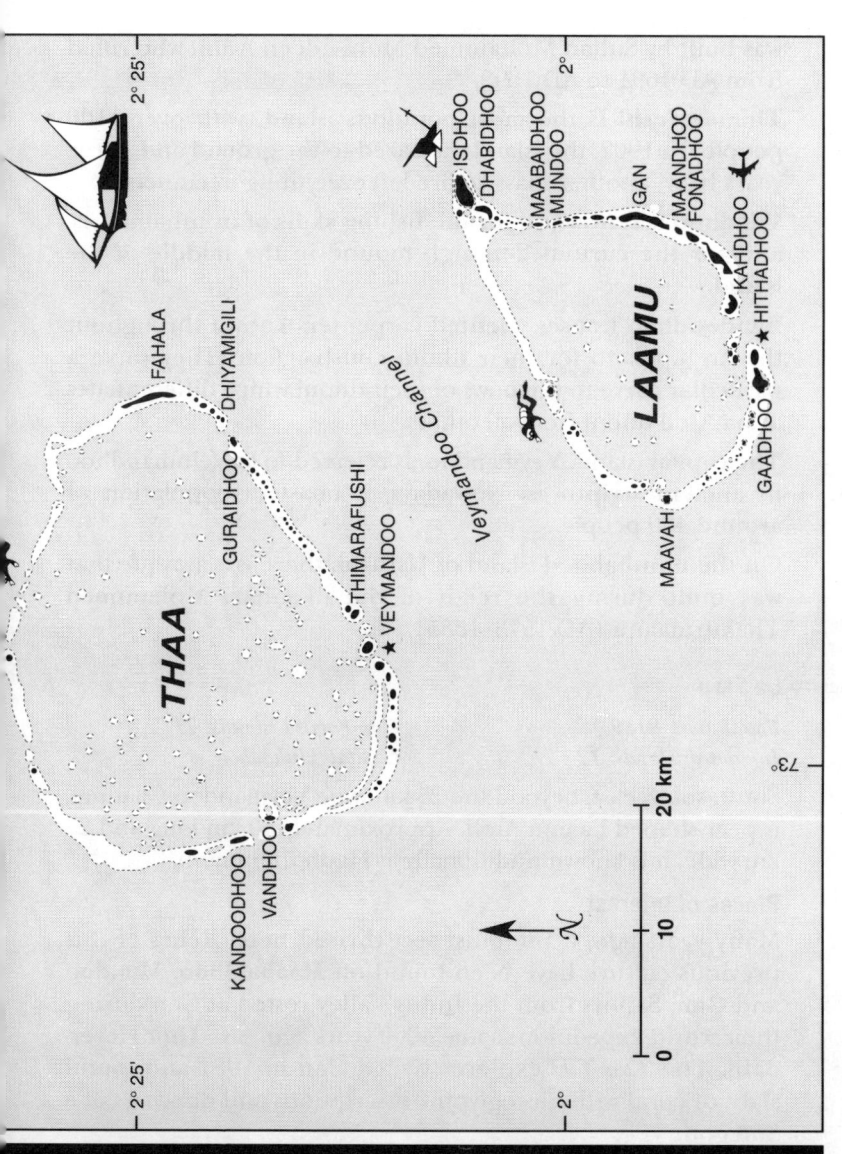

CENTRAL ATOLLS

was built by Sultan Mohammed Muhi-udeen Adhil who ruled from AD 1691 to AD 1692.

Thimarafushi is the most populous island, with over 1100 people. In 1902, the island was razed to the ground and, three years later, another massive fire left everything in cinders.

Vandhoo is renowned for the fishing skills of its inhabitants, and for the curious 2-m-high mound in the middle of the island.

Kandoodhoo houses talented carpenters known throughout the archipelago for their dhoni construction. They carve a particular curve to the bows of their dhoni which differentiates Thaa Atoll dhoni from all others.

The capital island, **Veymandoo**, is referred to as Velumandhoo in ancient scriptures. Nowadays, it boasts a population of around 420 people.

On the uninhabited island of **Usfushi**, there is a mosque that was built during the reign of Sultan Ghazi Mohammed Thakurufaanu (AD 1573–1585).

▭ Laamu

Population: 8189 *Uninhabited islands: 71*
Inhabited islands: 12 *Capital: Hithadhoo*

South-south-east, beyond the 25-km-wide Veymandoo Channel, is pear-shaped Laamu Atoll. Approximately 40 km long and 25 km wide, it is known traditionally as Hadhdhunmathi.

Places of interest

Many years ago, a Buddhist sect thrived here. Relics of this previous culture have been found on **Maabaidhoo**, **Mundoo** and **Gan**. Sailors from the Indus Valley rested at Gan during their world expeditions some 4000 years ago, says Thor Heyerdahl. The *Kon Tiki* explorer visited Gan in 1981 and found slabs of coral with hieroglyphic inscriptions and drawings of a Sun god.

While these early-day travellers may indeed have passed by in their reed ships, modern-day travel is by dhoni or Dornier.

Manoeuvring a dhoni through the reef

Now you can stop trying to imagine paradise

Bandos is the largest, most luxurious resort island in the Maldives. We call it paradise. You can dive, sail or snorkel in waters that are out of this world. Dine à la carte, dance at the disco and, if you get time, sleep in your luxury air-conditioned room.

Bandos Island is just a 4-hour flight from Singapore and a million miles from nowhere. Talk to your travel agent now and let them organise your ticket to paradise.

Bandos Island Resort

Telephone (960) 440088 Facsimile (960) 443877
Telex (896) 66050 BANDOS MF

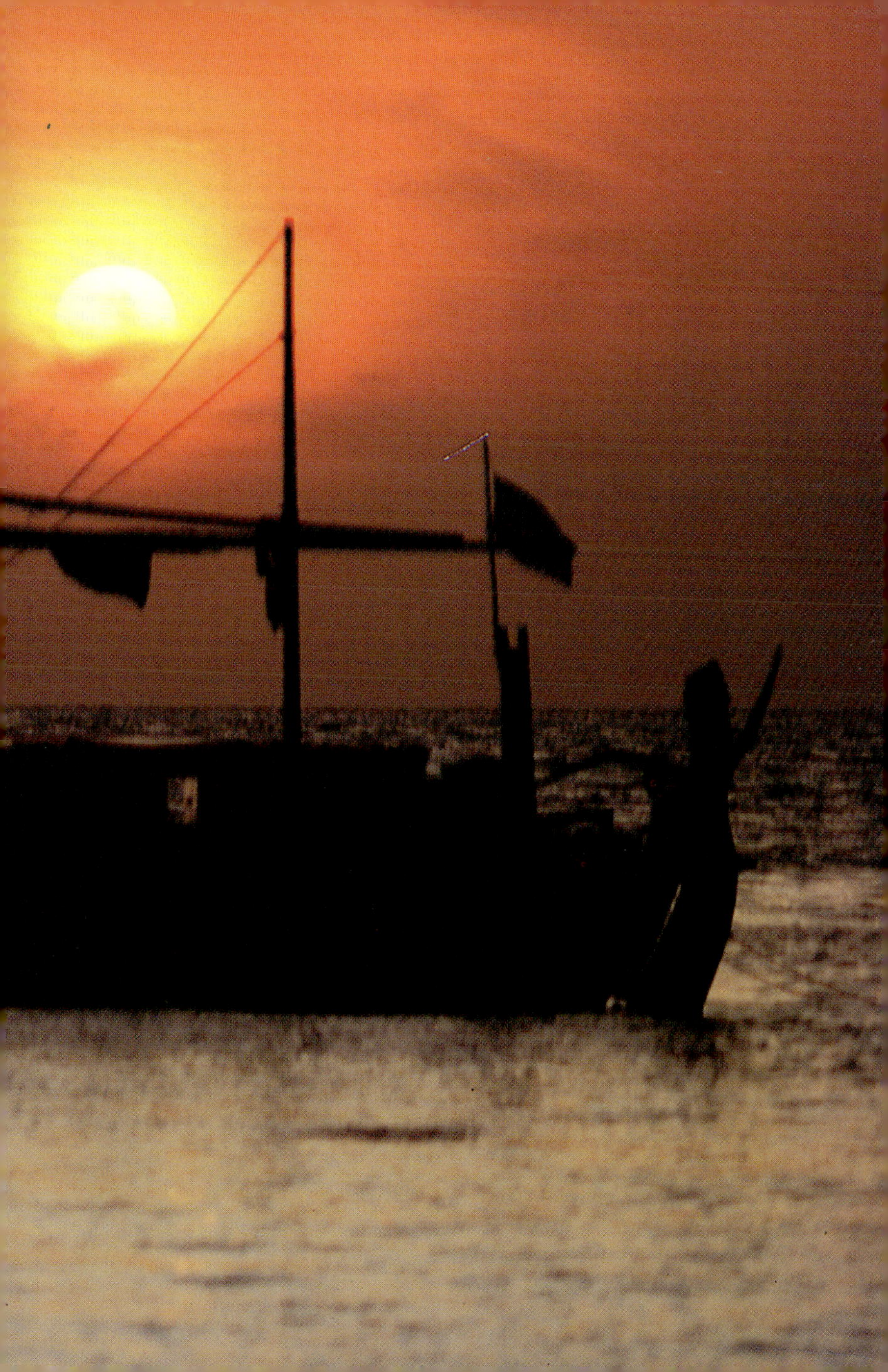

Weaving baskets

There is an airport on **Kahdhoo** which services regular flights to and from the international airport on Hulhule. Kahdhoo is linked to **Fonadhoo** and **Maandhoo** by a man-made causeway, and another causeway extends between Maandhoo and Gan.

On 10 January 1970, two brass statues were uncovered on the inhabited island of **Gaadhoo**. Found enclosed in an earthen pot, they were each just over 10 cm high.

The island of **Isdhoo** houses two separate villages. In January 1938, the British boat *Lagan Bank*, carrying a cargo of jute, tea and gunnies, was wrecked on the reef of this island. A Chinese fishing vessel named *Yuang Haing* ran aground here in February 1969, and was refloated and renamed *Isdhoo Muli.*

Dhabidhoo was once the capital of Laamu and also appears prominently in historical literature, where it is referred to as Dhadudhoov. A few mounds, indicating ancient habitation, have been discovered on the island.

The now deserted **Fushi** was the first capital of Laamu, but has been uninhabited since early 19th century.

About 400 people live on the capital island of **Hithadhoo**. Note the 2-m-high *us fas gandu* (stupa) on the eastern shoreline.

Maavah has a population of around 800 people. The menfolk are noted for their fishing skills. Many years ago, on 22 June 1873, a barque called the *François* was wrecked on the reef. None of the 22 crew members were killed.

Boat building, Raa Atoll

NORTHERN ATOLLS

Lhaviyani 178

Baa 179

Raa 184

Noonu 186

Shaviyani 187

Haa Dhaalu 195

Haa Alifu 196

LHAVIYANI

Population: 7725
Inhabited islands: 4
Uninhabited islands: 48
Capital: Naifaru

Skirt the maze of reefs and resort islands scattered north of Male', and then cruise across the renowned Kaashidhoo Channel, and you come to Lhaviyani Atoll, or Faadhippolhu as it is still sometimes called.

Getting there

It takes 45 minutes by helicopter from the international airport on Hulhule to reach Kuredu, and about 8 hours by engine dhoni. Fares vary accordingly: $US179 by air, $US100 by sea.

Places of interest

Only four of the 60 islands are inhabited. Many Lhaviyani residents are affluent. Some own fleets of engine dhoni, often employing a staff of 10 or more to attend to their domestic and business affairs. Everyone reaps the benefits of the nearby factory on **Felivaru**, where tonnes of fish are processed and canned. It was the first fish cannery in the Maldives. The canned fish is exported in large quantities to UK, France, Holland and Italy.

Naifaru is the capital island and, with a dense population of over 2000 and a harbour packed with motor cruisers, launches and dhoni, it is affectionately known as 'Kuda Male', the nation's 'little capital'.

Hinnavaru is similar to Naifaru. Densely populated with over 2000 people, it has an air of well-being and self-satisfaction. Many families on the island enjoy the luxuries of running water and electricity, and some operate flourishing fishing

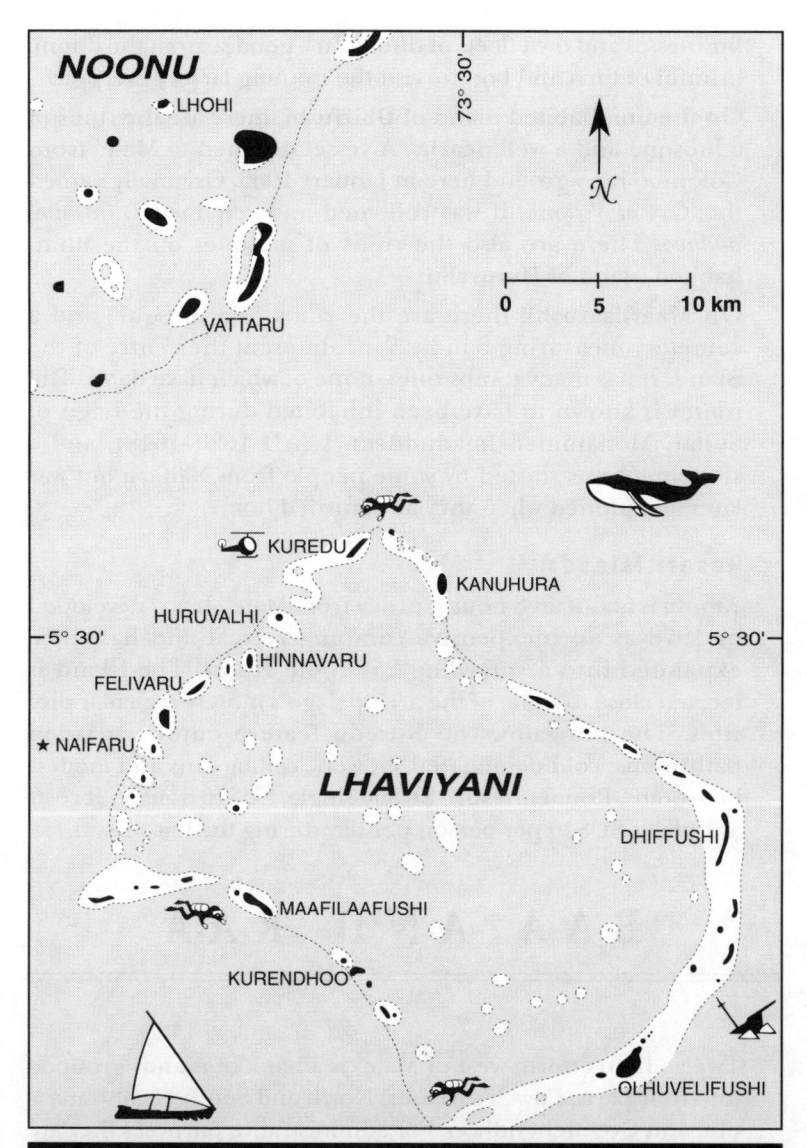

LHAVIYANI

businesses and own fleets of dhoni. In a good season, the dhoni, brimful of tuna and bonito, visit the canning factory every day.

On the uninhabited island of **Dhiffushi**, there are the ruins of a mosque and a well nearby. A vessel destined to Male' from Colombo ran aground here in January 1966. Originally named the *City of Victoria*, it was refloated and renamed *Diffushim-aadhoo*. There are also the ruins of mosques on the uninhabited island of **Huruvalhi.**

On **Maafilaafushi**, there are the ruins of a mosque, and a cemetery measuring 6 m by 5 m, almost at the centre of the island. It has many tombstones, none of which have dates. The island is known to have been inhabited during the reign of Sultan Mohammed Imaduddeen I (AD 1620–1648), and a settlement was started by some people from Naifaru but was later abandoned when they all returned home.

Resort islands

Kuredu is about an 8-hour journey from Male'. It was developed in 1978 as an inexpensive camping retreat and has since expanded into a sprawling 250-room resort. The island is located close to some of the archipelago's most spectacular dive sites. The bungalows on Kuredu feature outdoor garden bathrooms, cold desalinated showers, ceiling fans and modest bedrooms. Room rates are $US50 single, $US70 double. It costs as little as $US40 per person per day during the low season.

BAA AND RAA

Twelve hours north-west of Male' is a bank of islands grouped into four parts: Powell's Islands, North and South Maalhosmadulu, and Goifufehendhoo. For administrative purposes they are grouped into two sections and called, more simply, Baa and Raa.

Getting there

There is a helipad on Kunfunadhoo in Baa Atoll if you are keen to get there quickly. Expect to pay over $US200, one way.

Baa

Population: 7716 *Uninhabited islands: 62*
Inhabited islands: 13 *Capital: Eydhafushi*

Places of interest

To cruise north-west across the Kaashidhoo Channel seemingly leads nowhere. But just over the horizon are a few sandbanks and, further on, the isolated villages of **Goidhoo**, **Fuladhoo** and **Fehendhoo**. Many criminals live here, having been exiled from their families and friends. François Pyrard (a Frenchman who was shipwrecked in the Maldives in 1602 and who was subsequently detained for over five years) spent some days on these islands. A current resident is a German tourist who was banished here for life after stabbing his girlfriend to death in Male'. He was offered a transfer to a German prison but chose to be exiled to Fuladhoo. He has since married, had children and goes fishing and island hopping as he pleases. Goidhoo holds the remarkable record for the largest number of flying fish landing on an island—more than 3800 landed on the island on 13 November 1962!

Sailing north, beyond a 10-km-wide channel, you come to the main bank of Baa Atoll—a 40-km-long chain of islands. **Thulaadhoo**, in the south-west pocket, houses the nation's best wood carvers. Every day, the men of the village carve small wooden boxes with knives, then coat them with strands of red, black and yellow lacquer. They finish off their work by deftly engraving each box with an abstract design. Their specialty are the *maaloodh foshi,* large circular boxes used to store family feasts during religious festivities. Small jewellery boxes are whittled for the ever-growing tourist market.

Eydhafushi is the capital island. It sits on the eastern fringe of the atoll and boasts the country's first Atoll Community School. Affluent families enjoy the luxury of portable generators which light their homes. And a select few still practise the age-old craft of *feyli* weaving. The *feyli*, a heavy white cotton sarong with brown and black strands, was once the traditional Maldivian costume. Nowadays, it is worn by only a few of the older generation or sold to tourists. Unfortunately, the spinning and weaving of cloth in the islands is all but gone today as imported cloth is far cheaper. The main mosque on this island was originally built during the reign of Sultan Mohammed Mueenudheen I (AD 1799–1835) and has since been renovated.

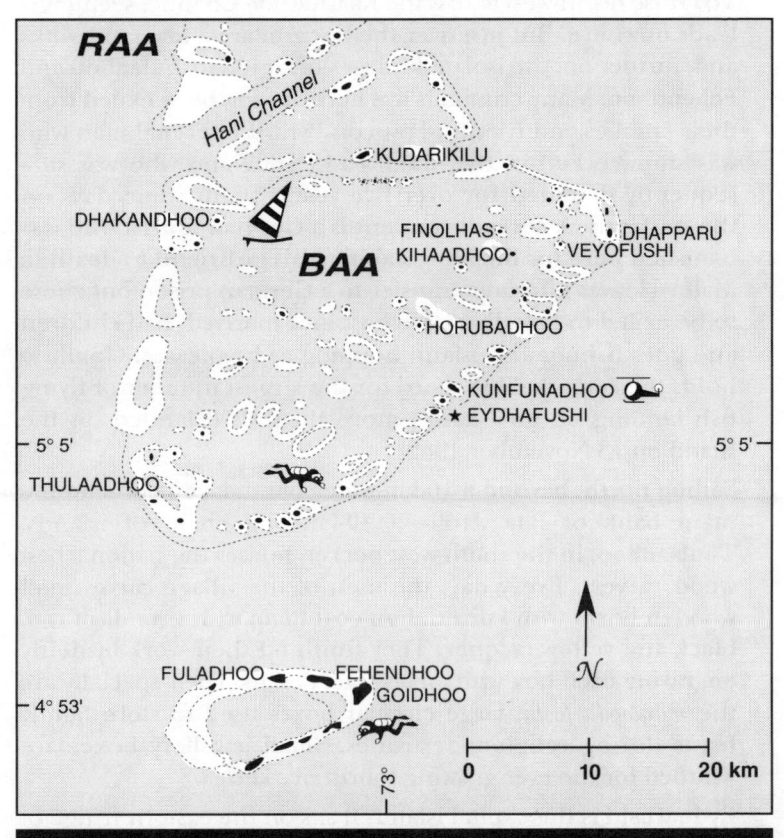

BAA

The small uninhabited island of **Horubadhoo** is nearby. There is little sign of the village that once existed here before the people were forced to flee and settle on neighbouring islands when an epidemic raged the island. A large bathing tank still stands, there are the ruins of an old mosque and there is a cemetery (the tombstones have no inscriptions).

Early settlers on **Kihaadhoo** built their village on the eastern side of the island. In October 1931, the village was shifted to the opposite side of the island after many people had died within a short period of time.

In February 1918, a group of fishermen from **Kudarikilu** sighted a floating mine and, not knowing what it was, towed it ashore. After much tampering, the mine exploded, killing six people. The blast was so powerful that the remains of the bodies were later found on neighbouring islands. The large crater on the island is a testimonial to the explosion.

Veyofushi, a small pristine deserted island, was once a thriving retreat for backpackers. During the 1970s, sand-floor thatch-roof huts and three meals a day cost as little as Rf20 per day.

Dhapparu, once inhabited, now holds the silent remains of two mosques and a large cemetery with many gravestones.

The uninhabited island of **Finolhas** was inhabited before the reign of Sultan Hassan Nooraddeen I (AD 1779–1799). All that remains now are the ruins of a mosque, a well and a cemetery.

The uninhabited island of **Dhakandhoo** has been permanently seared, since a fire broke out in May 1972 and burned for two weeks.

Resort islands

Kunfunadhoo sits opposite the capital island and has been on the drawing boards for major tourist development for some time.

Raa

Population: 11303
Inhabited islands: 70
Uninhabited islands: 16
Capital: Ugoofaaru

Places of interest

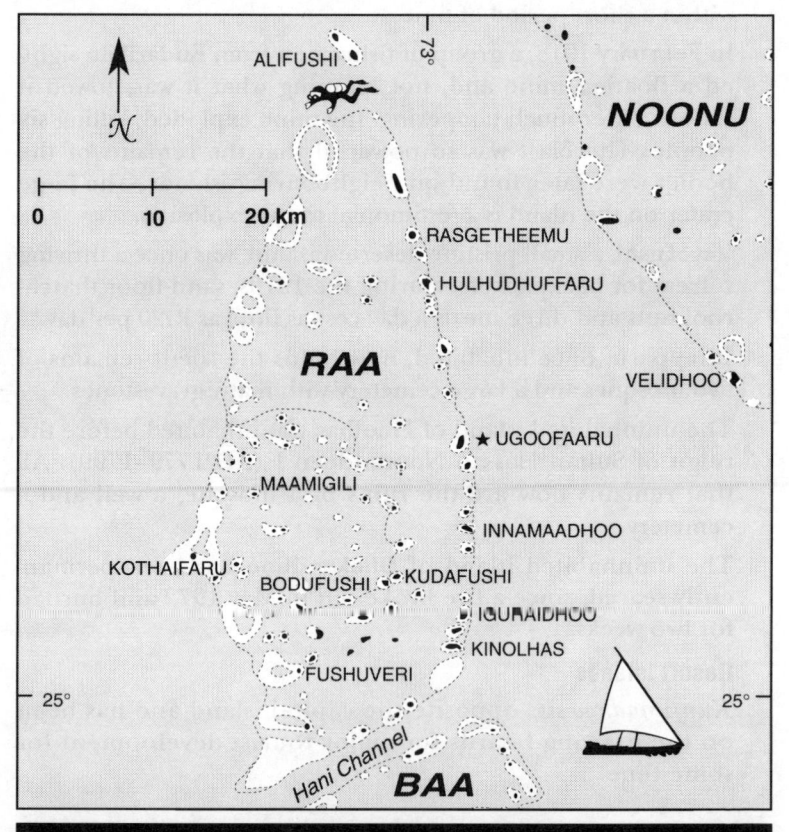

Baa becomes Raa, a 60-km-long chain of islands, after crossing the 2-km-wide Hani Channel and entering the northern part of Maalhosmadulu. Here live the master boat builders and carpenters of the Maldives. Locals travel from all parts of the archipelago to employ a boat builder from **Alifushi**, **Iguraidhoo** or **Innamaadhoo**, as craftsmen elsewhere do not seem to have the ability to produce the fine lines, curves and joins that distinguish Raa Atoll dhoni from all others.

It is only a short hop to **Kinolhas**, where Ibn Batuta, the famous 14th-century Arab traveller, once stayed. From here, heading north beyond the capital, **Ugoofaaru**, it is a skip and a jump to **Rasgetheemu**, the original 'King's Island' where Koimala Kalo lived some 2000 years ago.

On **Kudafushi**, a single tumbledown coral house, a freshwater well and a school of young basking sharks in the lagoon make for an idyllic Robinson Crusoe location. In 1946, for reasons unknown, the small community of people who once lived here moved to other nearby islands.

On the uninhabited island of **Bodufushi**, there are the ruins of a mosque built of coral-stone slabs and a cemetery. The tomb of Sultan Jalaludeen Umar Veeru (AD 1306–1335) can also be found on this island but there are no inscriptions on the stone. Similarly, on Hulhudhuffaaru, there are wells and tombstones without any markings.

Deserted **Fushuveri** houses the ruins of a mosque with two wells nearby. Writing on one tombstone in the graveyard gives the date of AD 1736.

On the once inhabited **Kothaifaru**, there are two octagonal wells and a cemetery. The inscription on one tombstone states: 'In rememberance of Mohammed Katheeb Thakurufaanu, son of Ibrahim Kuda Badeyri Thakurufaanu who died on Tuesday 21 Shawaal 1145 AH.'

Formerly inhabited, **Luboakandhoo** became uninhabited during the reign of Sultan Mohamed Mueenudheen I (AD 1799–1835). There are the ruins of a mosque and a bathing tank, well and cemetery nearby. Similarly, on **Maamigili**, two wells, one circular and the other octagonal, and a cemetery bear testimony to the fact that the island was once inhabited.

NOONU TO HAA ALIFU

Mind-boggling tongue-twisting names like Miladhunmadulu, Thiladhunmathi and Ihavandhippolhu traditionally define these northernmost atolls. For practical purposes, this 140-km-long chain of 209 islands is grouped into four and called Noonu, Shaviyani, Haa Dhaalu and Haa Alifu. Many visitors claim this to be the most awe-inspiring destination in the Maldives. It is certainly the heart of the archipelago, where island hopping, diving and simple lifestyles reign supreme.

Life here is completely dependent on the whims of nature, and the people living in these parts do so at the mercy of the Indian Ocean. Calm seas turn into thunderstorms overnight and roofs are uplifted and trees uprooted. In order to survive, the people of the north are far more interdependent than their southern brothers and sisters. They crisscross frequently from island to island and atoll to atoll, to trade with their neighbours.

Getting there

Air Maldives operates flights every day except Friday between the international airport on Hulhule and Hanimaadhoo in Haa Dhaalu Atoll. The return fare is Rf 900.

Noonu

Population: 8437 *Uninhabited islands: 59*
Inhabited islands: 13 *Capital: Manadhoo*

According to many locals, and it is difficult to disagree with them, no part of the archipelago is as beautiful as Noonu, with its series of reefs, agglomeration of islands and kaleidoscopic marine life. Travellers and anthropologists have also noted that the people of Noonu are more expressive in their music, laughter and play than those living in other atolls.

Places of interest

If you are historically inclined, take a day tour to **Landhoo** and the uninhabited **Lhohi**. Here you will see mounds of coral debris—burial grounds for ancient Buddhist relics. The old mosque on Lhohi was built by Sultan Ibrahim Iskandar II (AD 1720–1750).

On uninhabited **Iguraidhoo**, there are the remains of a mosque with a well and many tombstones nearby. Similarly, on **Kuredhivaru**, which was inhabited up to June 1943, there is a small mosque with the date 1121 AH inscribed on its coral-stone slabs, and the remains of a minaret close by.

Kudafari houses a small settlement of around 300 islanders who are best known for their fishing skills. A mosque was built on this island during the reign of Sultan Mohammed Shamshuddeen III (AD 1904–1934).

On 10 November 1966, minor earth tremors were experienced on the islands of **Maafaru** and **Velidhoo**.

Shaviyani

Population: 9022　　　　*Uninhabited islands: 37*
Inhabited islands: 15　　*Capital: Farukolhufunadhoo*

Beyond the artificial border that marks the end of Noonu and the beginning of Shaviyani, the islands become remarkably more fertile.

Places of interest

The capital of the atoll is **Farukolhufunadhoo**, known affectionately as Funadhoo. It is long, thickly vegetated, sparsely populated, and lies engulfed in a wide deep turquoise lagoon which provides perfect anchorage for dhoni en route north and south, to and from Male'. In January 1955, a severe storm struck the island and formed three small islands in its lagoon. Each of the islands is called **Aahuraa**. On Farukolhufunadhoo there are the remains of an old mosque and a large cemetery nearby.

Map of Maldives — Haa Alifu and Haa Dhaalu Atolls

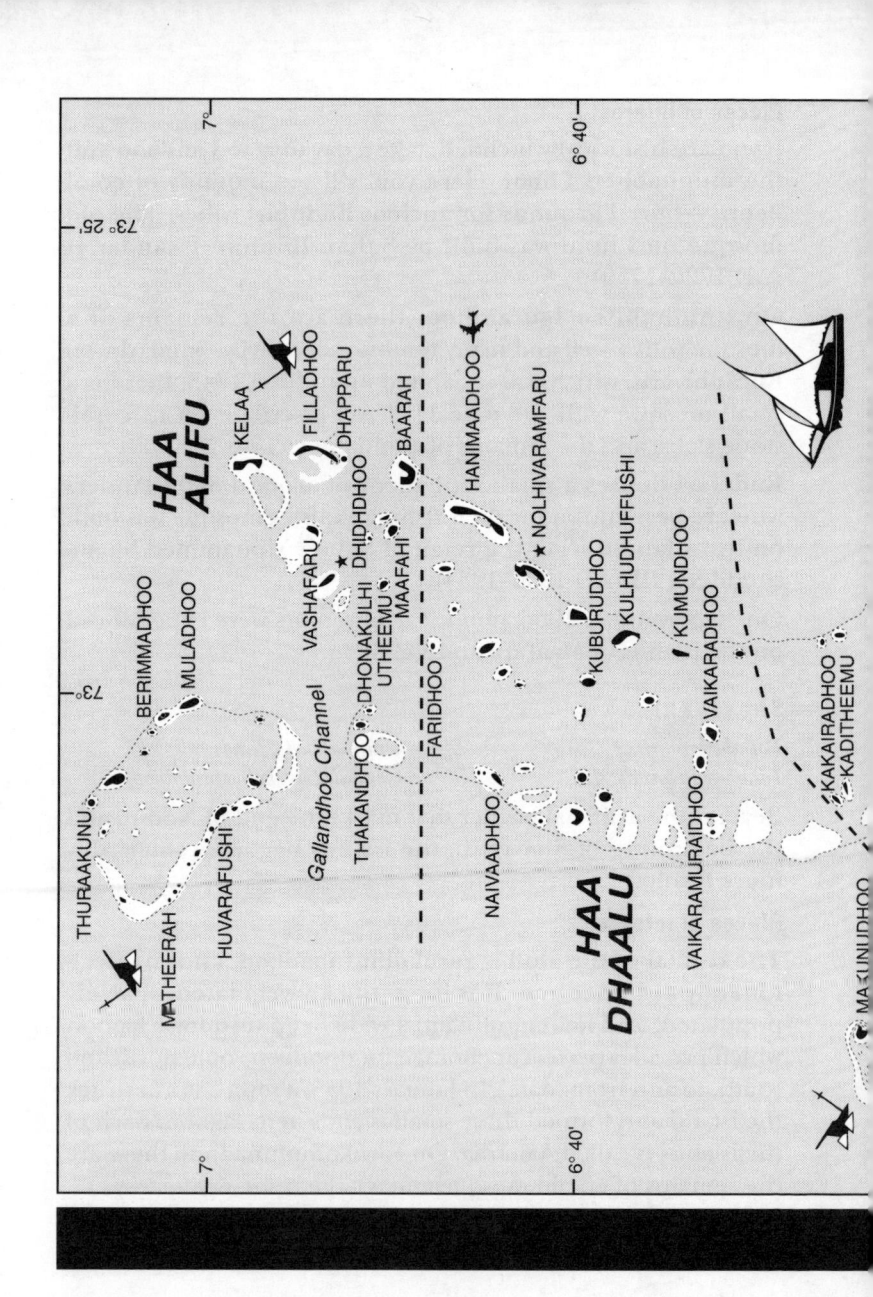

HAA ALIFU
- THURAAKUNU
- MATHEERAH
- HUVARAFUSHI
- BERIMMADHOO
- MULADHOO
- KELAA
- FILLADHOO
- VASHAFARU
- DHIDHDHOO
- DHAPPARU
- THAKANDHOO
- DHONAKULHI
- UTHEEMU
- MAAFAHI
- BAARAH
- HANIMAADHOO

Gallandhoo Channel

HAA DHAALU
- NOLHIVARAMFARU
- FARIDHOO
- KUBURUDHOO
- KULHUDHUFFUSHI
- KUMUNDHOO
- NAIVAADHOO
- VAIKARADHOO
- VAIKARAMURAIDHOO
- KAKAIRADHOO
- KADITHEEMU
- MAKUNUDHOO

73° 25'
73°
7°
6° 40'

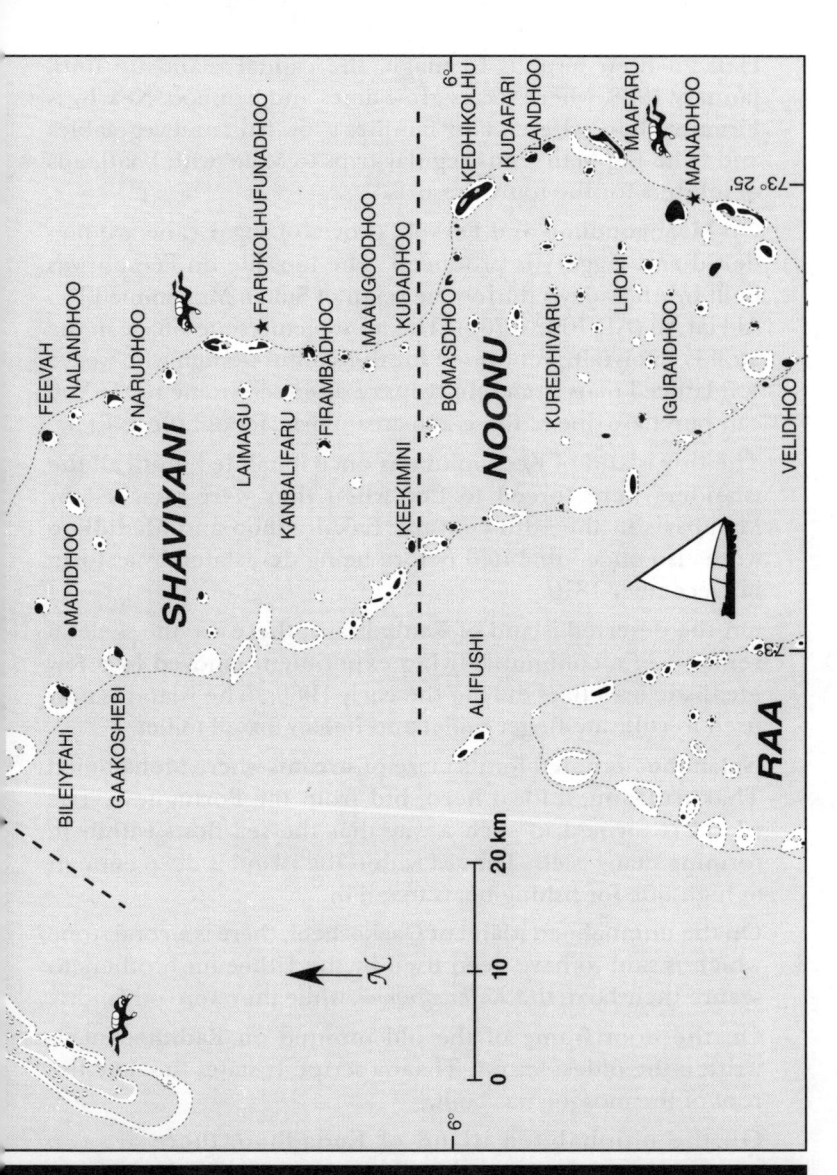

NORTHERN ATOLLS

Half an hour away is **Liamagu**, the capital island up until January 1968, where locals grow limes and bamboo. Nearby is **Firambadhoo**, where many families grow fruit and vegetables and 'The Big Man' runs regular trips to Male' with boatloads of lobsters for the tourist resorts.

On **Maaugoodhoo** and **Feevah**, groves of sugar cane are tendered and jaggery is produced. The mosque on Feevah was built by Ali Badeyri during the reign of Sultan Mohammed Ibn Al-Haj Ali (AD 1692–1701). The most picturesque village in the atoll is **Bileiyfahi**, renowned for the skillful women who weave soft latticed mats from thin strips of dried screwpine reeds. You can purchase one of these 2-m cream mats for as little as Rf 5.

The tiny island of **Keekimini** was once inhabited, until all the islanders were forced to flee when they were attacked by Malabaris in the 18th century. **Kakairadhoo** and **Madidhoo** were also once inhabited before being devastated by a storm in December 1819.

On the deserted island of **Kanbalifaru**, there are the skeletal remains of a communal-living experiment enjoyed by a few idealistic travellers during the early 1980s. The island is now used to cultivate finger millet and Italian foxtail millet.

Nalandhoo is noted for its maze of streams where Mohammed Thakurufaanu, a local hero, hid from the Portuguese. The island is formed in such a way that the sea flows within it, forming many islets. The sea within the island is deep enough at high tide for fishing boats to sail in.

On the uninhabited island of **Gaakoshobi**, there is a coral stone which is said to have been used by the Utheemu brothers to secure their boat, the *Kalhuoffummi*, while they were on land.

On the door frame of the old mosque on **Kaditheemu**, is written the oldest known Thaana script. It states the date the roof of the mosque was built.

On the uninhabited island of **Kudadhoo**, there are two mysterious underground hiding places said to be built in the 16th century.

IF HEAVEN IS A PLACE ON EARTH...

LAGUNA BEACH RESORT. MALDIVES.

If you've never heard of Laguna Beach Resort it's probably because it's one of the best kept secrets in the Indian Ocean.

Laguna Beach Resort, in the marvellous Maldives, seductive and surrounded by white sandy beaches. Far from the madding crowd, yet totally civilised. With all the modern amenities one could wish for. Great food at 3 superb restaurants. Lots of lovely things to do in, on, and under the crystal clear waters.

And the best suntan you've ever had. Laguna Beach Resort. If there is a heaven on earth, this has to be it.

Universal Enterprises Ltd., 38, Orchid Magu, Male' 20-02, Republic of Maldives. Tel: 322971; Telex: 66024 UNIENT NF; Fax: (960) 322678; Cable: Universal or contact your travel agent.

LAGUNA BEACH RESORT

Island children

Grinding curry paste

Relax!

Allow us to take care of you when you stop over in Male'. We are located only 3 minutes speed-boat ride from the airport and only 1 minute walk from the jetty.

At **Relax Inn** we offer:
- air-conditioned rooms with private facilities
- hot and cold fresh water
- satellite TV, local TV and in-house videos
- telephone service in every room
- spectacular views of the harbour and airport
- elevator service to all floors
- a souvenir shop on the ground floor
- fine food in our top-floor restaurant.

Relax Inn. Ameer Ahmed Magu, Henveiru, Male'.
Tel: (960) 314531/314532   Fax: (960) 314533

Shells for sale

The old mosque on the inhabited island of **Narudhoo** was built during the reign of Sultan Hassan Nooradeen I (AD 1779).

Haa Dhaalu

Population: 12,890 *Uninhabited islands: 19*
Inhabited islands: 17 *Capital: Nolhivaramfaru*

In 1958, the 77 northernmost islands in the Maldives were grouped into two administrative atolls called Haa Dhaalu and Haa Alifu. Be wary—tropical storms are common in these parts and entire villages have been destroyed by storms and tidal waves.

Places of interest

Along the eastern fringe of the reef, not far beyond the imaginary Shaviyani–Haa Dhaalu border, is one of the country's most populous villages—**Kulhudhuffushi**. The 3000 or so inhabitants practise a wide range of occupations, such as weaving coir and cadjan, and shark fishing. In 1965, following a national contest, the islanders were acknowledged as being the best makers of rope in the country. Long high-bowed dhoni laden with tonnes of rope, thatch and shark fins ply regularly between Kulhudhuffushi and Male'.

Diving enthusiasts often visit the isolated 25-m-long reef that sits west of the main bank of islands. It is a renowned graveyard for many foreign freighters. At the tip of the reef is **Makunudhoo**, a large island with a 600-strong population.

On **Kumundhoo**, you will find ancient ruins with circular foundations, and a mosque built during the reign of Sultan Mohammed Shamshuddeen III (AD 1904–1934).

Heading north, you will see **Faridhoo**, the highest island in the archipelago. It is about 3 m above sea-level! It is difficult to land on Faridhoo because of its stony beach. The island was depopulated in 1971, but the entire population returned in 1975. It is also difficult to land on **Kuburudhoo**, where boats have to be hauled ashore as there is practically no lagoon.

Nolhivaramfaru, the capital island, has good anchorage and supplies large amounts of copra for export. Radiotelephone contact with Male' was established here in 1962.

The island of **Vaikaradhoo** became uninhabitable after a severe storm in May 1812. Settlements were started by one Maamakunudhoo Thukkoi-be, who leased the island for 18,000 cowrie shells per year! The mosque on this island was built during the reign of Sultan Mohammed Shamshuddeen III (AD 1904–1934). Vaikaradhoo is agriculturally rich in comparison to its neighbours and provides easy landing in all seasons.

Vaikaramuraidhoo, which was inhabited up until 1819 when it was devastated by a severe storm, is dotted with wells and there are the ruins of a mosque with a cemetery.

Haa Alifu

Population: 12,031 *Uninhabited islands: 26*
Inhabited islands: 16 *Capital: Dhidhdhoo*

Places of interest

Historically and culturally, Haa Alifu is outstanding. **Utheemu** is the birthplace of Mohammed Thakurufaanu and still today Thakurufaanu's family home is regularly renovated as a mark of respect for his unmatched leadership of the late 16th century. It contains many relics of that period. Bamboo is grown on this island, from which fishing rods are made, and the women weave *saanthi* (reed mats).

Kelaa, on the protruding tip of Thiladhunmathi, also lays claim to significant forebear. Here, island chiefs traditionally played an important role in the coronation of a sultan and, from September 1934 until the end of World War II, the island was a major Indian Ocean air base operated by the British. Nowadays, Kelaa's attractions are its abundance of yams and its main mosque, built during the reign of Sultan Mohammed Ibn Ali (AD 1692–1701).

The tomb of Utheemu Ali Thakurufaanu, who was beheaded by the Portuguese, is found on the inhabited island of **Thakandhoo**.

Baarah provides good anchorage. To one corner of its main mosque are the ruins of an old minaret. And to the southern end of the uninhabited area of the island is a large stone slab with many carvings.

Vashafaru has a large lagoon and landing is fairly easy. The village has a population of around 350 and the mosque on this island was built during the reign of Sultan Mohammed Shamshuddeen III (AD 1904–1934).

The island of **Berimmadhoo** was depopulated in 1968 but the entire population returned in 1975. There is a mosque here which was built during the reign of Sultan Mohammed Shamshuddeen II (AD 1904–1934) and tombstones with no inscriptions. It is difficult to land on this island during the south-west monsoon.

The inhabited island of **Filladhoo** is joined to the uninhabited island of Dhapparu. The *Captain Pentalis* was wrecked on Filladhoo's reef in 1963. **Dhapparu** has the remains of two mosques, and a cemetery with many gravestones.

There is an abandoned well near the ruins of a mosque on the uninhabited island of **Maafahi**. The famous tomb of Sayid Shareef Ali of Mecca can be found on the uninhabited island of **Matheerah**. On the main flag post is written a single date— 1306 AH.

The capital island of **Dhidhdhoo** is renowned for making square sails from coconut leaves. It is said that this island was once two islands which merged naturally.

Dhonakulhi was prominent during the wars of the 18th century against the South Indian Malabars. All that remain now are mosque ruins and a cemetery.

Muladhoo has a large and deep lagoon, and bamboo grows well here.

Tacking north-west, across the Gallandhoo Channel, you come to the final group of islands in the Maldives. This 20-km-long chain of islands is known traditionally as Ihavandhippolhu. On the western fringe is the former atoll capital, **Huvarafushi**. The young girls of these islands are known to be the best dancers in the country, while the young boys are avid soccer fans. The adults of the village are known for their fishing (a fish-freezing plant was founded on Huvarafushi in 1981) and rope-making expertise. And, in 1966, the island came first in a national cowrie-collecting contest!

Further north is **Thuraakunu**, the northernmost island in the Maldives. It is 290 km from Minicoy, the southern part of the Indian island state of Lakshadweep, where the people also speak Dhivehi and wear traditional Maldivian dress. The Maldivian government still asserts that Minicoy is part of the Maldives, despite the fact that it is beyond its maritime boundary. Thuraakunu is a difficult island to approach because it has no lagoon large enough and there is a swell outside the reef.

Tuna to take home

SOUTHERN ATOLLS

Gaafu Alifu 201
Gaafu Dhaalu 204
Gnyaviyani 205
Seenu 206

GAAFU ALIFU TO SEENU

Not surprisingly, lifestyles are significantly different beyond the massive Huvadhoo Channel, an 85-km expanse of ocean. Popularly known as the One and Half Degree Channel, it separates the central atolls from those further south.

There is little interdependence between these atolls as they are geographically isolated from each other as well as from the rest of the archipelago. Fortunately, the climate in the south is conducive to cultivating a variety of crops, and many of the islands, particularly around the Equatorial Channel, are more luxuriantly vegetated than their neighbours to the north. Small plantations of bananas, yams, taro and manioc, as well as the ubiquitous coconut tree, are commonplace.

Given that these atolls are largely self-sufficient, you will find that each one has its own peculiarities. Most obvious of these are the dramatic differences between the languages spoken from atoll to atoll. They vary so much, in fact, that the Male' dialect is used when people from other atolls visit.

There has long been inherent jealousy between southern and northern islanders. The relationships became even more strained when, during the 1950s, 1960s and 1970s, southerners were forced to sell their fish to the government rather than to Colombo merchants, as they had done so profitably for so long. Coupled with this, the government forbade any islander to be employed at the British staging post on Gan. Conflict was imminent. The southerners formed the United Suvadive Islands and proclaimed their secession from the rest of the archipelago. Abdullah Afif Didi was made president of the new island state. This move by the southerners received international publicity but was, nonetheless, short-lived.

Since these controversial times, the new government has worked hard to appease the southern islanders. The Male'-based Addu Development Authority keeps a watchful eye on developments in the south and encourages foreign investment. Garment factories have begun operating on Gan and the old RAF barracks are now known as the Ocean Reef Club and used as holiday accommodation for tourists.

⇒ Getting there

Air Maldives operates six flights a week between Hulhule and Gan. The 1½-hour flight costs Rf1600 one way and offers passengers stunning aerial views of the archipelago.

The majority of locals take the 60- to 80-hour sea voyage. Large boats ply regularly between Male' and Seenu. Passengers are seated on the upper deck while bags of rice, vegetables, chickens, bicycles and all manner of odds and ends are stored on the lower deck. Previously, these boats were quite overcrowded but, while the trip is definitely not for the faint-hearted, Addu can now be reached by sea with some degree of comfort. The trip costs Rf150, one way. Contact the Addu Development Authority in Male' (tel: 323101) for further information.

⇒ Gaafu Alifu

Population: 79101 *Uninhabited islands: 76*
Inhabited islands: 10 *Capital: Viligili*

The downfall of the secessionist movement brought about the creation of two atolls as the gigantic Huvadhu Atoll was split arbitrarily to form Gaafu Alifu and Gaafu Dhaalu. Huvadhu Atoll, or Suvadive as it is still widely known, measures 70 km long and 55 km wide, making it the largest atoll in the world.

The majority of the population inhabit the islands around the perimeter of the atoll and their livelihoods are dependent on fishing. The horizon is invariably dotted with the billowing sails of hundreds of dhoni as they tack to and fro in search of tuna.

Maldives — 202 —

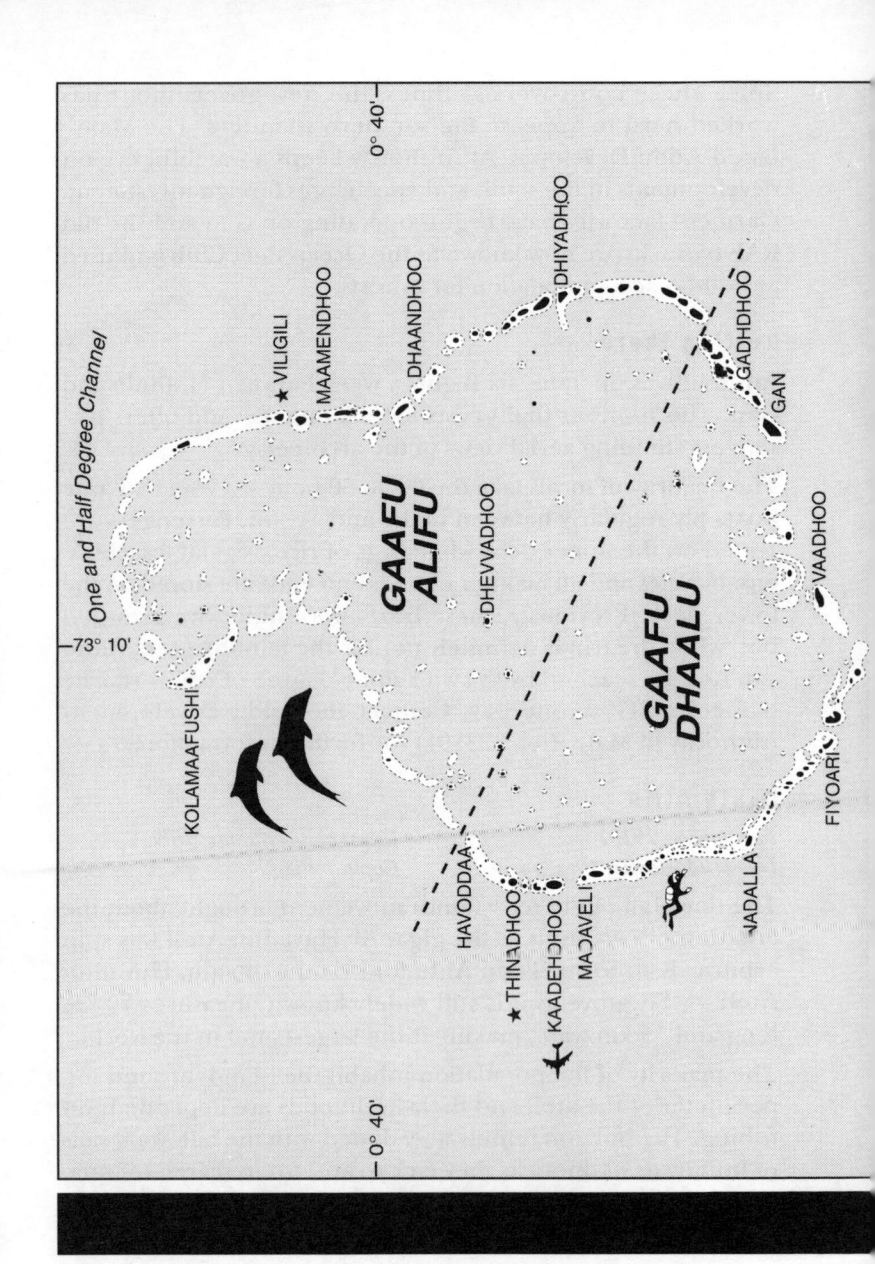

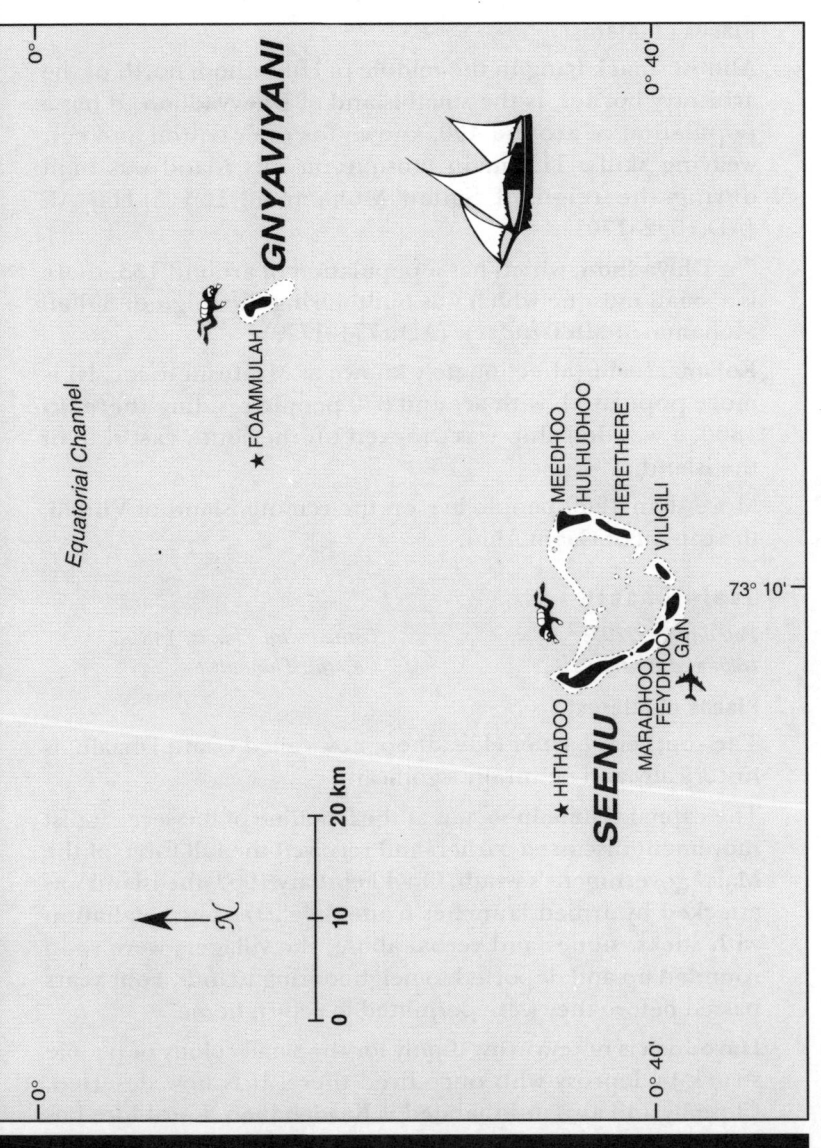

SOUTHERN ATOLLS

GNYAVIYANI

★ FOAMMULAH

Equatorial Channel

SEENU

★ HITHADOO

MEEDHOO
HULHUDHOO
HERETHERE
VILIGILI
MARADHOO
FEYDHOO
GAN

73° 10'

0° 40'

0°

Places of interest

Almost smack bang in the middle of Huvadhoo, north of the arbitrary border, is the small island of **Dhevvadhoo**. It has a population of around 400, known for their cotton and coir weaving skills. The main mosque on this island was built during the reign of Sultan Mohammed Ibn Al-Haj Ali (AD 1692–1701).

On **Dhiyadhoo**, which has a population of around 133, there is a small mosque which was built during the reign of Sultan Mohammed Mu'izzudeen (AD 1774–1779).

Kolamaafushi (affectionately known as Maafushi to locals) is more populated, with around 670 people residing there. In 1800, a wooden ship was wrecked off the south-east side of the island.

More than 1200 people live on the remote island of **Viligili**, the capital of Gaafu Alifu.

Gaafu Dhaalu

Population: 7295 *Uninhabited islands: 148*
Inhabited islands: 10 *Capital: Thinadhoo*

Places of interest

The southern part of Huvadhoo, now called Gaafu Dhaalu, is historically and culturally significant.

The capital, **Thinadhoo**, was at the frontline of the secessionist movement discussed earlier, and received the full force of the Male' government's wrath. On 4 February 1962, the island was attacked by armed launches from Male'. Despite retaliation with sticks, stones and verbal abuse, the villagers were soon rounded up and deported to neighbouring islands. Four years passed before they were permitted to return home.

Havoddaa is noteworthy, if only for the small colony of people struck by leprosy who once lived there. It is now deserted. Close by and also uninhabited is **Kaadehdhoo**. Local lore has it that its entire population was killed during a war with islanders from neighbouring Vaadhoo. Kaadehdhoo now has an airport with flights arriving three times a week from Male' (the return fare is Rf1300).

Vaadhoo is best noted, however, as once being the home of Mohammed Dumaaluddeen, a revered sheik who had studied Islam overseas. He was beckoned to become the nation's leading judge but he preferred a reclusive life on Vaadhoo. His tombstone is still cared for lovingly by the local muezzin. Another fondly remembered forefather is Sultan Mohammed Ibn Al-Haj Ali, a 17th-century sultan who reigned for eight years, bestowing many favours on his friends and family on Vaadhoo. He built numerous mosques on the island, some of them still in use today.

Gadhdhoo is known nationwide as the island for *thundu kunaa*, the beautiful tan-black-and-cream woven prayer mats. In days gone by, every ruler had their stock of *thundu kunaa* from Gadhdhoo to present to visiting diplomats and VIPs. The men of the village collect the reeds used to make these mats from the nearby island of **Fiyaori**. They bundle and strip the reeds before preparing them to be soaked in natural dyes. The women then weave the mats, charging around Rf100 for a standard 2-m mat into which an elaborate geometric design has been woven. The tourist shops in Male' charge Rf400 each for the same mats.

At the centre of uninhabited **Gan** is a large mound, said to have once been a Buddhist place of worship. Another mound is located on the western shore of the island and yet another on the north-eastern shore.

⇒ Gnyaviyani

Population: 710,4171   *Uninhabited islands: 0*
Inhabited islands: 1   *Capital: Foammulah*

Gnyaviyani lies isolated at the centre of the Equatorial Channel, about 40 km south of Gaafu Dhaalu Atoll. It consists of a single island, the largest island in the Maldives, which is 6 km long, surrounded by a barrier reef, luxuriantly vegetated and commonly called **Foammulah**.

In the middle of Foammulah are two lakes. As the island's encircling reef grows outwards and the island becomes older, the centre is expected to subside even more, forcing the lakes to become one large lagoon and a proper atoll to form.

For ease of administration, the 6000 or so inhabitants of this island congregate in seven suburbs: *Dhadi Magu; Dhiguwaadu; Hoadhadu; Miskiiymagu; Malegamu; Dhoodigamu; Funaadu*. The chief landing place is at Rasgefannu in the village of Malegamu. There are also landing areas at Maaneru (Miskiiymagu) and Dhiyarehifaadu (Funaadu).

Many households throughout the island have flourishing gardens of taro, fruits and vegetables and, in some places, pineapple and orange groves abound. Their healthy diet coupled with a temperate climate affords the islanders of Foammulah a longer life expectancy than any of their Maldivian counterparts.

Beyond the coarse coral beach that surrounds the island, are several ancient monuments. During his visit to Foammulah in 1922, HCP Bell unearthed the stone head of a Buddha, a crystal casket and some oval-shaped beads. In the past, Foammulah was also visited by Jean and Raoul Parmentier, two Frenchmen who landed in their ships, *Pensce* and *Sacre*, in 1529. In 1559, a Dutchman, Fredrick De Houtman, visited the island and wrote that he had seen many temples and alters, one of which was an ancient structure made of blue lazulite. And Ibn Batuta spent over two months here in the 13th century. Academics are still pondering the fascinating pre-Muslim history of Foammulah. For many years it was known only for its isolation, which made it an ideal island for political prisoners.

▬ Seenu

Population: 6160   *Uninhabited islands: 32*
Inhabited islands: 6   *Capital: Hithadoo*

Nearly 600 km from Male' and 3 hours' cruising from Foammulah is Seenu, traditionally called Addu, the southernmost atoll in the Maldive archipelago. It has long been regarded as the economic and political hub of the south. During the 1960s, it was an engine room for rebellion, and the people living there still refer to themselves as Addu people rather than Maldivian people. Coupled with this, 25 years of British presence in the atoll has had an inevitable impact. English is widely spoken throughout Seenu, and many of the atoll's young men are recruited by resort operators from the north because they are better versed in the ways and wonders of the western mind.

Places of interest

Gan is the gateway to Seenu. It has a domestic airport and the *Ocean Reef Club* (the former RAF barracks) is situated there. The barracks, part of a British air base during World War II and again from 1956–1977, have been converted into 20 comfortable fan-cooled rooms with facilities including a restaurant and bar, swimming pool and untended golf course. Despite being attractively priced at $US90 per day for two (including meals), few tourists ever venture this far from Male'.

The main activity on Gan comes from the hum of sewing machines in the two garment factories. About 1500 local women arrive by bus each day to work at the factories, and some 500 Sri Lankan women are employed on yearly contracts, living in the barracks and working nightshifts.

Also on Gan is a *bodhi* tree, the sole remnant of the days of Buddhism in this area. Many Buddhist remains were destroyed when the runway was built.

Feydhoo is connected artificially to **Maradhoo** by a causeway which opened in April, 1970. Another causeway, opened in September 1981, connects Feydhoo to Gan. Together these causeways make up the longest road in the Maldives, some 16 km long.

Apart from its fishing expertise, the people of the capital island, **Hithadoo**, are renowned blacksmiths and jewellers. On the island is the Koruvalu Miskiiy, built during the reign of Sultan Mohamed Imaduddeen I (AD 1620–1648), and the grave of Sultan Hassan X (AD 1701), in the graveyard of the

Thakurufaanu Miskiiy, who died in 1765, having spent 60 years here in exile. In all, there are 20 mosques on Hithadoo and, at the northern extremity of the island, lies the ruins of a fort. In 1944, the *British Loyalty* was wrecked on the island's south-west reef.

The inhabited island of **Meedhoo** has a cemetery with the tombs of many *gaazee* and 15 mosques.

Island woman

ADDITIONAL INFORMATION

Travel directory 210
Further reading 226
Gadabout Guides 229
Glossary 235
Dhivehi dictionary 243
Index 257
Photo credits 265

TRAVEL DIRECTORY

⇒ Travel agents (Male')

Beach Travel and Tours
Coconut Villa, Henveiru
(tel: 320507/fax: 324572)

Cosmos International
Labulaage
Ameer Ahmed Magu,
Henveiru
(tel: 313797/fax: 313798)

Crossworld Maldives
Karankaa Villa, Henveiru
(tel: 320912/fax: 3209143)

Cyprea Hotels and Travel
25 Boduthakurufaanu Magu,
Henveiru
(tel: 322451/fax: 323523)

Deen's Orchid Agency
Jazeera,
Boduthakurufaanu Magu,
Henveiru
(tel: 328437/fax: 323779)

Dhirham Travels
Fareedhee Magu, Maafanu
(tel: 323371/fax: 324752)

Galena Maldives
Orchid Magu, Maafanu
(tel: 324743/fax: 324465)

Imad's Agency
Jawahiriyya, Chandani Magu,
Machchangolhi
(tel: 324845/fax: 324835)

Jet Wing
70 Orchid Magu
(tel: 314037/fax: 314038)

Landmark Travel
52 Boduthakurufaanu Magu
(tel: 324369/fax: 328424)

Phoenix Travel
Fasmeeru,
Boduthakurufaanu Magu,
Henveiru
(tel: 323181/fax: 325499)

Safari Tours
Chandani Magu,
Machchangolhi
(tel: 323524/fax: 322516)

Seasand Enterprises
Gadha Shop,
Majeedi Magu, Galolhu
(tel: 324922/fax: 320730)

Seasan Tours
Sunny Coast, Maafanu
(tel: 325634/fax: 325633)

Scorpion Travels
37 Boduthakurufaanu Magu
(tel: 327443/fax: 327442)

Sun Travel and Tours
Manaage, Machchangolhi
(tel: 325975/fax: 320419)

Sultan Park, Male'

Resort island, Kaafu Atoll

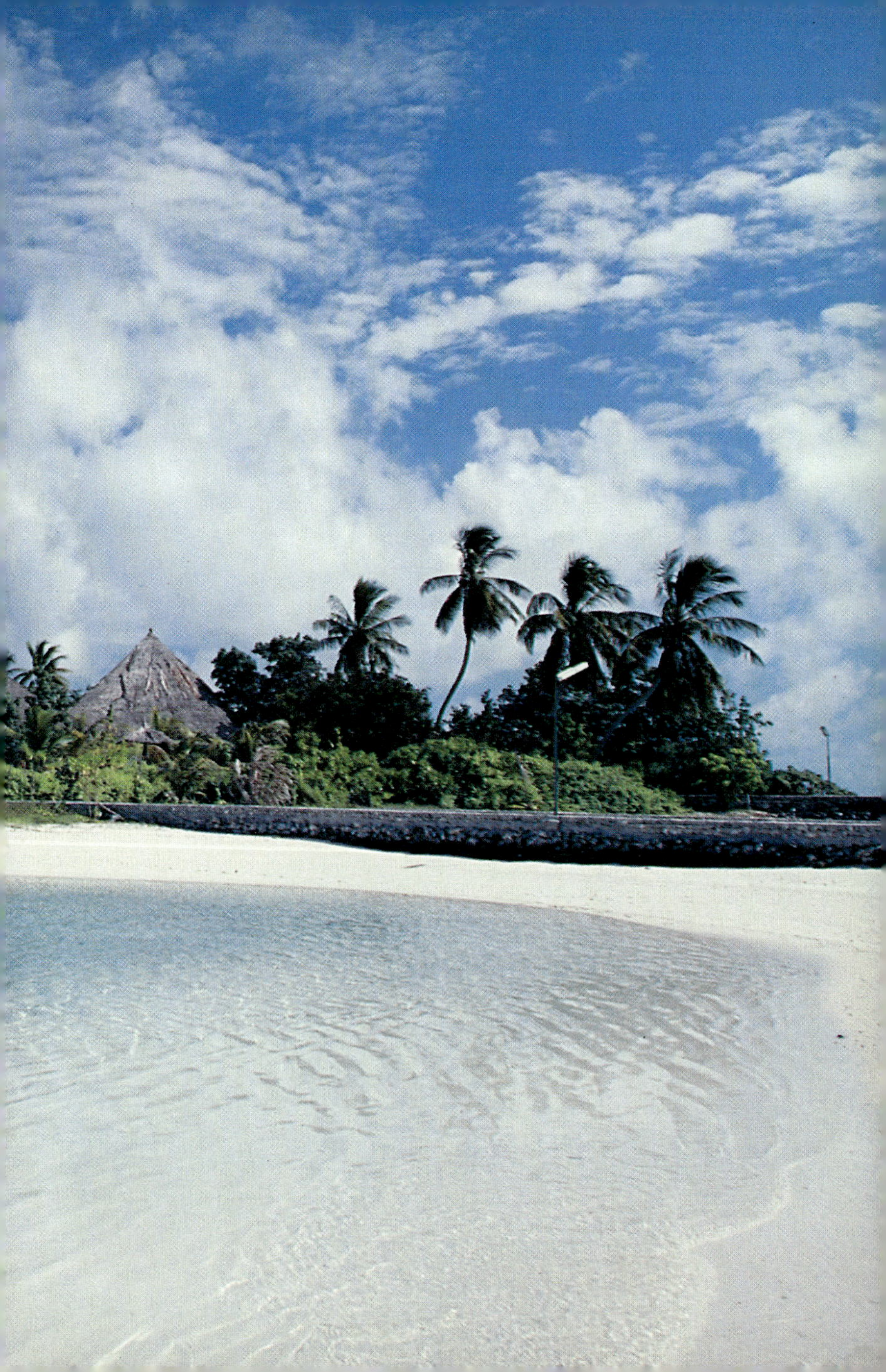

Above: Island flora
Below: Bandos Island Resort

Sunland Travel
MTCC Building
(tel: 323467/fax: 325543)

Universal Enterprises
38 Orchid Magu, Maafanu
(tel: 323080/fax: 322678)

The Travel Bureau
Maldives Air Services,
Boduthakurufaanu Magu
(tel: 322438/fax: 325056)

Voyages Maldives
Fareedhee Magu, Maafanu
(tel: 323019/fax: 325336)

Resorts

The following directory lists for each resort: the number of rooms; full-board, low-season (May–October) and high-season (November–April) room rates; distance from the airport; return transfer fare from the airport per person, by air or sea; accepted credit cards; an office address in Male'; and telephone and facsimile numbers at the resort (unless indicated otherwise).

Please note that return transfers by sea range from engine dhoni to cabin cruisers, and prices vary accordingly.

Alimatha Aquatic Resort (70 rooms)
Low season: $US80 single/$US100 double. High season: $US95 single/$US145 double. 61 km from the airport. Transfer by sea: $US80. Credit cards: AE. Male' office: Safari Tours, SEK No 1, Chandani Magu. Tel: 450544. Fax: 450575.

Angaga Island Resort (50 rooms)
Low season: $US75 single/$US85 double. High season: $US100 single/$US120 double. 69 km from the airport. Transfer by sea: $US90. Credit cards: AE, VC MC. Male' office: Mithulhaagiri, Male'. Tel/Fax: 450520.

Ari Beach Resort (76 rooms)
Low season: $US49 single/$US73 double. High season: $US98 single/$US122 double. 97 km from the airport. Transfer by sea: $US110. Credit cards: AE, VC, MC. Male' office: 52 Boduthakurufaanu Magu. Tel: 450513. Fax: 450512.

Asdu Sun Island (30 rooms)
Low season: $US60 single/$US90 double. High season: $US90 single/$US130 double. 37 km from the airport. Transfer by sea: $US75. Credit cards: AE, VC, MC. Male' office: Shoanary, Henveiru. Tel: 445051.

Athurugau Island Resort (42 rooms)
Low season: $US120 single/$US130 double. High season: $US170 single/$US180 double. 68 km from the airport. Transfer by sea: $US157. Credit cards: AE, VC, MC, DC. Male' office: Voyages Maldives, Fareedhee Magu. Tel: 450508. Fax: 450574.

Avi Island Resort (28 rooms)
Low season: $US75 single/$US100 double. High season: $US90 single/$US150 double. 64 km from the airport. Transfer by air: $US300. Credit cards: AE, VC, MC. Male' office: Shoanary, Henveiru. Tel/Fax: 450595.

Bandos Island Resort (203 rooms)
Low season: $US134 single/$US169 double. High season: $US162 single/$US192 double. 8 km from the airport. Transfer by sea: $US40. Credit cards: AE, VC, MC. Male' office: Jazeera, Boduthakurufaanu Magu, Henveiru. Tel: 443310. Fax: 443877.

Baros Holiday Resort (56 rooms)
Low season: $US50 single/$US60 double. High season: $US110 single/$US120 double. 16 km from the airport. Transfer by sea: $US40. Credit cards: AE, VC, MC, JCB. Male' office: Universal Enterprises Ltd, 38 Orchid Magu. Tel: 442672. Fax: 443497.

Bathala Island Resort (37 rooms)
Low season: $US60 single/$US65 double. High season: $US85 single/$US90 double. 58 km from the airport. Transfer by sea: $US150. Credit cards: AE, VC, EM. Male' office: 55 Boduthakurufaanu Magu. Tel: 450587. Fax: 450558.

Bi Ya Doo Island Resort (96 rooms)
Low season: $US115 single/$US125 double. High season: $US130 single/$US140 double. 29 km from the airport. Transfer by sea: $US35. Credit cards: AE, VC, MC, JCB, DC. Male' office: Prabalaji Enterprises (Pvt) Ltd, Maarandhooge, Henveiru. Tel: 443516. Fax: 443742.

Boduhithi Coral Isle (87 rooms)
Low season: $US90 single/$US130 double. High season: $US110 single/$US165 double. 29 km from the airport. Transfer by sea: $US70. Credit cards: AE, VC. Male' office: Safari Tours, SEK No 1, Chandani Magu. Tel: 445905. Fax: 442634.

Bolifushi (32 rooms)
Low season: $US55 single/$US75 double. High season: $US65 single/$US90 double. 15 km from the airport. Transfer by sea: $US20. Credit cards: AE, VC, MC. Male' office: Seesan Goalhi. Tel: 443517. Fax: 445924.

Club Little Huraa (43 rooms)
Low season: $US35 single/$US60 double. High season: $US77 single/$US118 double. 16 km from the airport. Transfer by sea: $US25. Credit cards: AE, VC, MC. Male' office: Bahaareege, Kalhu Huraa Magu, Galolhu. Tel: 445934. Fax: 444231.

Club Med (152 rooms)
Low season: $US130 single/$US260 double. High season: $US130 single/$US260 double. 2 km from the airport. Transfer by sea: $US20. Credit cards: AE, VC, MC, JCB, SS. Male' office: No 1 Ibrahim Hassan Didi Magu, Majeedi Bazaar. Tel: 444552. Fax: 442415.

Cocoa Island (8 rooms)
Low season: $US270 single/$US270 double. High season: $US390 single/$US390 double. 32 km from the airport. Transfer by air: $US200. Credit cards: AE, VC, MC, EM. Male' office: Gulisthaanuge, Fiyaathoshi Magu, Maafanu. Tel: 443713. Fax: 441919.

Dhiggiri Tourist Resort (30 rooms)
Low season: $US70 single/$US90 double. High season: $US70 single/$US105 double. 60 km from the airport. Transfer by sea: $US80. Credit cards: AE, VC, MC. Male' office: Safari Tours, SEK No 1, Chandani Magu. Tel/Fax: 450592.

Dhigufinolhu Tourist Resort (60 rooms)
Low season: $US100 single/$US130 double. High season: $US120 single/$US160 double. 19 km from the airport. Transfer by sea: $US50. Credit cards: AE, VC, MC. Male' office: Digufinolhu Male' Office, Orchid Higun. Tel: 443599. Fax: 443886.

Ellaidhoo Tourist Resort (50 rooms)
Low season: $US70 single/$US90 double. High season: $US70 single/$US100 double. 58 km from the airport. Transfer by sea: $US80. Credit cards: AE, VC, MC. Male' office: Safari Tours, SEK No 1, Chandani Magu. Tel: 450514. Fax: 450586.

Emboodhu Finolhu Tourist Resort (40 rooms)
Low season: $US75 single/$US95 double. High season: $US100 single/$US120 double. 8 km from the airport. Transfer by sea: $US30. Credit cards: AE, VC, MC, JCB. Male' office: Makhumaage, Galolhu. Tel: 444451. Fax: 445925.

Embudu Village (106 rooms)
Low season: $US60 single/$US85 double. High season: $US80 single/$US110 double. 15 km from the airport. Transfer by sea: $US25. Credit cards: AE, VC, MC. Male' office: Kaimoo Hotels and Travel Services (Pvt) Ltd, Roanuge. Tel: 442673. Fax: 442673.

Eriyadu Island Resort (46 rooms)
Low season: $US45 single/$US60 double. High season: $US65 single/$US80 double. 39 km from the airport. Transfer by sea: $US50. Credit cards: AE, VC, MC. Male' office: Eriyadu Male' Office, AAA Trading Co, Ibrahim Hassan Didi Magu. Tel: 444487. Fax: 445926.

Fesdu Fun Island (50 rooms)
Low season: $US50 single/$US60 double. High season: $US90 single/$US100 double. 64 km from the airport. Transfer by sea: $US100. Credit cards: AE, VC, MC, JCB, DC. Male' office: Universal Enterprises Ltd, 38 Orchid Magu. Tel: 450541. Fax: 450547.

Fihalhohi Tourist Resort (76 rooms)
Low season: $US68 single/$US84 double. High season: $US79 single/$US99 double. 45 km from the airport. Transfer by sea: $US30. Credit cards: AE, VC, MC. Male' office: Dhirham Ltd, Faamudeyri Magu. Tel: 442903. Fax: 443803.

Full Moon Beach Resort (156 rooms)
10 km from the airport. Transfer by sea: $US40. Credit cards: AE, VC, MC, JCB, DC. Male' office: Universal Enterprises Ltd, 28 Orchid Magu. Tel: 441976. Fax: 441979.

Fun Island Resort (100 rooms)
Low season: $US90 single/ $US100 double. High season: $US135 single/$US145 double. 39 km from the airport. Transfer by sea: $US70. Credit cards: AE, VC, MC, DC. Male' office: Villa Building, Ibrahim Hassan Didi Magu (PO Box 2073). Tel: 444558. Fax: 443958.

Gangehi Island Resort (25 rooms)
Low season: $US115 single/$US165 double. High season: $US130 single/$US190 double. 71 km from the airport. Transfer by air: $US198. Credit cards: AE, VC. Male' office: Holiday Club, Maizaandhoshuge, Henveiru. Tel: 450505. Fax: 450506.

Gasfinolhu Island Resort (38 rooms)
Low season: $US100 single/$US200 double. High season: $US100 single/$US200 double. 18 km from the airport. Transfer by sea: $US25. Credit cards: AE, VC, MC. Male' office: Imad's Agency, Chandani Magu. Tel: 442078. Fax: 445941.

Giraavaru Tourist Resort (48 rooms)
Low season: $US90 single/$US160 double. High season: $US110 single/$US190 double. 11 km from the airport. Transfer by sea: $US30. Credit cards: AE, VC, MC. Male' office: Phoenix Hotels and Resorts Pte Ltd, Fasmeeru, Boduthakurufaanu Magu. Tel: 440440. Fax: 444818.

Halaveli Tourist Village (40 rooms)
Low season: $US65 single/$US90 double. High season: $US110 single/$US150 double. 84 km from the airport. Transfer by sea: $US100. Credit cards: AE, VC, MC. Male' office: Eastinvest (Pvt) Ltd, Akiri, Boduthakurufaanu Magu. Tel: 450559. Fax: 450564.

Helengeli Tourist Village (30 rooms)
Low season: $US60 single/$US82 double. High season: $US82 single/$US120 double. 52 km from the airport. Transfer by sea: $US60. Credit cards: AE, VC, MC. Male' office: Manta Reisen, Boduthakurufaanu Magu. Tel/Fax: 444615.

Hembadoo Island Resort (44 rooms)
Low season: $US45 single/$US60 double. High season: $US65 single/$US75 double. 39 km from the airport. Transfer by sea: $US40. Credit cards: AE, VC, MC. Male' office: Transit Inn, Maaveyo Magu. Tel: 443884. Fax: 441948.

Holiday Island (125 rooms)
177 km from the airport. Credit cards: AE, VC, MC, DC. Male' office: Villa Building, Ibrahim Hassan Didi Magu. Tel: 450011. Fax: 450022.

Hudhuveli Beach Resort (44 rooms)
Low season: $US80 single/$US105 double. High season: $US90 single/$US120 double. 15 km from the airport. Transfer by sea: $US30. Credit cards: AE, VC, MC, DC. Male' office: Jazeera, Boduthakurufaanu Magu, Henveiru. Tel: 443396. Fax: 443849.

Ihuru Tourist Resort (40 rooms)
Low season: $US95 single/$US150 double. High season: $US100 single/$US160 double. 19 km from the airport. Transfer by sea: $US44. Credit cards: AE, VC, MC. Male' office: Ihuru Investments (Pvt) Ltd, Bodukosheege, Ameer Ahmed Magu. Tel: 443502. Fax: 445933.

Kandooma Tourist Resort (60 rooms)
Low season: $US50 single/$US65 double. High season: $US65 single/$US85 double. 27 km from the airport. Transfer by sea: $US35. Credit cards: AE, VC. Male' office: Zebey, Orchid Magu, Maafanu. Tel: 444452. Fax: 445948.

Kanifinolhu Tourist Resort (125 rooms)
Low season: $US115 single/$US125 double. High season: $US130 single/$US140 double. 19 km from the airport. Transfer by sea: $US30. Credit cards: AE, VC, MC, JCB. Male' office: 25 Boduthakurufaanu Magu. Tel: 443152. Fax: 444859.

Kudahithi Tourist Resort (6 rooms)
Low season: $US225 double. High season: $US225 double. 29 km from the airport. Transfer by sea: $US75. Credit cards: AE, VC. Male' office: Safari Tours, SEK No 1, Chandani Magu. Tel/Fax: 444613.

Kudarah Island Resort (30 rooms)
Low season: $US126 single/$US188 double. High season: $US150 single/$US225 double. 97 km from the airport. Transfer by air: $US300. Credit cards: AE, VC, MC. Male' office: 2/F Merry Side, Boduthakurufaanu Magu, Henveiru. Tel: 450549. Fax: 450550.

Kunfunadhoo
Closed for redevelopment.

Kuramathi Tourist Resort (190 rooms)
Low season: $US60–110 single/$US70–120 double. High season: $US80–140 single/$US90–150 double. 58 km from the airport. Transfer by sea: $US100. Credit cards: AE, VC, MC, JCB, DC. Male' office: Universal Enterprises Ltd, 38 Orchid Magu. Tel: 450527. Fax: 450556.

Kuredu Island Resort (150 rooms)
Low season: $US40 single/$US60 double. High season: $US50 single/$US100 double. 129 km from the airport. Transfer by sea: $US70. Credit cards: AE, VC, MC. Male' office: Champa Trade and Travels. Tel: 230337. Fax: 230332.

Kurumba Village (169 rooms)
Low season: $US105 single/$US115 double. High season: $US165 single/$US175 double. 3 km from the airport. Transfer by sea: $US12. Credit cards: AE, VC, MC, JCB, DC. Male' office: Universal Enterprises Ltd, 38 Orchid Magu. Tel: 443081. Fax: 443885.

Laguna Beach Resort (104 rooms)
Low season: $US95 single/$US105 double. High season: $US165 single/$US175 double. 11 km from the airport. Transfer by sea: $US40. Credit cards: AE, VC, MC, JCB, DC. Male' office: Universal Enterprises Ltd, 38 Orchid Magu. Tel: 443042. Fax: 443041.

Lhohifushi Tourist Resort (105 rooms)
Low season: $US88 single/$US103 double. High season: $US100 single/$US120 double. 18 km from the airport. Transfer by sea: $US30. Credit cards: AE, VC, MC. Male' office: Altaf Enterprises Ltd, Ibrahim Hassan Didi Magu. Tel: 441909. Fax: 441908.

Maayafushi Tourist Resort (60 rooms)
Low season: $US50 single/$US65 double. High season: $US75 single/$US110 double. 61 km from the airport. Transfer by sea: $US100. Credit cards: AE, VC, MC. Male' office: Star Resort, 2/7 Ameer Ahmed Magu. Tel: 450588. Fax: 450568.

Madoogali Resort (50 rooms)
Low season: $US120 single/$US200 double. High season: $US180 single/$US240 double. 79 km from the airport. Transfer by: sea $US180/air $US400. Credit cards: AE, VC, MC. Male' office: Madoogali Male' Office, Boduthakurufaanu Magu. Tel: 450581. Fax: 450554.

Makunudhoo Club (29 rooms)
Low season: $US105 single/$US135 double. High season: $US175 single/$US260 double. 35 km from the airport. Transfer by sea: $US140. Credit cards: AE, VC, MC. Male' office: Gelena Maldives, 7 Orchid Magu. Tel: 446464. Fax: 446565.

Meerufenfushi Island Resort (164 rooms)
Low season: $US35 single/$US55 double. High season: $US50 single/$US75 double. 40 km from the airport. Transfer by sea: $US50. Credit cards: AE, VC, MC. Male' office: Champa Trade and Travels. Tel: 443157. Fax: 445946.

Mirihi Marina (26 rooms)
Low season: $US65 single/$US94. High season: $US127 single/$US140 double. 89 km from the airport. Transfer by: sea $US100/air $US300. Credit cards: AE, VC, MC. Male' office: Velangali, 2 Muiveyo Magu. Tel: 450500. Fax: 450501.

Moofushi Island Resort (60 rooms)
Low season: $US90 single/$US160 double. High season: $US300 single/$US315 double. 89 km from the airport. Transfer by: sea $US150/air $US320. Credit cards: AE, VC, MC. Male' office: WDI, 1/7 Boduthakurufaanu Magu. Tel: 450598. Fax: 450509.

Nakatchafushi Tourist Resort (51 rooms)
Low season: $US60 single/$US70 double. High season: $US120 single/$US130 double. 23 km from the airport. Transfer by sea: $US50. Credit cards: AE, VC, MC, JCB, DC. Male' office: Universal Enterprises Ltd, 38 Orchid Magu. Tel: 443847. Fax: 442665.

Nika Hotel (26 rooms)
Low season: $US170 single/$US260 double. High season: $US285 single/$US440 double. 68 km from the airport. Transfer by air: $US250. Credit cards: AE, VC, MC, JCB, DC. Male' office: Nika Hotel Office, 10 Fareedhee Magu. Tel: 450516. Fax: 450577.

Ocean Reef Club, Gan
Low season: $US40 single/$US60 double. High season: $US70 single/$US90 double. Transfer by air: $US160. Credit cards: VC, MC. Male' office: Phoenix Hotels and Resorts. Tel: 323181. Fax: 325499.

Olhuveli View Hotel (125 rooms)
Low season: $US225 single/$US250 double. High season: $US275 single/$US300 double. 35 km from the airport. Transfer by sea: $US65. Credit cards: AE, VC, MC. Male' office: Onyx, 3/37 Chandani Magu. Tel: 442788. Fax: 445942.

Palm Tree Island (60 rooms)
Low season: $US135 single/$US170 double. High season: $US150 single/$US190 double. 19 km from the airport. Transfer by sea: $US50. Credit cards: AE, VC, MC. Male' office: Veligandu Hura Male' Office, Orchid Higun. Tel: 443882. Fax: 443886.

Paradise Island (140 rooms)
16 km from the airport. Transfer by sea: $US30. Credit cards: AE, VC, MC, DC. Male' office: Villa Building, Ibrahim Hassan Didi Magu. Tel: 440011. Fax: 440022.

Rannalhi
Closed for redevelopment

Ranveli Beach Resort (56 rooms)
Low season: $US61 single/$US122 double. High season: $US61 single/$US122 double. 77 km from the airport. Transfer by air: $US157. Credit cards: VC, MC. Tel: 450570. Fax: 450523.

Reethi Rah Resort (50 rooms)
Low season: $US62 single/$US104 double. High season: $US88 single/$US135 double. 32 km from the airport. Transfer by sea: $US45. Credit cards: AE, VC, MC. Male' office: Shaazeewin, Fareedhee Magu, Maafanu. Tel: 441905. Fax: 441906.

Rihiveli Beach Resort (46 rooms)
Low season: $US155 single/$US186 double. High season: $US195 single/$US230 double. 40 km from the airport. Transfer by sea: $US132. Credit cards: AE, VC, MC. Male' office: Imad's Agency, Chandani Magu. Tel/Fax: 443731.

Tari Village (24 rooms)
Low season: $US90 single/$US110 double. High season: $US120 single/$US160 double. 16 km from the airport. Transfer by sea: $US30. Credit cards: VC. Male' office: Phoenix Hotels and Resorts. Tel: 442881. Fax: 444650.

Thulhagiri Island Resort (58 rooms)
Low season: $US108 single/$US134 double. High season: $US144 single/$US1789 double. 11 km from the airport. Transfer by sea: $US30. Credit cards: AE, VC, MC. Male' office: Jazeera, 15 Boduthakurufaanu Magu, Henveiru. Tel: 445929. Fax: 445939.

Thundufushi Island Resort (44 rooms)
Low season: $US165 single/$US220 double. High season: $US210 single/$US280 double. 76 km from the airport. Transfer by: sea $US160/air $US290. Credit cards: AE, VC, MC. Male' office: Voyages Maldives, Fareedhee Magu. Tel: 450583. Fax: 450515.

Twin Island (32 rooms)
Low season: $US115 single/$US125 double. High season: $US165 single/$US175 double. 81 km from the airport. Transfer by air: $US240. Credit cards: AE, VC, MC, DC. Male' office: Universal Enterprises Ltd, 38 Orchid Magu. Tel: 450524. Fax: 450596.

Vaadhoo Diving Paradise (31 rooms)
Low season: $US90 single/$US130 double. High season: $US100 single/$US140 double. 8 km from the airport. Transfer by sea: $US30. Credit cards: AE, VC, MC. Male' office: Maarandhooge, Irumatheebai, Henveiru. Tel: 443976. Fax: 443397.

Vabbinfaru Paradise Island (31 rooms)
Low season: $US120 single/$US180 double. High season: $US180 single/$US250 double. 16 km from the airport, Transfer by sea: $US50. Credit cards: AE, VC. Male' office: Dhirham, Faamudheyri Magu. Tel: 443147. Fax: 443843.

Veligandu Island (63 rooms)
Low season: $US80 single/$US120 double. High season: $US100 single/$US140 double. 56 km from the airport. Transfer by sea: $US80. Credit cards: AE, VC, MC. Male' office: Crown Company, Orchid Magu. Tel: 450519. Fax: 450519.

Villi Varu Island Resort (60 rooms)
Low season: $US115 single/$US125 double. High season: $US130 single/$US140 double. 29 km from the airport. Transfer by sea: $US35. Credit cards: AE, VC, MC, JCB, DC. Male' office: Prabalaji Enterprises (Pvt) Ltd, Maarandhooge, Henveiru. Tel: 447070. Fax: 447272.

Ziyaaraiyfushi Tourist Resort (79 rooms)
Low season: $US55 single/$US70 double. High season: $US70 single/$US85 double. 40 km from the airport. Transfer by sea: $US40. Credit cards: AE, VC, MC. Male' office: Phoenix Hotels and Resorts Pte Ltd, Fasmeeru, Boduthakurufaanu Magu. Tel: 443088. Fax: 441910.

Tourist hotels

Hotel Alia (Haveeree Higun, Male')
Low season: $US35 single/$US50 double. High season: $US40 single/$US55 double. Credit cards: AE, VC. Tel: 322080. Fax: 322197.

Nasandhura Palace Hotel (Boduthakurufaanu Magu, Male')
Low season: $US55 single/$US75 double. High season: $US55 single/$US75 double. Credit cards: AE, VC, MC. Tel: 323380. Fax: 320822.

Relax Inn (Ameer Ahmed Magu, Male')
Low season: $US25 single/$US40 double. High season: $US25 single/$US40 double. Credit cards: AE, VL. Tel: 314531. Fax: 314533.

Growing taro, Foammulah

FURTHER READING

Adeney, M and Carr, WK. *The Maldives Republic: The Politics of the Western Indian Ocean Islands*. Praeger Publishers, London.

Agassiz, A. *Memoirs of the Museum of Comparative Zoology at Harvard College Vol XXLX: The Coral Reefs of the Maldives*. Cambridge University Press, USA 1903. A topographical survey of the Maldivian atolls.

Baksi-Lahiri, Sudeshna. *Women's Power and Ritual Politics in the Maldives*. Fulbright-Hays Doctoral Dissertation Program, 1981. An academic view of the role of women in Maldivian society.

Batuta, Ibn (author) and Gray, Albert (editor). *Ibn Batuta in the Maldives and Ceylon*. Royal Asiatic Society, Colombo 1881. Memoirs of a 14th-century traveller.

Bell, HCP. *The Maldive Islands: An Account of the Physical Features, Climate, History, Inhabitants, Production and Trade*. Government Printer, Colombo 1883.
Report on a Visit to Male'. Government Printer, Colombo 1920.
The Maldive Islands: Monograph on the History, Archaeology and Epigraphy. Government Printer, Colombo 1940.
The most important available journals on Maldivian history.

Bowder, Jim. *Maldive Island Money*. Society for International Numismatics, California 1969. A look at ancient Maldivian currency.

Butany, WT. *Report on Agricultural Survey and Crop Production*. UNDP, Rome 1974. A review of the major Maldivian crops and agricultural problems.

Colton, Elizabeth. 'Maldives Looks to the Future'. *Far Eastern Economic Review* (October 1979), Hong Kong. An interview with the President of the Maldives.

Crowe, Philip K. *Diversions of a Diplomat in Ceylon*. Macmillan and Co, London 1957. A short chapter on life in Male' by a former British Ambassador to Ceylon.

de Silva, MWS. *Some Observations on the History of the Madivian Language*. The Philological Society, Oxford 1970.

Didi, MA. *Ladies and Gentlemen: The Maldive Islands*. Ministry of External Affairs, Male' 1949. Written by a former President of the Maldives.

Forbes, Andrew DW. 'Weaving in the Maldive Islands'. Occasional Paper No 9, British Museum, London. A look at the mat industry in Suvadive Atoll.
Southern Arabia and the Islamicisation of the Central Indian Ocean Archipelagoes. Archipel 21, Paris 1981. An account of how Islam spread to the Maldives.
Archives and Resources for Maldivian History. University of Khartoum, Sudan. A review of the best literature on Maldivian history.

Gardiner, Stanley J. *The Fauna and Geography of the Maldive Islands.* Cambridge University Press, USA 1906.

Gupta, Ranjan. *The Indian Ocean.* Marwah Publications, Bombay. A short chapter on the geopolitics of the Maldives.

Hass, Hans 'Central Subsistence: A New Theory of Atoll Formation'. *Atoll Research Bulletin,* Pacific Science Board, Washington DC 1962. A possible alternative to Darwin's theory.

Health, Ministry of. *On the Way Toward Health for All Vol 1.* UNICEF, Male' 1980. A program of health statistics.

Heyerdahl, T. *The Maldive Mystery.* George Allen and Unwin, London 1986. Thought by many to be an archaeological masterpiece.

Hockly, TW. *The Two Thousand Isles.* H F and G Witherby, London 1935. An account of the people, history and customs of the Maldives.

Information, Department of. *The Maldive Islands Today.* Male'. A brief look, by various local authors, at different facets of Maldivian society.

Innes, Hammond. *Sea and Islands.* Collins, London 1967. A fictional story set in the southern Maldivian atolls.

Kurian, George Thomas. *Encyclopaedia of the Third World Vol 2.* Mansell, London 1979. A basic fact sheet.

Lateef, K. *An Introductory Economic Report.* The World Bank, Washington DC 1980. A documentary on the Maldivian economy.

Maloney, Clarence. *The Maldives: New Stresses in an Old Nation.* University of California Press, California 1976.
People of the Maldive Islands. Orient Longman, New Delhi 1980. A sociological dissection of the Maldivian people.

Maniku, Hassan. *The Maldives: A Profile.* Department of Information, Male' 1977.
The History of the Maldivian Constitution. Department of Information, Male' 1982.
Some of the books by today's most prolific Maldivian author.

Moresby, Robert. *Nautical Directions for the Maldive Islands.* Allen and Co, London 1840.

Mukerjee, Dilip. *Maldives Diversifies Contacts with Big Neighbours*. Pacific Community, London 1975. A look at 'Big Troubles Thursday'.

Munch-Peterson, N F. *Background Paper for Population Needs Mission*. UNDP, Rome 1981. A brief resume of Maldivian society.

Phadnis, Urmila and Luithui, Ela Dutt. 'The Maldives Enters World Politics'. *Asian Affairs* (January 1981).

Pyrard, François. *The Voyages of François Pyrard of Laval to the East Indies, the Maldives, the Moluccas and Brazil Vol 1*. Hakluyt Society, London 1887. A detailed account of 17th century Maldivian customs.

Reynolds, CHB. *The Maldive Islands*. Royal Central Asian Society, London 1974.

Linguistic Strands in the Maldives. School of Oriental and Asian Studies, London 1978.

Rosset, CW. *The Maldive Islands*. The Graphic, London 1886. Impressions of Male' by a 19th-century visitor.

Seidler, Helen. *Report on the Survey of Island Women*. National Planning Agency, Male' 1980. A statistical overview of a woman's role in Maldivian society.

Smallwood, C. *A Visit to the Maldive Islands*. Royal Central Asian Society, London 1961. A review of the Maldives by a former captain of the British Air Force.

Stoddard, TL. *Area Handbook for the Indian Ocean Territories*. American Unviersity, Washington DC 1971.

Villiers, Alan. *Give Me a Ship to Sail*. Hodder and Stoughton, London 1958.

'The Marvellous Maldive Islands'. *National Geographic* (June 1957), National Geographic Society, Washington DC.

Young, IA and Christopher, W. *Memoir on the Inhabitants of the Maldive Islands*. Bombay Geographical Society, Bombay 1844. Important memoirs by two 19th-century naval officers.

Zuhair, M. *Practical Dhivehi*. Novelty, Maldives, 1991. A handy language guide.

GADABOUT GUIDES

Street scene, Himmafushi

Other Gadabout Guides

Cook Islands
Rugged beauty and friendly Polynesian people ensure that most visitors fall in love with Rarotonga and her 14 sister Cook Islands. This informative guide is full of essential travel tips and stunning photographs.

Fiji
Myths, facts and practical travel tips are interspersed with colour photographs, useful maps and illuminating descriptions. This book is a vital source of information about an island paradise that suits all pockets and persuasions.

Mauritius
Discover the remote and cosmopolitan island of Mauritius with the help of this comprehensive guidebook. Superb colour photographs, interesting cultural and historical text, and travel tips for all budgets.

Tahiti
Often called the 'island of love', Tahiti is just one of the 115 islands that comprise French Polynesia. John Borthwick's love affair with these islands is reflected in the pages of this book. You'll discover anything from the finest French restaurants to black-pearl farms on far-flung Manihi.

Tasmania
Written by David McGonigal, this delightful fact-packed text covers everything from green politics to quaint country cottages, from alpine lakes to deserted beaches, lush rainforests and mountain treks.

Vanuatu
Stuart Bevan's book on Vanuatu takes you from active volcanoes to ancient ceremonies, from fascinating cargo cults to death-defying land dives. Bound to whet your appetite for a new travel adventure.

Male' harbour

Fish on their way to the teashop table

Island graveyard

Parking station, Male

GLOSSARY

aduba	a liquid measure equivalent to four *laahi*
aigaadia	a pushcart used to transport luggage and cargo
asaara	a side-dish to rice and curry and, more often than not, a pickled mixture of onion, chilli and lime juice
atholhu verin	Atoll Chief, responsible for the economic and political welfare of an administrative atoll
badhige	means 'kitchen' and in the far-flung atolls is usually a small, thatch-roof coral room with no windows which is separate from the living quarters and contains little more than a bare limestone floor with two or three dug-outs for stoves, a stack of firewood, some pots, pans and homemade wooden cooking utensils. Here, fillets of boiled fish smoke over a burnt-out fire and the women, sometimes whole families, squat on the floor to eat their meals
bandiyaa jehun	a popular traditional dance performed by young girls who writhe as they tap out a rhythm on metal water containers called *bandiyaa*
bas	language
baththeli	high-bowed dhoni, around 20 m long, many with two masts and a deckhouse, some propelled by inboard engines and others by lateen cloth sails, and mostly used for long-distance travelling
baiskal baththi	a battery-operated lamp available for less than Rf10 from most island stores and a must if you intend riding a bicycle after dark. They are also very handy to have in

	your luggage for dark moonless nights in far-flung villages without electricity
beyfulhu	the so-called 'noble class', the close friends and relatives of former sultans
bidi	a local cigarette made from newspaper and imported tobacco leaf
bileiy	a pungent green leaf eaten after and between meals with areca nut and spices
bimbi	a black millet regarded locally as 'poor people's food' despite its nutritional value
bodu beru	a drum made from hollowed coconut wood and the hide of a stingray
boki	light bulb
dhaani	an aluminium can attached to a long stick, used to take water from a well for drinking and showering purposes
dhandi jehun	similar to the *bandiyaa jehun*, except that it is performed by men beating out a rhythm with sticks
dharifulhu	offspring
dhathuru	voyage
dhekunu buri	the southern part
dhiyaa hakuru	smooth and golden coconut honey made by cooking and stirring *raa* for several hours
Dhivehi	the spoken language
Dhivehin	the appellation used by Maldivian citizens
Dhivehi Raajje	the 'Island Kingdom', the local term for the Maldives
dhon meehaa	literally means 'white person' and generally applies to all tourists
dhufani	chewing areca nut
faathihaa	a memorial service for a deceased friend or family member
fanditha	a sort of religious magic
fan	cadjan, made by plaiting dried palm leaves together and securing them with rope
faru	reef

fihaara	means 'shop'. Island stores in the far-flung atolls are often no more than small rooms in people's houses which are usually lined with shelves of condensed milk, cordial, toothpaste, sweets, sacks of rice, flour and sugar and, if you're lucky, shampoo. Beyond Male', these stores add a 10-per-cent mark-up to their prices
finolhu	a sandbank with little or no vegetation
foah	areca nut, usually eaten with *bileiy*
fulhi baththi	a local invention which consists of a small glass jar, a strip of recycled aluminium, and a piece of thread suspended in kerosene, providing the flickering lights which burn in most island homes
garudhia	fish broth, best eaten with rice, a piece of boiled fish, *asaara* and a dash of *rihaakuru*
gaazee	the locally trained, highly regarded Islamic judges who preside over common matters, such as marriage, divorce and petty crime
gifili	island-style garden bathrooms which have high coral or thatch fences, deep wells and *dhaani*
Giraavaru	local aboriginal people, said to be descended from the Indian Tamils but also believed (by some academics) to have descended from the same tribe as the Australian Aborigines
goalhi	a narrow lane, running off a wider *magu*
goathi	a plot of land granted by the government to all indigenous families
hadith	the sayings of Prophet Mohammed, regarded as a supplement to the scriptures of the *Quran*
Hajj	the pilgrimage to Mecca, made by only a few affluent Maldivian citizens or those assisted by the government
Hajji	the title acquired by anyone who

	accomplishes the ultimate goal of all true Muslims—to make the pilgrimage to Mecca
hakeem	local medicine man
Hijra	Mohammed's flight from Mecca to Medina in AD 622 (the Mohammedan Era and the Islamic calendar are reckoned from this time). It is the Arab word for 'departure from one's country
hiki mas	rock-hard fillets of tuna commonly referred to as 'Maldive fish' (thin slices of *hiki mas* eaten with chunks of *kaashi* is a local favourite)
hulhangu	the south-west monsoon
iloshi fathi	hundreds of coconut leaves are stripped to their thin flexible spines and tied together to form brooms which are particularly effective on sand floors (women are seen at any time of day, backs bent, sweeping the roads, their yards and the mosques, until once again their islands are neat and tidy)
iruvai	the north-east monsoon
jinni	demonic spirits
jorli	wonderful hammock chairs found outside most homes or suspended from trees
kaashi	old coconuts, usually grated and used to make coconut milk
kaashi kiru	coconut milk, made by soaking grated coconut in water and squeezing out the pulp (used as the base for local curries)
kahambu	specific type of turtle seen floating around the coral reefs and sometimes lumbering along island shores
kanamadhu	a nutritious nut which grows wild on many islands
kandiki	black sarong skirt worn by a woman under her *libaas*
kandu	sea
kandu mas	skipjack, easily identified by their long thin stripes

kanneli	yellowfin tuna, usually the largest species of the tuna family
karu hakuru	thick and creamy coconut honey, made by cooking *dhiyaa hakuru* with added sugar (there are many grades, the quality depending on the strength of the cook in charge of stirring
katheeb	island Chief, elected every two years
kaaveni sai	wedding reception
keyolhu	captain of a fishing crew
kuda katheeb	island Deputy Chief
kudhi baiy	a locally grown brown millet
kurumba	young coconuts, ideal for drinking
laahi	a standard grain and liquid measure which is approximately equivalent to 250 g of rice or 255 ml of honey
latti	mackerel, which has the darkest flesh of all the tuna species and is easily identified by three spots near its pectoral fin
libaas	long-sleeved brightly coloured dress worn by women over their *kandiki*. It is worn tight across the arms and chest and loose around the stomach and legs, so whether a woman is active, inactive or pregnant makes little difference
lonu mas	fillets of fish coated with salt and left to dry in the sun (rarely eaten by locals but exported in large quantities to neighbouring countries)
maavadi	chief carpenter
maavaharu	ambergris, from the gut of the sperm whale (a valuable substance used in the manufacture of expensive perfumes and cosmetics, and sometimes found along island shores or floating on top of the ocean)
madhiri dhundhandi	mosquito coils
magu	street

makthab	traditional, privately owned schools which teach young island children simple arithmetic and how to read and write Dhivehi and Arabic
mas	fish
miskiiy	mosque, usually no more than a large coral building with a corrugated iron roof
maaloodh	a Muslim lore recital
muh	a standard linear measure most often used when buying cloth, approximately equal to 45.7 cm
mudhim	muezzin, the person responsible for calling people to prayer
mundu	sarong (traditional attire for men)
nakaiy	intervals of 13 or 14 days in which the weather patterns are consistent
namaadhu	prayer
odi	large cargo boats that ply between Male' and the southern atolls
oi	ocean current
Quran	the sacred scripture of Islam, which contains revelations made in Arabic by Allah directly to Prophet Mohammed
raa	delicious sweet toddy, tapped from coconut trees
raaveri	toddy tapper
raagondi	bluefin tuna, usually found wherever there's a flock of birds hovering close to the ocean surface
raivaru	a sort of poetic chant
raveri	anyone who leases an uninhabited island
rian	a standard measure used when building boats, approximately 68.5 cm (or about the length of an adult's arm from fingertip to shoulder blade)
rihaakuru	dark brown concentrated fishpaste, made by the continual boiling of large amounts of *garudhiya*, fish and salt

roanu	coir rope, made from the stringy insides of coconut husks after they have been buried in sand for several days
roshi	unleavened bread
sai	tea, the national beverage
saanthi	a soft, latticed mat woven from thin strips of dried screwpine reed
salavaath	popular religious ritual, often practised as a deterrent to evil spirits
Shari'ah	Islamic legal code, the system of justice practised in the Maldives
sifain	police officers, easily identified by their khaki uniforms
suthuli	the best type of thread for a *fulhi baththi*
Thaana	local script
Tarikh	a history of the Maldivian sultans, originated by Hasan Tajaldin, continued by his nephew, completed by his grandson, and later destroyed when the Sultan's Palace was burnt down in 1752 (a copy has since been prepared but it is as yet unavailable to the public—academics rely on a translated copy prepared by HCP Bell)
undhoali	a wooden swinging bed, usually found suspended from huge breadfruit trees in the gardens of many island homes
us fas gandu	mounds of coral debris found on only a handful of islands, invariably the burial grounds for ancient Buddhist relics
uthuru buri	the northern part
valhi	knives of all shapes and sizes, from a small mas valhi used for cutting fish to a large kathi valhi for collecting firewood (Maldivian children learn to handle knives at a very early age)

An islander from Foammulah

DHIVEHI DICTIONARY

Pronunciation

a	as in	c*u*t	ai	as in	*eye*
eh	as in	r*e*d	ee	as in	tr*ee*
i	as in	f*i*t	th	as in	*th*rough
o	as in	h*o*t	dh	as in	*the*
u	as in	p*u*t	eiy	as in	ob*ey*
aa	as in	f*a*ther			

above	*mateega*
ache, to	*rihenee*
acquaintance	*rattehi*
across	*huras*
active	*muraali*
advice	*naseyhaiy*
advertisement	*ishthihaaru*
aeroplane	*mathindhaa boatu*
after	*fahun*
afternoon	*mendhuru*
again	*alun*
age	*umuru*
alcohol	*bangu raa*
all	*mulhin, hurihaa*
also	*ves*
anchor	*nagili*
ancient	*eveyla*
angel	*malaaikathu*
angry	*rulhi*
animal	*janavaaru*
ankle	*thambi*
anniversary	*munaasiba*
annoy, to	*undhagu kuranee*
answer	*javaab*
ant	*hini*
anyone	*kommes meehaku*
anything	*kommes echcheh*
apply, to	*ungulhanee*
arm	*aiy*
ascend, to	*machchah aranee*
arsenic	*korkadi*
ash	*alhi*
ashtray	*alhi-kendi*
ask, to	*ahan*
astrology	*nakaiy terikan*
attire	*hedhun*
baby	*kuda kujjaa*
backbone	*maibadha*
bacon	*ooru mas*
bad	*nubai*
bag	*dhabas, cothalhu*
bail, to	*hikkanee*
bait	*en*
bake, to	*fihanee*

— 243 — *Additional information*

balanced	*hama hama*	blade	*thila*
balloon	*fuppaa han*	blanket	*rajaa*
banana		blind	*kanu*
—cooking	*maalhoskeyo*	blood	*ley*
—ripe	*dhonkeyo*	blow, to	*fumenee*
barbeque, to	*fihanee*	blue	*noo kula*
barber	*bor koshaa meehaa*	bluebottle	*bodu mehi*
		blunt	*koshi*
basket	*vashi gandu*	body	*hashigandu*
bathe, to	*fen vuranee*	boil, to	*kakani*
beach	*athiri mathi*	bone	*kashi*
beacon	*neru baththi*	book	*foiy*
bean	*tholhi*	bottle	*fulhi*
beard	*thumbulhi*	bow (of ship)	*dhirumbaa*
beautiful	*reethi*	bowels	*kuda gohoru*
bed	*endhu*	box	*foshi*
bedbug	*thaiy makunu*	bracelet	*ulhaa*
beef	*geri mas*	brain	*sikundi*
beer	*biaru*	bread	*paan*
before	*kurin*	breadfruit	*bambukeyo*
beg, to	*salaam jahanee*	breakfast	*hendhunu sai*
begin, to	*fashani*	breast	*ura mathi*
believe, to	*gabool kuranee*	breathe, to	*neyvaa lanee*
bellows	*girumbaa*	bright	*ali gadha*
belongings	*thakethi*	bring, to	*gennanee*
below	*thireega*	broad	*fulhaa*
beside	*kaireega*	broom	*iloshi fathi, fihigandu*
best	*evvana*		
betel		brush	*burus*
—leaf	*bileiy*	build, to	*ahanee, raananee*
—nut	*foah*	burn, to	*aadhanee*
between	*demedu*	bury, to	*valhulanee*
bicycle	*baiskalu*	but	*ekamaku*
big	*bodu*	butter	*bataru*
bird	*dhooni*	butterfly	*kokaa*
birthday	*ufan dhuvas*	button	*goh*
bite, to	*dhaiy alhani*	cage	*koshi*
bitter	*hithi*	cake	*keyku*
black	*kalhu*	calm	*madu*
black coral	*endheri*	call, to	*govanee*

Maldives — 244 —

camphor	*kaafuru*	coconut	
can (container)	*dhalhu*	—old	*kaashi*
candle	*ubbaththi*	—scrapings	*kaashi huni*
cannot	*nuvaane*	—shell	*naashi*
captain	*nevi kalege*	—tree	*ruh*
cardamom	*kaafurutholi*	—young	*kurumba*
cargo	*aagu*	coffin	*sandhoah*
cat	*bulhaa*	cold	*fini*
ceiling	*fangi filaa*	colour	*kula*
certain	*yageen, gaimu*	comb	*funaa*
chair	*gondi*	come, to	*annanee*
change, to		comfort	*araamu*
(money)	*maaru kuranee*	common	*aadhaige*
cheap	*agu heyo*	compass	*samuga*
cheat	*makaru, vagu*	condensed milk	*geri kiru*
cheek	*kor*	constipation	*bodu kamu*
chef	*bodu kakkaa*		*nudevun*
chess	*raazuvaa*	container	*alhaa echcheh*
chest	*mey mathi*	contract	*ebbasvun*
chew, to	*hafani*	cook, to	*kakani*
chicken	*kulkulhu*	copper	*rathuloa*
child	*kujjaa*	copy, to	*nakalu kuranee*
chilli	*mirus*	coral	*akiri*
—dried	*hiki mirus*	corpse	*gaburu*
—raw	*ror mirus*	cottonwool	*kafa*
chin	*dhaiy dholhi*	cough, to	*kessanee*
chisel	*vadaan kashi*	count, to	*gunanee*
chop, to	*koshanee*	country	*raajje*
cigar	*suttaa*	cow	*geri*
cinnamon	*fonitoshi*	cowrie	*kuda boli*
circumcise, to	*hithaanu kuranee*	crab	
clean	*saafu*	—sea	*kakuni*
clean, to	*saafu kuranee*	crazy	*moya*
close, to	*lappanee*	create, to	*ufadhdhanee*
closed	*lappaafa*	crime	*kuh*
clothes	*hedhun*	crooked	*gudhu*
cloves	*karamfu*	crow	*kaalhu*
cock	*haa*	cruel	*ihaanethi*
		cry, to	*ronee*
		cucumber	*bodu kekuri*

cunning	*makaru veri*	doubt	*shakku*
cup	*jordu*	down	*thiri*
cupboard	*alamaari*	dragonfly	*dhon dhooni, loafindhu*
curry	*riha*		
—paste	*havaadu*	draw, to	*kurahanee*
custard-apple	*atha*	dream	*huvafen*
cut, to	*kandanee*	drill	*buruma*
damaged	*halaaku vefa*	drink, to	*bonee*
dance, to	*nashanee*	drum	*beru*
danger	*nurakkaa*	dry	*hiki*
dark	*andhiri*	duck	*asdhooni*
dates	*kadhuru*	dumb	*mammanu*
dawn	*fathis*	ear	*kanfaiy*
dead	*maruvefa*	early	*avas*
debt	*dharani*	earth	*bin*
deep	*fun*	east	*irumathi*
demonstration	*muzaahiraa*	easy	*faseyha*
dentist	*dhathuge doctor*	eat, to	*kanee*
desire, to	*edhenee*	eel	*ven*
devil	*iblis*	egg	*bis*
dew	*shabnam*	eggplant	*bashi*
diarrhoea	*beyrah hingun*	elbow	*ulham bashi*
die, to	*maruvanee*	empty	*hus*
different	*tafaatu*	end	*kolhu, nimun*
difficult	*undagu*	enemy	*dhushminun*
dig, to	*konnanee*	enough	*heyo*
dirty	*hadi*	enter, to	*vannanee*
disgraceful	*huthuru*	envelope	*sitee ura*
dish	*thashi*	equal	*evvaru*
dishonest	*makaru veri*	evening	*haveeru*
distance	*dhurumin*	everything	*hurihaa eche*
dive, to	*feenanee*	exact	*baraabaru*
divide, to	*bai bai kuranee*	example	*misaalu*
		exchange, to	*badhalu kuranee*
divorce	*vari*	exit	*nukunna than*
do, to	*kuranee*	expense	*kharadhu*
dog	*kuththaa*	expensive	*agu bodu*
dolphin	*kormas*	extinct	*nethi vedhiun*
donkey	*himaaru*	extinguish, to	*nivanee*
door	*bodu dhoru*	eye	*lor*

Maldives — 246 —

eyebrow	*buma*	flour sifter	*fureyni*
eyelash	*esfia*	flower	*maa*
eyelid	*lolubondi*	fly	*mehi*
face	*moonu*	forehead	*niyy kuri*
fair (skin)	*dhon*	foreigner	*beyru meehaa*
fall, to	*vettenee*	forget, to	*handhaan nethunee*
family	*aai'laa*		
famous	*mash'hooru*	frog	*boh*
fan	*fanka*	front	*kuri*
fantastic	*fakkaa*	fry, to	*thelulanee*
far	*dhuru, dhurugai*	full	*furifa, furijje*
		game	*kulhivaru*
fare	*agu*	garbage	*kuni*
fast	*avas, baaru*	garden	*bageecha*
fasten, to	*assanee*	garlic	*lonumedhu*
fat	*fala*	gentle	*madu maithiri*
fate	*iraadha*	get away!	*dhurah dhey!*
fear	*biru*	get out!	*nukume!*
feather	*fiya*	get up!	*teduve!*
feel, to (think)	*hivani*	ghee	*githeyo*
feet	*faithila*	gecko	*hornu*
fever	*hun*	gift	*hadhiyaa*
few	*madhu*	ginger	*inguru*
field	*dhandu*	give, to	*dhenee*
fight, to	*thalhaa folhanee*	glass	*billoori*
find, to	*hoadhanee*	glove	*ura*
finger	*ingili*	glue	*theras*
finished	*nimunee*	go, to	*dhanee*
fire	*alifaan*	goat	*bakari*
firewood	*dharu*	gold	*ran*
first	*evvana*	grass	*vina*
fish	*mas*	green	*fehi kula*
fish, to	*mas baananee*	grey	*alhi kula*
fishing line	*vadunanu*	grill, to	*fihani*
flag	*dhidha*	grind, to	*fundani*
flat	*fathaa*	grow, to	*hadhanee*
flip-flops (thongs)	*faivaan*	government	*sarukaaru*
		guava	*feyru*
floor	*binmathi*	gums	*hiru gadu*
flour	*godhan fuh*	gun	*badi*

— 247 — *Additional information*

hair	*istashi*	hungry	*bandufai*
half	*bai*	hurry	*avas*
hammer	*marutheyo*	hurt	*thadhu*
hang, to	*eluvani*	ice	*gandu fen*
hand	*aiythila*	idiot	*gamaaru*
handkerchief	*kuda rumaa*	if	*nama*
handsome	*chaalu*	ill	*bali*
happy	*ufaa*	illegal	*manaa*
hard	*haru*	illegitimate	*nahalaalu*
hat	*thaakihaa*	image	*soora*
have, to	*huri*	incense	*dhundhadi*
head	*boa*	infection	*balivun, nubaivun*
head lice	*ukunu*	ink	*dheli*
healthy	*sihathu ragalhu*	inheritance	*vaarutha mudhaa*
heart	*hiyy*	innocent	*thedhuveri*
heat, to	*hoonu kuranee*	inside	*ethere*
heaven	*suvaruge*	insult	*badhunaamu*
heavy	*baru*	intelligent	*visnun thoonu*
heal	*funaabu*	into	*ethere ah*
hell	*naraka*	invisible	*nufenna*
herbs	*faipilaaveli*	invitation	*dhau vathu*
heron	*maakana*	iron	*dhagaddu*
hide, to	*filanee*	island	*rah*
high	*us*	jar	*fulhi*
hold, to	*hifaatani, hifani*	jasmine	*huvadhu maa*
holiday	*bandhu dhuvas, chuttee*	jaw	*dhaiydholi*
		job	*wazeefa*
home	*ge*	joke	*samaasa*
honour	*aburu*	jump, to	*fummanee*
hook (fish)	*bulhi*	jungle	*valu*
horizon	*udhares*	kerosene	*saafu theyo*
horse	*as*	key	*thalhu dhadi*
hot		kill, to	*maraalanee*
—spicy	*kulhi*	kiss	*dhon*
—temperature	*hunu*	kitchen	*badhige*
house	*ge*	kite	*madi*
how?	*kihineiy?*	knee	*kakoo*
how much?	*kihaavarakah?*	knife	*valhi*
how many?	*kithah?*	labourer	*masakkathu meehaa*
hit, to	*jahanee*	ladder	*harugandu*

lamp	*fulhi baththi*	loud	*adugadha*
lantern	*bigaru*	love	*loabi*
large	*bodu*	low	*thiri*
late	*las, lasvi*	lung	*fuppaamey*
laugh, to	*henee*	lucky	*naseebu*
lavatory	*faahaanaa*		*gadha*
lawyer	*vakeelu*	mad	*moya*
lazy	*kanneiy*	magic	*jaadhoo*
leaf	*fai*	maggot	*fani*
leak, to	*foo elhun*	make, to	*hadhanee*
learn, to	*dhas kuranee*	mango	
leave, to	*dhanee*	—green	*hui am'bu*
leg	*fai*	—ripe	*dhon am'bu*
legitimate	*haalaalu*	many	*baivaru*
leisure	*araamu*	map	*chaatu*
lentils	*mugu*	marriage	*kaiveni*
letter	*sitee*	mast	*kumbu*
lid	*mathi gadu*	mat	*kunaa*
lies	*dhogu*	matches	*alifaan dhadi*
lie down, to	*oshoan nanee*	mate, to	*joaduvanee*
life	*dhiri ulhun*	mattress	*godhadi*
light	*ali*	measure, to	*minanee*
lightweight	*lui*	medicine	*beys*
lightning	*vidhun*	medium	*medhu*
lime	*lumboa*	meet, to	*badhalu kuranee*
limestone	*uva*	melon	*karaa*
limp	*koru*	menstruate, to	*hailuvanee*
line	*ron'gu*	middle	*medhu, medhuge*
linoleum	*tharafaalu*	midnight	*mendhamu*
listen, to	*adu ahanee*	milk	*kiru*
little	*kuda*	mirror	*loagan'du*
live, to	*ulhenee*	miscarriage	*hayyarun nettun*
liver	*mey*	mix, to	*ekkuranee, modenee*
lizard	*bon'du*	money	*faisaa*
loan	*dharanyah negun*	monkey	*raamaa makunu*
lobster	*ihi*	moon	*han'dhu*
lonely	*ekaniveri*	more	*gina'adhi*
long	*dhigu*	morning	*hedhunu*
look, to	*balanee*	mortar	*van*
loose	*dhoo*		

mosquito	*madhiri*	octopus	*borva*
—coil	*madhiri dhundhadi*	odd	*thafaathu*
—net	*madhirige*	offensive	*hadi*
mountain	*farubadha*	oil	*theyo*
moustache	*mathimas*	okay	*varihama*
mouth	*anga*	old	
much	*gina*	—objects	*baa*
murder, to	*maraalanee*	—people	*muskulhi*
must	*majubooru*	omelette	*bis gandu*
mutton	*bakari mas*	onion	*fiyaa*
nail	*mohoru*	open	*hulhuvifa*
naked	*oriyaan*	open, to	*hulhuvanee*
name	*nan*	opinion	*hiyaalu*
narrow	*hani*	opium	*afihun*
nasty	*nubai, goas*	or	*noonee*
nature	*gudhrathu*	orange	
naughty	*siyaasa*	—colour	*orenju*
nautilus shell	*foo en'buri*	—fruit	*foni lumbor*
neat	*saafu, thaahiru*	out	*beyru*
near	*kairi*	outside	*beyrufavaai*
necklace	*haaru*	over	*matheegai*
needle	*thinoas*	page	*gan'du, sofhaa*
nest	*haali*	painful	*thadhuvanee*
net	*dhaa*	paint	*dhavaadhu*
never	*dhuvahakuves nuvaane*	painting	*kurehun*
		pair	*jordu*
new	*aa*	palm	*aiythila*
news	*habaru*	paper	*karudhaas*
nice	*reethi*	papaya	*falhoa*
noon	*mendhuru*	part	*bai*
nose	*neyfaiy*	passionate	*loabi*
not bad	*goaheh noon*	peanut	*badhan*
not good	*ragalheh noon*	peel, to	*mashanee*
nothing	*evves echeh noon*	peg	
nutmeg	*thakoo vaiy*	—metal	*kabila*
now	*mihaaru*	—wooden	*ili*
oar	*fali*	pen	*galan*
oath	*huvaa*	pencil	*fansuru*
obey, to	*thabaa vun*	people	*meehun*
occupation	*masakkaiy*	pepper	*aseymirus*

Maldives — 250 —

perfect	*baraabaru*	puss	*dhos*
person	*meehaa*	put, to	*bahattanee*
perspire, to	*dhaahillun*	putrid	*kuni vefa*
pestle	*mor*	quantity	*adhadhu*
pig	*ooru*	quarrel, to	*araarun vanee*
piece	*ethikolheh*	quay	*faalan*
pill	*beys gulha*	queen	
pillow	*baalis*	—cards	*bibee*
pimple	*bihi*	—chess	*manthiri*
pineapple	*alanaasi*	—title	*raanee*
pink	*fiyaathoshi kula*	question	*suvaalu*
place	*than*	quick	*avahah*
place, to	*bahattanee*	quiet	*hamahimeyh*
plane	*mathindhaa boatu*	rabbit	*musalhu*
plate	*thashi*	race, to	*vaadha jahanee*
pliers	*kakuni*	rain	*vaarey, vissaara*
poison	*viha*	rain, to	*vaarey vehenee*
police	*sifain*	rainbow	*visaara dhuni*
polish, to	*ofu aruvani*	rainwater	*vaarey fen*
pomegranate	*annaaru*	raisin	*meybiskadhuru*
poor	*fageeru*	rat	*meedhaa*
pot	*theli*	razor blade	*reyzaru thila*
potato	*aluvi*	read, to	*kianee*
pound, to	*talani*	reason	*sababu*
pork	*ooru mas*	receipt	*raseedhu*
prayer	*dhuvaa*	recipe	*kakkan vee gioy*
present (gift)	*hadhiyaa*	red	*raiy kula*
pretty	*reethi*	reef	*faru*
pregnant	*balive indefi*	refrigerator	*ais alamaari*
previous	*kureege*	relax, to	*araamu kuranee*
price	*agu*	remember, to	*hadhaan kuranee*
problem	*massala*	remove, to	*naganee*
profit	*faidhaa*	rent	*kuli*
prohibited	*manaa*	repair, to	*hadhanee, mara-*
proud	*foni*		*amaathu kuranee*
pull, to	*dhamanee*	repeat, to	*alun hadhanee*
pulse	*vindhu*	repent, to	*thaubaa vanee*
pumpkin	*barabor*	reply	*javaabu*
punishment	*adhabu*	rescue, to	*salaamai kuranee*
push, to	*koppanee*		

rest, to	araamu kuranee, varu bali filuvanee	scissors	kathuru
		scrape, to	gaananee
reward	inaamu	scratch, to	kahanee
rib	meykashi	screwpine	kashikeyo
rice		search, to	hoadhanee
—cooked	baiy	season	moosun
—raw	han'doo	secret	sirru
rich	mussadhi	see, to	fennanee
ride, to	dhuvvanee	seed	oh
ridiculous	sakaraai, goas	selfish	foni
ring	an'goti	sell, to	vikkanee
rip, to	veedhanee	send, to	fonuvanee
ripe	dhon	sentence	jumla
roast, to	fihanee	sew, to	fahanee
roof	furaalhu	shell	boli
room	kotari	shirt	gamis
rope	roanu	shoes	faivaan
rotten	kunivefa	shop	fihaara
rose	finifenmaa	short	kuru
round	vah	show, to	dhakkanee
row, to	fali jahanee	shut, to	lappanee
rub, to	ugulhanee	shadow	hiani
rubbish	kuni	shallow	thila
rudder	hungaanu	share, to	bahanee
ruler	fathigadu	shark	miaru
run, to	dhuvanee	sharp	thoonu
rust	dhabaru	short	kuru
sad	dhera	shy	ladhu
safe	rakaatheri	sick	balive
sail	riyaa	side	faraai
sail, to	dhuvvanee	sideburns	kanhulhi
salad	satani	sign, to	soi kuranee
salary	musaara	signature	soi
salt	lonu	silly	seyku
sand	veli	silver	rihi
sandbank	finolhu	similar	ehgoiy
sandpaper	hila karudaas	simple	faseyha
sarong	mundu	sin	faafa
say, to	bunanee	sing, to	lava kiani
school	madhurasaa	sit, to	isheenanee

skin	*han*	stomach	*bandu*
sky	*udu*	stone	*hila*
slave	*alhu*	stop, to	*huttaalani*
sleep, to	*nidhanee*	storeroom	*bandaha ge*
slow	*las, lasvee*	storm	*kolhi gandu*
small	*kuda*	story	*vaahaka*
smile, to	*henee*	stove	*undhun*
smooth	*omaan*	straight	*thedhu*
smell	*vas*	strike, to	*jahani*
smoke	*dhun*	string	*vaa kolheh*
smoke, to	*borni*	strong	*varugadha*
snail	*baraveli*	studious	*ilmuveri*
snake	*harufa*	stupid	*seyku*
sneeze, to	*kimbihi alhanee*	success	*kaamiaabu*
soap	*saiboani*	sugar	*hakuru*
socks	*istaakeenu*	sun	*iru*
soft	*madu*	sunshade	*hiaa*
some	*eh bai, ekathikolhu*	sure	*gaimu, yageen*
something	*kommes echcheh*	swallow, to	*diruvaialani*
song	*lava*	sweet	*foni*
sore	*thadhu*	sweet potato	*kattala*
sorry	*maaf kurey*	swim, to	*fathanee*
sort, to	*tharutheeb kuranee*	swing, to	*hellanee*
sound	*adu*	swordfish	*hibaru*
soup	*suruvaa*	table	*meyzu*
sour	*hui*	tablet	*gulha*
speak, to	*vaahaka dhakkanee*	tailor	*fahaa meehaa*
spear, to	*hifani*	take, to	*naganee*
spectacles	*ainu*	tall	*dhigu*
spicy	*kulhi*	tank	*thaangi*
spider	*faidhigu makunu*	taro	*ala*
spit, to	*kulhu jahanee*	taste	*raha*
spoon	*samsaa*	tasty	*meeru*
square	*hathareskan*	tea	
stand, to	*thedhuvanee*	—cup	*jordu*
star	*thari*	—cup of	*sai*
start, to	*fashanee*	—leaves	*saifaiy*
stay, to	*hunnanee*	—pot	*saikuraa*
steal, to	*vakkan kuranee*	—strainer	*saifureyni*
stingray	*madi*	telescope	*dhurumee*

— 253 — *Additional information*

tell, to	*bunani*	toothache	*dhathuga rihun*
temperature	*fini hoonumin*	toothpaste	*dhaiy un'gulhaa beys*
terrific	*baraabaru*		
that	*e*	tortoise	*kanzu kahambu*
thatch	*fan*	tortoiseshell	*kahambu faiy*
therefore	*veemaa*	touch, to	*aiy lanee*
these	*mi*	towel	*thuvaali*
thick	*boa*	translator	*tharujamaanu*
thief	*vagu*	tray	*thabah*
thigh	*fala mas gandu*	tree	*gas*
thin		trial	*shariah*
—objects	*hani*	triangle	*thinkan*
—people	*hiki*	trousers	*fatuloonu*
think, to	*visnanee*	true	*thedhu veri*
thing	*echcheh*	trust	*ithubaaru*
this	*mi*	turmeric	*reen'dhoo*
thongs (flip-flops)	*faivaan*	tuna	*kandumas*
those	*e*	turtle	*velaa*
thread	*rodhi*	twins	*eh maabandu*
throat	*karu*	two-faced	*dhefun keheri*
through	*therein*	ugly	*huthuru*
throw, to	*ellanee*	umbrella	*kuda*
thunder	*gugurun*	unavailable	*libeykah neiy*
tide	*dhiyavaru*	under	*dashuga*
tidy	*thaahiru*	underground	*bimu adi*
tight	*baaru*	undress, to	*hedhun baalanee*
tiller	*hungaanu*	unfinished	*nunimey*
timber	*la kudi*	unhappy	*dheravefa*
time	*vaguthu, gadi*	unlock, to	*thalhu hulhuvanee*
tin	*dhalhu*	unlucky	*badhu nasoibu*
to	*ah*	unmarried	*hus nashi bai*
tobacco	*dhun faiy*	unravel, to	*niulhanee*
today	*miadhu*	unripe	*githi*
toe	*faige ingili*	untidy	*nuthaahiru*
together	*ekugai*	upper	*mathi*
tomorrow	*maadhamaa*	use, to	*beynun kuranee*
tongue	*dhoo*	vacant	*husvefa*
tonight	*mirey*	vegetables	*tharukaaree*
tooth	*dhaiy*	veins	*naaru*
		very	*varah*

vinegar	*raahui*	wheat	*godhan*
voice	*adu*	wheel	*furolhu*
vomit, to	*hodulanee*	when?	*kon ira kun?*
vowel	*fili*	where?	*kon thaakah?*
voyage	*dhathuru*	which?	*kon?*
wage	*musaara*	white	
waist	*una gandu*	—colour	*hudhu*
waste	*kuni*	—skin	*dhon*
wait, to	*madu kuranee*	who?	*kaaku?*
walk, to	*hinganee*	whose?	*kaakuge?*
wall	*faaru*	why?	*keevve?*
want, to	*beynun vanee*	wide	*fulhaa*
war	*hanguraama*	wind	*vai*
wash, to	*dhonnanee*	window	*kuda dhoru*
watch, to	*balanee*	wipe, to	*fuhenee*
water		wire	*naru*
—rain	*vaarey fen*	wise	*budhdhi vari*
—well	*valhu fen*	wish, to	*edhenee*
watermelon	*karaa*	with	*eku, ekugai*
waves	*raalhu*	without	*nulaa*
wax	*uh*	witness	*heki veriyaa*
weak		wok	*thaas*
—objects	*bali*	wooden spoon	*undhulhi, dheyfaiy*
—people	*varu dhera, bali kashi*	wool	*keheri*
		world	*dhuniye*
weapon	*hathiyaaru*	work	*masakkaiy*
weather	*moosun*	worm	*fani*
weave, to	*viyanee*	wrist	*kuda hulhu*
wedding	*kaiveni*	write, to	*liyanee*
weight	*baru*	yellow	*reen'dhoo kula*
well		young	
—health	*gadha*	—objects	*lha*
—water	*valhu*	—people	*zuvaan*
wet	*theiy*	zoo	*haivaanu bagicha*
what?	*korcheh?*	zuchini	*thoraa*

— 255 — *Additional information*

INDEX

Aahuraa 187
aborigines 25, 238
Al-Barakat, Abu 26, 119
accommodation 89, 90, 96
Addu 201, 206, 207
Addu Development Authority 201
agriculture 66
Ahmedi Bazaar 88, 118
Air Maldives 97, 130, 164, 186, 201
airlines 84, 130
Ali Rajas 26, 27
Ali Rasgefaanu Ziyaaraiy 119
Alia Hotel 123, 127, 224
Alifu 81, 98, 99, 155, 156, 157
Alifushi 184
Alimatha 162, 215
ambergris 108, 109, 239
Angaga 160, 215
anniversaries 58, 62
Araarootuge 124
Arabs 25, 26, 56
Ari 81, 156, 161
Ari Beach 156, 215
Asdu 215
Asgar Tours 126
Athurugau 215
atoll formation 6, 7
Avi 216
Baa 49, 50, 81, 99, 107, 108, 180, 181, 182
Baarah 196
Badidhoo 167
bakeries 130
Bandos 138, 216
banks 88, 103, 130

Baros 140, 216
Bathala 160, 216
Batuta, Ibn 25, 42, 185, 206, 225
Beach Travel and Tours 98, 125, 210
Beach Travel Tourist Lodge 125
Bell, HCP 23, 24, 42, 43, 116, 117, 148, 162, 206, 225, 241
Berimmadhoo 197
Bi Ya Doo 144, 216
bicycles 122, 235
Big Troubles Thursday 36
Bihuros Kamana Mosque 119
Bileiydhoo 166
birds 18, 19
birth 60
blacksmiths 49, 207
Blue Lagoon Club 157
boat builders 184
Bodu Eid 59
Bodufinolhu 145
Bodufolhudhoo 156
Bodufushi 162, 185
Boduhithi 141, 216
Bolifushi 145, 217
bookshops 135
Borahs 27, 28
British 25, 27, 28, 29, 30, 35, 36, 75, 148, 196, 200, 207
Buddhist 24, 156, 170, 187, 205, 207, 241
Buruneege Guesthouse 124
business hours 103
Camy Cool Spot 129
carpenters 43, 49, 170, 184, 239

— 257 — *Additional information*

carvers 181
Cheers 128
Christopher 25, 42, 228
cinemas 106, 129, 135
circumcision 61
Citizens Majlis 63
Club Little Hura 142, 217
Club Med 138, 217
Cocoa Island 142, 217
coconut milk 70, 238
commemorations 58
consulates 99, 135
coral 6, 7, 19, 20, 21, 22, 107
Cosmos International 210
Cottage Club 157
cottage industries 66
coups 26, 29, 36, 38
courier services 135
Crossworld Maldives 210
cult centre 166
currency 25, 88
customs 85, 87, 104, 136
Cyprea Hotels and Travel 210
dance 56, 57, 235
Dawn Cafe 129
death 61
Deen's Orchid Agency 210
Dhaalu 49, 55, 81, 99, 166
Dhabidhoo 175
Dhakandhoo 183
Dhapparu 183, 197
Dharanboodhoo 165
Dhewadhoo 204
Dhidhdhoo 196, 197
Dhiffushi 147, 180
Dhiggaru 164
Dhiggiri 162, 217
Dhigufinolhu 145, 217
Dhirham Travels 210

Dhivehi 24, 70, 75, 81, 150, 198, 236, 241
Dhiyadhoo 203
dhon meehun 42, 146, 236
Dhonakulhi 197
dhoni 65, 96, 97, 99, 170, 185, 235
Dhoonidhoo 148
Didi, Mohammed Amin 30, 35
divorce 44, 237
Dragon Restaurant 128
duty-free 86, 105
dynasties 28, 167
electricity 104, 136
Ellaidhoo 160, 217
embassies 100, 117, 135
Emboodhu Finolhu 144, 145
Embudhoo 156
Embudu Village 142, 218
emergency services 136
Eriyadhoo 157
Eriyadu 218
Evening Glory 129
evil spirits 47, 57, 241
excursions 89, 98, 149
Eydhafushi 181
Faadhippolhu 81, 178
Faafu 81, 99, 165, 167
Fahala 167
fanditha 47, 55, 236
Faridhoo 195
Farukolhufunadhoo 187
Farukolufushi 37, 138
fauna 17
Feevah 190
Fehendhoo 181
Fehividhuvaruge 125
Felalee 166
Felidhe 81, 161
Felidhoo 161, 162

Felivaru 65, 178
Fenfushi 157
Fesdu 159, 218
festivals 48, 58
Feydhoo 149, 207
feyli 108, 182
Fihalhohi 218
Filladhoo 197
film 95, 104, 105
Finolhas 183
fishes 19, 20, 21, 30, 43, 65, 79, 108, 157, 178
Fish Market Hotel 129
Fisherman's Day 62
fishing 62, 64, 146, 157
fishing villages 98, 104, 106, 146
flying fish 20, 181
Foammulah 81, 205, 206
Fonadhoo 175
foreign investors 36, 105
Fotheyobodufushi 162
Pyrard, François 25, 42, 49
De Houtman, Fredrick 206
Fuladhoo 181
Full Moon Beach Resort 140, 218
Fun Island Resort 145, 218
Funadhoo 149, 187
Fushi 175
Fushuveri 185
Gaafaru 147
Gaafu Alifu 81, 99, 200, 201
Gaafu Dhaalu 38, 50, 81, 97, 99, 107, 201, 204
Gaakoshebi 190
gaazee 63, 237
Gadhdhoo 50, 107, 205
Galena Maldives 98, 210
Gan 35, 36, 97, 170, 175, 201, 205, 207

Gangehi 160, 219
Gasfinolhu 219
Gayyoom, Maumoon Abdul 36, 37, 38, 63
Giraavaru 24, 25, 138, 219, 237
Gnyaviyani 81, 99, 205
Goidhoo 181
Goifufehendhoo 180
government 22, 30, 35, 36, 37, 62, 106, 198
government offices 103, 117, 136
Grand Friday Mosque 118
Green Lin 126
Ground Six 128
guesthouses 3, 90, 96, 122
Gulhi 148
Guraidhoo 142, 146, 148, 162, 167
Haa Alifu 81, 87, 99, 186, 195, 196
Haa Dhaalu 57, 81, 87, 97, 99, 186, 195
Hadhdhunmathi 81, 170
hadith 48, 237
hakeem 43, 61, 238
Halaveli 160, 219
Handhuvaru Hotel 129
Hangnaameedhoo 157
Hanimaadhoo 97, 186
Havoddaa 204
health 101
Helengeli 219
helipads 137, 156, 161, 181
Hembadoo 219
Heyerdahl, Thor 23, 166, 170
Higaakulhi 162
hiki mas 108, 165, 238
Himithi 166
Himmafushi 147
Hinnavaru 178
Hithadhoo 170, 175

Holiday Island 219
holidays 58
Horubadhoo 183
Hudhuveli 81
Hudhuveli Beach Resort 138, 140, 220
Hukuru Miskiiy 119
hulhangu 10, 15, 238
Hulhudheli 166
Hulhule 36, 85, 86
Hummingbird Helicopters 98
Hura 147
Huravee Day 62
Huruvalhi 180
Huvadhu 81, 201
Huvarafushi 197, 198
Iguraidhoo 38, 185, 187
Ihuru 141, 220
Imad's Agency 210
Imaduddeen 29, 30, 167, 180, 207
Independence Day 62
Indian Restaurant 129
Innamaadhoo 185
Intimate Restaurant 128
Intime 128
iruvai 10, 238
Iruvai Cafe 129
Isdhoo 175
Iskandar 157, 187
Islam 24, 26, 28, 45, 46, 47, 48, 49, 240
Islamic calendar 58, 238
Islamic Centre 118
Izzuddeen 147
jaggery 190
Jet Wing 210
jewellery 55, 107, 146, 166, 181
Jumhooree Maidan 118
Junction Hotel 129
Kaadehdhoo 38, 97, 204

Kaafu 81, 90, 96, 98, 99, 137, 146
Kaashidhoo 148
Kaashidhoo Channel 148, 178, 181
Kaditheemu 190
Kahdhoo 97, 164, 175
Kaimoo Harbour Inn 123
Kakaahuraa 164
Kakairadhoo 190
Kalo, Koimala 23, 116, 185
Kana Oiy Hura 141
Kanbalifaru 190
Kandholhudhoo 156
Kandoodhoo 170
Kandooma 146, 220
Kanifinolhu 141, 220
Karankaa Villa 123, 210
katheeb 63, 239
Keekimini 190
Kelaa 196
Keyodhoo 162
keyolhu 43, 239
Kihaadhoo 183
Kinolhas 185
Kolamaafushi 204
Kolhumadulu 81, 167
Kolhuvaariyafushi 164
Kon Tiki 23, 170
Kosheege 125
Kothaifaru 185
Kuburudhoo 195
Kuda Bandos 149
Kuda Eid 59
kuda katheeb 63, 239
Kuda Rah 161
Kudadhoo 190
Kudafari 187
Kudafushi 185
Kudahithi 142, 220
Kudahuvadhoo 166, 167
Kudarah 220

Kudarikilu 183
Kulhudhuffushi 36, 57, 195
Kumundhoo 195
Kunfunadhoo 181, 183, 220
Kuramathi 98, 157, 159, 220
Kuredhivaru 187
Kuredu 178, 180, 221
Kurumba 99, 140, 221
Laamu 81, 97, 99, 163, 170, 175
lacquer work 50
Laguna 145, 221
Lakshadweep 27, 198
Landhoo 187
Landmark Travel 210
Lhaviyani 36, 65, 81, 99, 178, 180
Lhohi 187
Lhohifushi 221
Liamagu 190
libraries 101, 137
Lif-Sham Guest House 125
lingams 166
Little Troubles Thursday 36
Lohifushi 141
Luboakandhoo 185
Maabaidhoo 170
Maadheli 166
Maafahi 197
Maafaru 187
Maafilaafushi 81, 180
Maafushi 148, 204
Maafushivaru 156, 161
Maagiri Tourist Lodge 124
Maalhaveli 165
maaloodh 47, 55, 61, 181, 240
Maamigili 157, 185
Maandhoo 175
Maaugoodhoo 190
Maavah 175
Maayafushi 160, 221
Madidhoo 190

Madivaru 138
Madoogali 221
Magoodhoo 165
Mahibadhoo 96, 156, 157
Makunudhoo 195, 221
Makunufushi 142
Maldivian Air Taxi 98
Maldivian cuisine 67
Male' 24, 36, 37, 89, 99, 115, 117
Male' Atoll 81, 137
Male' Tour Inn 125
mammals 19
Manadhoo 186
Maradhoo 207
markets 16, 66, 79
Martyr's Day 62
Mathiveri 157
mats 50, 107, 190, 196, 205
Mazaage 126
media 106
Meedhoo 167, 208
Meemu 81, 99, 164, 165
Meerufenfushi 81, 222
mercenaries 36, 37, 38, 62
Mermaid Inn 126
Minicoy 27, 198
Ministry of Tourism 3, 89, 90, 101, 137
Mirihi Marina 222
Moofushi 222
Moon Cafe 129
MTCC 98
muezzin 46, 119, 205, 240
Muladhoo 197
Mulah 165
Mulaku 81, 164
Muli 164
Mundoo 170
Naifaru 178, 180
nakaiy 10, 240

— 261 — *Additional information*

Nakatchafushi 140, 222
Nalandhoo 190
Narudhoo 195
Nasandhura Palace Hotel 122, 127, 225
Nasir, Ibrahim 35, 36, 149
national anthem 57, 58
National Day 62
national flag 64, 118
National Museum 119
Newport Restaurant 128
night-life 129
Nika Hotel 159, 222
Nilandhoo 165
Nivico 126
Nolhivaramfaru 195, 196
Noofaru Tourist Lodge 124
Noonu 81, 99, 186, 187
North Huvadhu 81
North Maalhosmadulu 23, 81, 180
North Miladhunmadulu 81
North Nilandhe 81, 165
North Thiladhunmathi 81
Nuruddeen 30
Ocean Reed 126
Ocean Reef Club 201, 207, 222
Olhuveli View Hotel 146, 222
Palm Tree Island 145, 222
Paradise Island 223
Park View Restaurant 127
Parmentier, Jean and Raoul 206
permits 91
Phoenix Travel 210
photography 104, 162
Portuguese 26, 27, 28, 62, 75, 190, 196
post office 30, 103, 136
Powell's Islands 180
prayer 47, 59, 61, 103, 118, 240

pronunciation 70, 76, 243
Queen of the Night 129
Quench 128
Quran 38, 46, 48, 49, 58, 61, 106, 237, 240
raa 102, 148, 150, 236, 240
Raa 23, 43, 81, 99, 180, 184
raaveri 44, 150, 240
raivaru 57, 240
Raiymandhoo 165
Rakeedhoo 162
Ramadan 58, 59, 103
Rangali 156
Rannalhi 223
Ranveli Beach Resort 223
ras roanu 166
Rasdhoo 98, 156
Rasgetheemu 23, 24, 185
Raskamuge Dhevana Majlis 28
Raskamuge Is Majlis 28
Raskamuge Thinvana Majlis 28
recipes 68
Reethi Rah 223
Relax Inn 123, 225
religion 46, 47
republic 35, 38, 62
resort islands 90, 137, 157, 162, 180, 183
restaurants 127
Rihiveli 144, 223
Safari Tours 210
safaris 89, 98, 118
Sakeena Manzil 126, 136
salavaath 47, 61, 241
Sandbank Cafe 129
Scorpion Travels 210
Seagull Airways 97
Seagull Cafe House 128
Seasan Tours 210

Seasand Enterprises 210
Seenu 18, 81, 97, 99, 199, 201, 206, 207
Selvio 126
Shamshuddeen 29, 30, 148, 195, 196, 197
Shanghai Restaurant 128
Shari'ah 63, 241
Shaviyani 81, 99, 186, 187
shopping 106
Singapore Bazaar 118
Slice 128
social classes 43
Sony 125
South Huvadhu 81
South Maalhosmadulu 81, 180
South Miladhunmadulu 81
South Nilandhe 81, 166
South Thiladhunmathi 81
stamps 104
stupas 24, 175
Sultan Park 119
sultanas 28
Sultanate 28, 29, 35, 116
sultans 26, 28, 29, 43, 55, 56, 85, 116, 119, 236, 241
Sun Travel and Tours 99, 210
sunburn 102
Sunland Travel 99, 215
Sunrise Lodge 125
Suvadive 201
table manners 88
Tari Village 141, 223
Tarikh 24, 241
taxis 122
Tea Centre, The 129
teashops 67, 105, 117, 127, 147
telecommunications 103, 104, 149
Tetra Guest House 124

Thaa 81, 99, 167, 170
Thaana 75, 190, 241
Thaburudhoo 149
Thakandhoo 196
Thakurufaanu, Mohammed 26, 27, 118, 119, 190, 196
Thimarafushi 170
Thinadhoo 204
Thoddoo 156
Thulaadhoo 50, 181
Thulhagiri 138
Thulusdhoo 223
Thundufushi 223
Thuraakunu 198
time 77, 103
tipping 105
Tomb of Abu al-Barakat 119
tourism 50, 55, 65, 66, 149
tourist hotels 87, 90, 95, 225
travel agents 87, 98, 118, 210
Travel Bureau, The 215
turtles 20, 55, 107, 157, 164, 165
Twin Island 161, 224
Twin Peaks 128
Ugoofaaru 184, 185
United Suvadive Islands 35, 200
Universal Enterprises 215
Usfushi 170
Utheemu 26, 196
Vaadhoo 144, 204, 205, 224
Vaavu 81, 99, 161, 163
Vabbinfaru 224
vaccinations 86, 102
Vaikaradhoo 196
Vaikaramuraidhoo 196
Vandhoo 170
Vashafaru 197
Vattaru Reef 161, 162, 164
vegetation 7, 17

Velassaru 145
Velidhoo 187
Veligandu 160, 224
Veligandu Hura 145
vessels 96
Veymandoo 167, 170
Veyofushi 183
Veyvah 165
Victory Day 62
Viligili 201, 204

Villi Varu 144, 224
Villingili 149
visas 86
Voyages Maldives 98, 215
water sports 89
wildlife 18
women 25, 38, 45, 46, 61, 108
Young 25, 42
Ziyaaraiyfushi 142, 224
ZSS 98

Photo credits

Colour
Gadabout Guides 13, 91, 94, 214B, 33

Virginia Greig 12A, 12B, 73B, 151, 171, 174, 193, 212, 233, 267,

Philippe Metois FC, IFC, 11, 32, 72, 73A, 112, 113, 132, 134, 152, 153, 192, 211, 214A, 231, 232, 234, IBC

Robbie Newman 0, 51, 191

Black-and-white
Bernard Koechlin 40, 45, 109, 110, 176, 225, 242

Philippe Metois 79, 82, 198   *Najeeb Studio* 4, 39, 208

Stuart Bevan was born in England and grew up in the suburbs of Sydney. During the 1970s, he set off on a venture that took him through Europe, the Middle East and Asia. He settled for some years in the Maldives, rented an island and wrote a book. That was how Gadabout Guides began. Stuart has been writing and travelling ever since.

Clown fish